Rear Admiral
Larry Chambers, USN

Rear Admiral Larry Chambers, USN

First African American to Command an Aircraft Carrier

Ric Murphy

McFarland & Company, Inc., Publishers
Jefferson, North Carolina

Photographs noted as "(personal collection)" are
from the collection of Rear Admiral Larry Chambers

LIBRARY OF CONGRESS CATALOGUING-IN-PUBLICATION DATA

Names: Murphy, Ric, author.
Title: Rear Admiral Larry Chambers, USN : first African American to command an aircraft carrier / Ric Murphy.
Other titles: First African American to command an aircraft carrier
Description: Jefferson, North Carolina : McFarland & Company, Inc., Publishers, 2018 | Includes bibliographical references and index.
Identifiers: LCCN 2017049329 | ISBN 9781476667270 (softcover : acid free paper) ∞
Subjects: LCSH: Chambers, Larry, 1929– | Admirals—United States—Biography. | United States. Navy—Officers—Biography. | United States. Navy—African Americans—Biography. | Midway (Attack aircraft carrier)—Biography. | African American sailors—Social conditions—20th century. | African American sailors—Civil rights—History—20th century. | Vietnam War, 1961–1975—Aerial operations, American. | Vietnam War, 1961–1975—Naval operations, American. | United States—History, Naval—20th century.
Classification: LCC E840.5.C53 M87 2018 | DDC 359.0092 [B] —dc23
LC record available at https://lccn.loc.gov/2017049329

BRITISH LIBRARY CATALOGUING DATA ARE AVAILABLE

ISBN (print) 978-1-4766-6727-0
ISBN (ebook) 978-1-4766-2753-3

© 2018 Ric Murphy. All rights reserved

No part of this book may be reproduced or transmitted in any form or by any means, electronic or mechanical, including photocopying or recording, or by any information storage and retrieval system, without permission in writing from the publisher.

Front cover: Rear Admiral Larry Chambers, United States Navy (Ret.)

Printed in the United States of America

McFarland & Company, Inc., Publishers
　Box 611, Jefferson, North Carolina 28640
　　www.mcfarlandpub.com

To Janet Faye Murphy Chambers

Acknowledgments

My research owes much to the cooperation of archivists, librarians, and historians who freely shared their time and expertise. I wish to thank the wonderful and supportive staff of the USS *Midway* Museum, including Rod Atteberry, Exhibit's Audio Visual Technician; Dave Hanson, Collection Manager; and Karl Zingheim, Historian, for their guidance and direction. I would also like to thank Lisa Crunk and the staff of the Naval History and Heritage Command and Holly Reed, Archives Specialist, NWCS-Stills, National Archives.

I would like to thank Rear Admiral Chambers for allowing me to interview him and review his personal pictures, files and artifacts, and for his knowledge and patriotism. I am also grateful to Larry's wife, Sarah Jones-Chambers, who made the logistics possible to conduct the interviews with Larry and helped sort through the nautical terms used herein. Sarah's personal knowledge helped bring life to several of the stories that may have been forgotten to history.

Finally, I wish to thank the men of USS *Midway*, who without question or doubt saved the lives of the Americans, foreign nationals and Vietnamese refugees on that hot, momentous day of April 29, 1975. While they may never have gotten the medals they so richly deserve, they are truly unsung heroes worthy of our nation's praise and sincerest of accolades. Thank you for your service.

Table of Contents

Acknowledgments   vi
Preface   1
Glossary   3
Introduction   5

1. The First Thirty Days   9
2. The Dunbar Years   23
3. The Annapolis Years   34
4. Cold War   49
5. Vietnam War   74
6. Civil Unrest   86
7. Fall of Saigon   101
8. Operation Frequent Wind   116
9. "Bird Dog on Final"   141
10. Port of Sattahip   157
11. Rear Admiral   172

Epilogue   187
Chronology   193
Chapter Notes   205
Bibliography   211
Index   215

Preface

I became interested in the career of Rear Admiral Lawrence Chambers during the Vietnam War when I learned that he was the captain of the USS *Midway* and the first African American to command an aircraft carrier in the United States Navy. And, like millions of others worldwide, I was captivated by the events in South Vietnam during the Fall of Saigon, when the largest helicopter evacuation on record took place as part of the United States military action known as Operation Frequent Wind.

During Operation Frequent Wind, as communist-led North Vietnamese were entering the city, there were countless American military personnel who courageously rescued American civilians, military personnel, other foreign nationals and South Vietnamese sympathizers by helicopter and ferried them out to awaiting American aircraft carriers. This included the *Midway* where Captain Chambers displayed tremendous courage and leadership including ordering that millions of dollars of military helicopters be pushed over the side of the ship so that a South Vietnamese Air Force Major could safely land on board in a small Cessna aircraft with his family, saving their lives.

While many articles, journals and books have been written about the Vietnam War and the events surrounding the Fall of Saigon, I wanted to explore the leadership qualities of one of the many unsung heroes of the war, who had the temperament and judgment to make the right decisions during a period of crisis and humanitarian need. The minutes and hours leading up to, and every split-second during, the mission of Operation Frequent Wind aboard the *Midway* reflected a highly efficient organization managed by a skilled and calm commanding officer.

The intention of this book was not just to pay tribute to an American hero who became the first African American to graduate from the U.S. Naval Academy and reach the rank of flag officer, but to provide the life story of an extraordinary man who helped desegregate the United States Naval Academy and the United States Navy during a period of racial strife and international turmoil while consistently demonstrating great humility, sense of perspective and professional integrity, always with great honor.

Glossary

A&T	Agricultural and Technical
AFS	Combat Stores Ship (refrigerated stores, dry provisions, technical spares, general stores, fleet freight, mail and personnel for transfer at sea)
AIRPAC	Commander, Naval Air Forces Pacific
ARVN	Army of the Republic of Viet Nam (also known as South Vietnam's Army)
CDR	Commander
CIA	Central Intelligence Agency
CIC	Combat Information Center
CINCPAC	Commander in Chief U.S. Pacific Command
CO	Commanding Officer
CVA	Aircraft Carrier with Fighter & Attack Squadrons (with number indicates the hull number of the vessel)
DEFCON	Defense readiness condition
FBI	Federal Bureau of Investigation
HELO	Helicopter
JROTC	Junior Reserve Officer Training Corps
KGB	Russian Military Security Force
NATO	North Atlantic Treaty Organization
NAVAIR	Naval Air Systems Command
NLF	National Liberation Front
NTDS	Naval Tactical Data System

RADM	Rear Admiral
ROTC	Reserve Officer Training Corps
RPM	Revolutions per minute
SAC	Strategic Air Command
SIOP	Single Integrated Operational Plan
U.S.	United States of America
USAF	United States Air Force
USN	United States Navy
USS	United States Ship

Introduction

In history there are events that align, creating historic moments in time. While these events may be small or isolated they become significant when they have a dramatic impact and affect countless lives. These moments are often supported by heroes whose lives would be forgotten if not recorded. This book is a collection of research, history and personal interviews with Rear Admiral Lawrence Chambers, a man with humble beginnings who became an American hero.

On 29 April 2015, the world celebrated the 40th Anniversary of Operation Frequent Wind, the successful evacuation of over 200,000 refugees from South Vietnam's capital city. Today, the evacuation is known as the "Fall of Saigon."

The Vietnam War was a complex geopolitical war that spanned from 1959 to 1975 and expanded the interests and administrations of five United States presidents. The war came alive on American television screens each evening during the supper-hour news broadcast and highlighted the inequities of race, class and geopolitical affairs in America and around the world.

Rear Admiral Lawrence Cleveland Chambers, the second African American in U.S. history to reach flag rank in the U.S. Navy, was the commanding officer of the aircraft carrier USS *Midway* (CV-41) in 1975 during the evacuation of Saigon. Then Captain Chambers, he was a key player in the evacuation of United States citizens, foreign nationals, and South Vietnamese who had worked closely with the American government during the war.

Chambers, who has been heralded as making key and pivotal decisions during the evacuation of Saigon and helping evacuees flee the repressive government of North Vietnam, had his own experiences with repression and oppression, having lived under America's own segregationist laws of the South.

His rise to the highest levels of the United States Navy is all the more compelling once his early life is examined. Chambers, son of a widowed, working mother, began his life in a segregated neighborhood in the South where he dreamed of becoming an aviator and an engineer. Hardworking and disciplined even before his days at Dunbar High School in Washington, D.C., Chambers consistently exhibited exceptional decision-making skills, bravery and compassion in the face of great challenges, most notably during his controversial decision to push overboard millions of dollars' worth of military equipment in order to save a South Vietnamese Air Force major, his wife and five children. Chambers has had his own challenges due both to outside forces such as prejudiced instructors at Annapolis and Pensacola, and forces beyond anyone's control, like the leukemia that took away his beloved wife Janet. He has endured trials with grace and will leave behind a career and legacy admired by many people, Black and white alike.

Chambers' success is not limited to the events that took place in Indochina at the close of the Vietnam War because it is the culmination of events, experiences and people's influences that shaped him into the man he was on that fateful April day in 1975. His life must be viewed not only through the lens of his youth but also through the prism of the entire Vietnam War, as well as the geopolitical relationship to the Cold War between the United States and the communist bloc nations of China and the Soviet Union.

In order to fully understand the complexity and the importance of Rear Admiral Chambers' career one must understand it in the context of the U.S. Navy in the performance of a wide range of missions that supported presidential doctrines that changed from administration to administration as international events unfolded. As the culmination of world events precipitated a change in presidential doctrines during the Cold War, these geopolitical events had a direct correlation to Chambers' career and the events that led to the evacuation of South Vietnam's capital city, Saigon, in 1975.

Chambers, who was trained as a naval aviator, worked with the U.S. Air Force during critical missions such as Rolling Thunder and Linebacker air campaigns against North Vietnam, as well as in air operations in Laos and Cambodia. He was assigned to aircraft carriers as they provided support missions against enemy targets, amphibious transport for Air Force and Marine personnel, squadron air attacks behind enemy lines to prevent the resupply of enemy forces and cover during offensive and defensive tactical maneuvers.

Chambers was a career military man who overcame adversity. Referred to by many as a "Navy man," Chambers' career was propelled by the events of the Cold War, particularly in Vietnam, at a time when his government needed bright young men with the capacity and intelligence to meet the growing challenges of a "new Navy" as it confronted the growth of communism worldwide under the constant threat of nuclear war.

The biography of Rear Admiral Lawrence Cleveland Chambers is a story of a man whose *endurance* enabled him to overcome the prejudices of the Jim Crow South where history dictated that the color of his skin should have defined him as a second-class citizen rather than as a graduate of the United States Naval Academy. It is the story of a man's *perseverance* which enabled him to reach the highest ranks of the United States Navy and to act as Commanding Officer on two major combatants. Lastly, Chambers himself provides a personal *reflection* of all the events that led up to a successful execution of Operation Frequent Wind, and how despite the challenges, his compelling life story enabled him to make the right decisions for all the right reasons.

Map 1. Southeast Asia

Chapter 1

The First Thirty Days

After eight years of combat on the Vietnam peninsula, the United States and North Vietnam signed the Paris Peace Accords in 1973. Two years later, North Vietnam launched a new invasion of South Vietnam, quickly overwhelmed its armed forces, and moved toward its capital city of Saigon. In preparation for a possible evacuation of United States citizens and in many cases their Vietnamese spouses and children, foreign nationals and Vietnamese who had worked closely with the American government during the war, the United States naval assets in East Asia were placed on high alert.

On March 26, 1975, during this period of escalating geopolitical turmoil in Southeast Asia Captain Lawrence C. Chambers assumed command of the aircraft carrier USS *Midway* (CV-41). Commissioned one week after the end of World War II, *Midway* was built to be the largest warship in the world and kept that standing until 1955. According to the records held by the *Midway* Museum the 70,000-ton vessel is 968 feet in length and supports a crew of 4,500. Its impressive flight deck is 1,001 feet long, the equivalent of more than three football fields, and spans an area of 4.02 acres.

Five days later, the ship and her crew got underway from Yokosuka, Japan, on what was supposed to be a routine cruise with visits scheduled for Hong Kong and Subic Bay in the Philippines. Shortly thereafter, Captain Chambers received word that the military and political situation in Southeast Asia was deteriorating and that *Midway* might be needed in the region. Before moving to the South China Sea, *Midway* was ordered to on-load two squadrons of U.S. Marine Corps helicopters off the coast of Okinawa and transports the helicopters and Marine crewmen to the Subic Bay operating area where they were transferred to other carriers destined to execute Operation Eagle Pull, the evacuation of Phnom Penh, Cambodia.

On April 15, *Midway* entered Subic Bay for a scheduled ten-day upkeep period in the Philippines. Just three days later she was ordered to get underway and steam at maximum speed toward Vietnam. Before leaving port, in anticipation of his mission's objective, Captain Chambers ordered the off-loading of over half of his aircraft wing and five hundred officers and crewmen to make room on board for the upcoming mission.

Several days later, after steaming to a position off the southern tip of Vietnam, *Midway* loaded ten U.S. Air Force HH-53 helicopters. For the next eight days, the Air Force crewmen from the 56th Special Operations Wing, the 21st Special Operations Squadron, and the 40th Aerospace Rescue and Recovery Squadron prepared for an operation that they knew could commence any minute. During preparations for an anticipated evacuation, a group of sailors was selected and trained to process evacuees upon arrival aboard *Midway*. The group, made up of petty officers and non-rated men, was assigned to work on the flight and hangar decks in designated handling areas.

On the afternoon of April 29 Captain Chambers received orders to execute Operation Frequent Wind, the evacuation of Saigon. As part of this operation, the carriers USS *Midway* (CV-41), USS *Hancock* (CV-19), and USS *Okinawa* (LPH-3) became part of the largest helicopter evacuation in United States history. Based on various sources, these aircraft carriers would be responsible for the immediate evacuation of as many as 200,000 Americans, foreign nationals and Vietnamese refugees from Saigon.

Upon receiving the evacuation order, Captain Chambers and the 4,500 crewmen of *Midway* went into action. The U.S. Air Force helicopters on board *Midway* immediately lifted off the flight deck and flew to the South Vietnamese capital city of Saigon to begin the evacuation. As the North Vietnamese approached Saigon on the afternoon of April 27 U.S. Air Force, Navy and Marine helicopters from the task force were joined by U.S. Army, Air America[1] and South Vietnamese helicopters to execute the arduous challenge of transporting Americans and Vietnamese refugees to the USS *Midway* and other carriers in the task force. The recently assigned Captain of *Midway* was now involved in one of the largest helicopter evacuations in history.

At that pivotal point in American history no other African American had reached the height of naval combat command then held by Captain Chambers of *Midway*. As he looked across the bow of the ship into the vast waters before him, and considered the military command now under his control, Chambers reflected on his youth and the journey that had brought him to that point.

Lawrence Cleveland Chambers was born in segregated Bedford, Virginia, to Lawrence and Charlotte Chambers and was the third of five children. When he was four years old his father, a World War I Navy veteran and a mortician, passed away prematurely from injuries acquired during the war, leaving his wife with four small children. To make matters worse, Charlotte was pregnant with their fifth child.

Although he passed away when Larry was only four, Larry retained vivid memories of his father, who remained a significant influence on Larry's life. Chambers remembers watching his father perform embalming services as an undertaker. He recalls that his father "had the ability, when given a photograph, to make perfect restorations of badly mangled people who were killed in accidents." As with most services in Bedford, Virginia, the mortuary services were segregated. One incident Chambers remembers in particular was when a young white man had been killed while being chased by federal revenue agents for "running whiskey." Though the young man's body was badly damaged, Chambers' father restored the body perfectly. According

Rear Admiral Larry Chamber's father, Lawrence Chambers, Sr., World War I Navy Seaman, circa 1915 (personal collection).

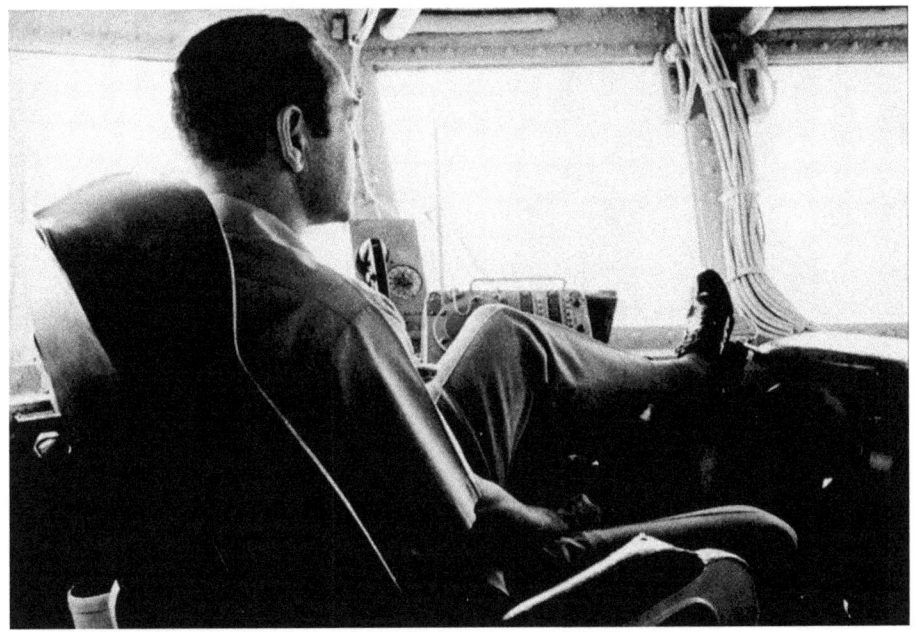

South China Sea, April 30, 1975. Captain Chambers observes the successful landing of the Cessna O-1 on the USS *Midway* (personal collection).

to Chambers, "in those days people didn't have a lot of cash … but the parents were so grateful for the restoration that they paid my father with moonshine. My daddy probably had a thousand-year supply of moonshine."[2]

After her husband passed away, faced with having to raise five young children, Charlotte Chambers made the difficult, heart-breaking decision to move

Bedford County, Virginia, 1930. Charlotte Chambers holding Larry Chambers as a toddler (personal collection).

1. The First Thirty Days 13

Bedford County, Virginia, 1934. Charlotte Selden Chambers, with four of her five children, Lauretta (seated at left), Andrew (on lap), Charlotte, and Larry (youngest son, Melvin not yet born) (personal collection).

four hours away to accept a clerical position in Washington, D.C., at the United States War Department. When the young, widowed mother left rural Bedford, Virginia, to move in with her sister Estelle and her husband, she left behind her five young children with her capable parents, Clement and Gladden Selden.

Larry's grandparents, particularly his grandfather, left a profound and ever-lasting impact on him. Larry has many fond memories of his grandfather and would often say that, as a child and young man, his grandfather taught him many lessons "that I drew upon later in life as a father, as a husband, and as a military leader."

His grandfather, Clement Selden, was born in 1884 and was the son of slaves. A man of strong character, Clement wanted to make sure that his grandchildren understood their family history and the many challenges that their ancestors were forced to endure as slaves. He often shared stories about his parents' lives during slavery and how they overcame obstacles through endurance, a lesson that his grandson Larry would often draw upon later in life.

With the passing of Larry's father at such a young age, his grandfather was an important role model and father figure in Larry's formative years. As a little kid, Larry would call his grandfather "Boo Pop," unable to pronounce his grandfather's nickname, "Booze Papa," correctly. With a tender smile Larry recalls how much his grandfather, Booze Papa, loved to hear the blues: "Booze Papa loved his music, and he loved to talk for hours to each of his grandkids. He didn't have what we would call today a formal education," but Larry's grandfather was extremely intelligent nonetheless. "He seemed to know a lot about a lot of things. He made each of us feel like we were ten feet tall, and that was a feeling I kept with me all through life's challenges," Chambers laughs. He adds, "This only created problems for me once I went to Annapolis because more times than not, I was knocked down to size." Chambers explained, "When they called and told us to stand in line according to height, I always stood at the rear of the line because my granddaddy told me I stood at ten feet tall, and I actually thought that was my height."

Once in Washington, D.C., Clement and his wife encouraged their daughter, Charlotte, to take clerical classes at the Cortez Peters Business School. They knew that in order for her to secure the future of her children, Washington was the best place to seek employment or Charlotte would end up like many of the other young and intelligent African American women in Bedford, Virginia, limited to the traditional employment opportunities of domestic housework. Clement and Gladden Selden did not want this for their daughter, nor did they want this to be the future for their grandchildren.

The Depression was a difficult period for the Selden-Chambers family. By 1940, Clement and Gladden Selden were raising the youngest three of their nine children, Eugene, Bernice, and William, alongside their grandchildren Charlotte (named after her mother), Lauretta, Lawrence, Andrew, and Melvin. Once or twice a month, Charlotte would leave her sister's home in Washington, D.C., and make the long journey on the bus to visit her children and parents in Bedford, Virginia.

1. The First Thirty Days 15

Bedford County, Virginia. Uncle Malakai Roper was very proud of his car, and he always kept it looking brand new. Above are Charlotte H. Chambers with all of her children before the move to Washington, D.C. What a wonderful reunion of the family. Sisters Charlotte and Lauretta, Larry and brothers Melvin and Andrew (personal collections.

In reflection, Larry Chambers remembers that Bedford was a nice place to live, particularly as a youngster. He remembers Bedford as being an industrial town of about 5,000 people with woolen and textile mills where the finished textiles were exported to Lynchburg and points beyond. One of the largest employers at that time, according to Chambers, was the Elks National Home, a retirement community for members of Elk Lodges.

Bedford was a solid community when the Great Depression hit hard where white and Black families worked for a living, and when they didn't have money, they paid for services with produce. Larry recalls that these were hard-working men and women and they did not want a free ride. He says, "My grandfather instilled that sense of self-worth and honesty in each of us. He drilled into each of us on a daily basis the importance of getting an education and working hard."

After passing a series of civil service exams and achieving several promotions despite the Depression looming over her head the tenacious Charlotte Chambers saved money from employment as a clerk with the United States War Department and moved the entire family from rural Bedford, Virginia, to the Shaw neighborhood of Washington, D.C., named after Colonel Robert Gould Shaw of the 54th Massachusetts Colored Infantry Regiment in the Civil War.

As with most children in the predominantly African American neighborhood in which the Selden-Chambers found themselves, Larry was now enrolled at the segregated Lucretia Mott elementary school in the fourth grade.

It is hard to imagine the Captain of *Midway*—a man who happened to be the first African American to become the commanding officer of a capital ship who was responsible for one of the world's largest floating cities, and who managed a crew of over 4,500 men, treating each equally without regard to race, color, or ethnicity—grew up in the segregated Jim Crow South. In formal discussions with men who served under Captain Chambers all commented on his leadership skills, strength and fairness.

Larry attributes these characteristics, in great part, to his grandfather's lessons of life. Larry and his siblings moved to Washington near the height of the world's great economic depression and the political and religious turmoil in Europe. In response to the need to monitor the escalating war in Europe, the War Department was becoming a very busy and active place. During this time while Charlotte Chambers worked long hours to support her family, her parents' influence over the grandchildren was profound. The ability of her parents to help raise her children was profound because it allowed her to spend the hours providing for her family while being assured her children were receiving the best of care and life lessons from their grandparents through loving discipline.

Even though he was extremely intelligent and worldly, as the son of a former slave, Clement Selden was a victim of his circumstances and would never have the opportunities that his grandchildren would have. But Clement knew that each of his grandchildren would be part of a promising future. His wisdom left an indelible mark on all of his grandchildren, particularly his grandson Larry.

At the dinner table, Clement Selden would challenge his grandchildren in discussions about the events in Europe and America. He would encourage them to read African American newspapers and to draw parallels between what was going on in the Jewish ghettos in Europe and the African American communities in America. He would then draw inferences between the harsh treatment of the Jews, being forcibly taken from their homes all across Europe and sent to concentration camps, and the Africans who were brought forcibly to America in the seventeenth, eighteenth and nineteenth centuries.

Chambers' grandfather Clement was always careful to express neither bitterness toward, nor hatred of, any particular group. Instead, he directed his grandchildren's discussion to the importance of self-worth and self-reliance in order to succeed in life. Clement wanted to make sure that his grandchildren were proud of where they came from, but also that they took personal responsibility for where they were going in life. Even though they were growing up in a segregated world they were as good as anyone else no matter where they lived.

While Larry's grandfather instilled in him a sense of honor and duty Larry's grandmother, of whom he has extremely fond memories, reminded

Bedford County, Virginia, circa 1888. Rear Admiral Larry Chamber's maternal great-grandmother, Alice Henry with her infant daughter Gladys Henry (Selden) (personal collection).

him to remain humble, respectful and pious. Chambers' speaks of his grandmother as a saint and believes that his mother and sisters inherited many of her traits. Of his grandmother Larry says, "She was fantastic. She was a midwife for a large number of births in the Black community back home and in Washington, D.C." He adds, "As far as I know, she may have also been midwife on some of the white births." Of the lessons his grandmother taught him Chambers believes the most important, which he still carries with him today, to be "keep your mouth shut, take your punishment, and be reverent."

Larry is Episcopalian, and as a child, his grandmother made sure he went to church regularly. When the family moved to D.C. everyone except Larry's grandfather went to St. George's Episcopal Church. To Gladden's annoyance Clement Selden insisted someone had to stay home to keep an eye on the house while the family was at church.

Bedford County, Virginia, circa 1925. Rear Admiral Larry Chamber's maternal grandmother, Gladys Henry Selden (personal collection).

For several summers Larry worked in the bishop's quarters at the National Cathedral in Washington, D.C., as a bus boy. He recalls it as a "delightful experience. When the Bishop entertained other religious heads or politicians, we supported him every way that we could." Larry's active participation in church encouraged the Bishop to write a letter of recommendation for Larry's college application. Larry was "touched and honored all at the same time."

Not until he was much older did Larry fully understand and appreciate all the challenges that his grandfather went through as the son of slaves. His grandfather's brother, Bob Selden, contin-

Bedford County, Virginia. At the end of each summer, before school started, Larry Chambers as a young teenager would visit with his Uncle Theodore Selden and family (Charlotte's brother) (personal collection).

ued to live in Bedford, Virginia. Larry's Great Uncle Bob shared with him the social and economic hardships their family had faced when they were growing up as well as stories of the treatment they had received as children of freedmen in the aftermath of the Civil War.

Uncle Bob told Larry that during the Depression hardly anybody had a job, and so everyone relied on the barter system. Although most were poor, nobody wanted a handout. When Larry's father buried somebody the farmers would pay him with the produce that they grew since they didn't have money to pay for the burial services. The community of Bedford, Virginia, as with most communities south of the Mason-Dixon Line, was a segregated community, and although Washington, D.C., was the nation's capital, it was also a segregated city. When the Chambers family moved to the African American neighborhood of 7th and T Streets Northwest, segregation was all that Larry knew. His neighbors were Black, his friends were Black and his teachers were Black. Life in a segregated city was difficult during the 1930s and 40s and D.C. was no different. For Larry, his siblings, and their friends, racial segregation was all that they knew of the world.

After the Civil War and Reconstruction the United States Supreme Court set the stage for the establishment of the Jim Crow laws based on several of its decisions, including the Court's landmark decision in *Plessey v. Ferguson* which affirmed that "separate but equal" was constitutional. The Jim Crow laws essentially made the segregation of races legal. The laws ensured that the Black population would be racially segregated, have limited access to educational opportunities and inadequate employment opportunities.

In Washington, D.C., wealthy whites lived west of Rock Creek Park, and everyone else lived on the other side of the park. It was a city where public accommodations, such as water fountains, were labeled "White Only," and entrances at the rear of the building were meant for African Americans. It was a city where the signs to those entrances read "Black Only," and where the foundation of public education was tiered into well-funded white schools and underfunded Black schools. It was a city where experienced teachers, new textbooks, and state-of-the-art facilities were always found in white neighborhoods and dilapidated facilities and worn textbooks were the norm in Black neighborhoods.

Although segregation was legal throughout all of Larry's youth, his mother and grandparents made sure that the Chambers children were exposed to more than just the segregated neighborhood of 7th and T Streets Northwest. Once he was able to travel on his own Larry and his friends would borrow the weekly passes for the streetcars and buses that were purchased by working families and would eagerly go to the museums. "During those days," Chambers shares, "we could go to the museums without being confronted with many racial problems, unlike the department stores or other public accommodations in the city where the old Jim Crow signs were strategically posted."

As teenagers, they spent "many, many Sundays going to the museums, including the Museum of Natural History, the Corcoran Art Gallery, and the

National Air Museum." Chambers says that he practically lived in the National Air Museum. Every month or two the exhibits changed, and with each change, Larry—who dreamed of becoming an aviator—always found something that fascinated him. He would study the airplanes for hours at a time only to return home and spend hours building models of his favorite military planes.

Once he became a teenager, neither his mother nor his grandfather would tolerate any misbehavior from Larry. But Grandmother Gladden Selden was the real disciplinarian in the family. Larry was often a good-natured troublemaker with his siblings, and since Gladden knew Larry was the instigator in the household, on many occasions Larry would be the one she punished even if she wasn't sure he was the one to blame. When he protested his innocence his grandmother would firmly state that the punishment was for today and "the yesterdays when I didn't catch you." The memory still makes Larry smile, and he believes that in the end "I got the better deal because I got away with more mischief than I got caught for."

As some of the boys were hotwiring cars to steal so that they could take their girlfriends out on dates, Larry was home studying. As older boys were sneaking beer and stronger alcohol, and sometimes engaging in drug use on the street corner, Charlotte Chambers gave Larry money to go see the latest movie at the Lincoln Theater or live entertainment such as Duke Ellington at the segregated Howard Theater. Though an "amiable rabble-rouser" at home Larry was never tempted by the vices of his peers.

Larry's grandfather always pointed to the looks of despair on relatively young Black men who seemed to be glued to the same corner day after day, week after week, and whose lives were being devastated by alcohol and drugs. Clement Selden consistently reminded Larry that he could accomplish more and was expected to accomplish more. Any type of behavior like the men on the corner would not be condoned or tolerated. Clement also told each of his grandchildren that one day it would be their responsibility to give back to the community and they would not be able to do that if they were behind bars or had a criminal record.

Larry shares that it never occurred to him that he wasn't going to be at the head of his class; after all, at home that bar was set so high that it was also expected of all his siblings. As a self-confessed "nerd" when he first moved to Washington, D.C., Larry was confronted by several bullies. But he soon befriended twin brothers in his class, Oscar and Arthur Walden. He became good friends with Oscar and says, "It was a mutually beneficial relationship because I helped him with his homework and he beat the crap out of the kids who were trying to bully me." Chambers adds, "Once that got established, nobody bothered me anymore and we all played together, and that was the end of it."

Larry Chambers, who would become the second African American to reach Flag rank in the U.S. Navy, firmly believed that his childhood years reflected an innate strength of character and were pivotal for molding him into the military leader that he would become.

The coded signal had been given and the largest helicopter evacuation in history was about to commence. Chambers' years of preparation and expert training would now be tested, and the world would see what he was truly made of. Just thirty days into his assignment as captain of one of the world's largest and most powerful aircraft carriers ever built, was Larry Chambers, the boy from Bedford, Virginia, and the segregated streets of Washington, D.C., ready to meet the challenge?

Chapter 2

The Dunbar Years

Rear Admiral Chambers' career as a Naval flag officer was grounded in the strong work ethic he had learned during the Depression in Bedford, Virginia. He attributes his ability to handle stressful situations such as the complex military maneuvers involving the evacuation of thousands of refugees during Operation Frequent Wind to the discipline learned during his years at Dunbar High School in Washington, D.C.

The Great Depression of the 1930s and the entrance of the United States into World War II in 1939 caused financial havoc in virtually every home in America. Having five teenagers getting ready to go off to college, every dollar was being stretched for Charlotte Chambers who was a clerical worker in the War Department.

As the war progressed, opportunities for Washington's growing African American population began to emerge as a result of the wartime economy. Slowly, government jobs, although most were low level, were now being made available due to a labor shortage caused by large numbers of men going off to war. Incrementally, a Black middle class began to take shape and the values of middle class America developed all across the city in several historically Black neighborhoods. With surplus money came the growth and expansion of social clubs, an increase of faith-based community and identity and a strong emphasis on education.

Charlotte Chambers, the smart, tenacious and beautiful widowed mother who had been denied opportunities as a younger woman because of her race in segregated Bedford, Virginia, would make sure that each of her children was not denied those same opportunities. Charlotte worked extra hours at the War Department because she wanted more for her children. By the 1940s, as with most African American communities across the nation, the lines of the segregated streets of Washington, D.C., were blurred between thriving working class and middle class neighborhoods and those streets where thugs, hoodlums, numbers runners and dealers roamed, looking for their next victims. Charlotte worked too hard to have her children engaged in what she believed to be "low-life behavior" that certainly would not be tolerated in her home. She took every measure possible to make sure that they would attend the best schools. She made sure that they participated in after school and weekend activities that would develop their bodies, minds and spirits.

Charlotte ensured that her children were academically prepared and attended the prestigious college preparatory African American Dunbar High School in Washington, D.C. Dunbar's reputation was known for its stellar educational rigor not only in Washington, but in elite African American circles nationwide. While many have credited Rear Admiral Chambers' excellent military training to his time at Annapolis, they didn't realize that the foundation of his military training started at Dunbar High School, and his mother Charlotte was instrumental in making sure he got the best education at one of the nation's premier high schools.

Dunbar High School was a "segregated and underfinanced institution that was an educational marvel." The faculty, populated entirely of Black teachers, had a surprising number of PhDs and could have taught at higher level universities were it not for segregation. In addition, the school's "achievement levels were well above the national average."[1] Dunbar students were expected to become national leaders in their chosen fields, and Larry recalls many of his teachers revealed that their coursework was being taught as a college level course by some of the nation's best teachers to provoke the expectation that if you could do well at Dunbar, you would excel at any college or university nationwide.

According to an article in *The New Yorker*, Dunbar High School was the first public high school for Blacks in the United States and educated more notable Black professionals and public servants than any other high school in America. Originally known as the Preparatory High School for Colored Youth, Dunbar "was founded by William Syphax, who would have called himself a person of color." In 1868, Syphax was employed as a copyist (he made skilled copies by hand before printing became prevalent) in the Department of the Interior and "Syphax was appointed the first chairman of the Board of Trustees of the Colored Public Schools in the District of Columbia." While initially colored public schools referred only to elementary schools, "two years after his appointment, [Syphax] used his office to organize the Preparatory High School."[2]

During segregation, according to *The New Yorker*, "advocates of segregated education [pointed] with relief to the example of Dunbar High, an all-black school." In contrast, "opponents of segregation [found] it hard to believe that an all-black school, especially in a southern town like Washington could have had such an exceptional record of achievement."³ An important part of the answer is that among segregated schools, Dunbar was unique, and became so almost by accident. It was not racially segregated education that made Dunbar the success it was, but a combination of its students' social class and a peculiar set of historical circumstances that existed in the early years of its development.⁴ These circumstances were what produced Dunbar's faculty, the best that any all-Black high school had ever had.⁵

As with most Dunbar graduates, Chambers boasted about the high caliber of teachers at the school and the instructors he had in particular, stating that all of the teachers at Dunbar High School had earned bachelor's, master's and doctoral degrees, a remarkable feat for southern schools, particularly for segregated southern schools. Chambers is proud of the stellar reputation of the school and the eminent qualifications of his high school teachers. He believes that his instructors were the best of the best and that they were truly qualified. No matter what classroom a student went into, there was a skilled teacher. Larry says, "My Math teacher had a Ph.D., my Biology teacher had a Ph.D., my Physics teacher had a Ph.D., and all of my English teachers had master's degrees." He continues, "I benefited from their knowledge and expertise. That's why when former Dunbar students went to the tough Ivy League colleges, we didn't have to take remedial classes, we trained and we were prepared." Chambers believes that he had better instruction in high school than he did when he went off to college and to graduate school.

As reported in *The New Yorker*, many of the stellar Dunbar teachers were members of Phi Beta Kappa society, the oldest honor society in the country that acknowledges collegiate academic excellence in liberal arts and sciences.

According to *The New Yorker*, this was made possible by several factors, including the fact that the federal government paid Black teachers in Washington the same salaries as white teachers, possibly the only place in the South where such parity existed—a policy alone that might have been enough to attract highly qualified teachers. Many of the exceptional Black teachers who came to Dunbar had turned to teaching only because there was not much else for them to do. In the early years of Dunbar's history, Black college graduates—however well trained, however brilliant—were seldom hired by white institutions in any serious intellectual capacity. Those who were not lucky enough to be lawyers or doctors, and who did not wish to be postal clerks, low-level government workers, soldiers, Pullman porters or manual laborers found that teaching was the most distinguished career open to them. Those who resorted to teaching either joined the faculty of a Black university like Howard University or headed for Dunbar High School.⁶

The success of Dunbar High was not limited just to the quality of its teachers, but also the dedication of the Dunbar parents. According to Chambers, students' grades were carefully monitored and when a student, for whatever reason, didn't do his or her work or wasn't doing well in school, the teachers called home, and in those days, "Home took care of home, and immediately took care of the problem no matter what it was." Charlotte Chambers, who understood the importance of an education to succeed in a segregated society, made sure that from the time her children entered elementary school that they got a solid educational foundation. The children's grandparents, Clement and Gladden Selden, further reinforced this when she was not at home.

The family lived on a regulated schedule with dinner at six every evening after school activities. After dinner, they all sat around the kitchen table to do schoolwork, regardless of their age. Charlotte, who received the strong support of her parents, would help the older children who in turn took responsibility to help the younger two. In the Chambers' household, academic achievement and competition was expected from each child. Saying that something was too hard was unacceptable and was never a valid excuse for not doing better.

The four younger Chambers children attended the prestigious Dunbar High in Washington, D.C., during the height of World War II. For Larry, Dunbar's curriculum was tough, but one that he was able to navigate. It was a prerequisite for all of the students to take a romance language so Larry took Latin for two years. He then studied German as a foreign language his junior and senior years in high school. While at Dunbar High, Larry, and his younger brother, Andrew, enrolled in the Reserved Officer Training Corps (ROTC) program. Chambers attributed much of the success in his personal and military careers to the academic and life lessons learned at Dunbar High School and its Cadet Corps.

The Reserve Officer's Training Corps began as early as 1819. In 1916, President Woodrow Wilson signed the National Defense Act of 1916, where he brought the program under a single federally controlled program. The Junior ROTC program encouraged promising high school students to develop positive citizenship skills and to pursue an education in one of the military academies upon completion of their high school education. With millions of American boys enlisting and being drafted into the military during World War II, many African American leaders across the country believed that the ROTC would provide exceptional young African American men the path to becoming officers within the segregated United States military.

In her book, *First Class: The Legacy of Dunbar, America's First Black Public High School*, Alison Stewart writes that hundreds of African American "high school [students] … learned discipline, integrity and perseverance…. More than an after school military training activity or a club, the Corps was a life experience, one that fed the Dunbar ecosystem of excellence." The U.S. Infantry Drill regulations and the training manual from which lessons were modeled can best sum up the goal of the Corps: "The object of all military training is to win battles. Everything that you do in military training is done with some immediate object in view, which, in turn, has in view the final object of winning battles." The immediate objective at Dunbar was getting a good education. The final object was advancing the opportunities for African Americans.

Military instruction or joining an athletic team was mandatory for Dunbar men. The intent was that a Dunbar man had to be well rounded. If you were going to succeed either at a prominent Ivy League institution or in the business world, you had to be well rounded. In between his military instruction, Larry ran cross-country track, joined the golf team and played scrimmage football. However, at 135 pounds, he was discouraged from competing against the bigger boys.

Dunbar was all about competition and discipline. Whatever was thrown at Larry and his fellow classmates, Dunbar would give them the training necessary to overcome. Larry's math, biology and history teachers were extremely tough and kept piling on course material, and according to Larry, "The more you did, the more they piled on new coursework." Larry and his good friend Bruce Gabriel took all of their classes together, studied together and challenged each other in their studies.

One of the main strengths of Dunbar was that the teachers were not only tough, but they were also nurturing. "If we fell every now and then," Chambers says, "they would pick us up, but once we were back on our feet, they threw us back into the game. It wasn't perfect, but they prepared us for life."

Dunbar also provided Chambers with role models. Several Tuskegee Airmen who were not much older than Larry and his classmates would come by Dunbar High School and watch the Dunbar Cadets march. "These guys were sharp!" says Larry. He adds, "They stood tall, they shared their adventures, and they provided us with tips on how to improve our drill formation." Larry admired these aviators and knew that one day he wanted to be just like them.

The ROTC cadets were required to participate in many drills—or, according to Larry, "Too many drills." They had close order drills. They had marching drills. It seemed to him that they had a minimum of two or three days a week of just marching drills. Larry recalls, "We were so indoctrinated into just doing military drills that we thought it was part of the game." When the cadets were reprimanded for even small mistakes, Larry says, "We just stood there and took the verbal abuse.... Just like they did in the movies, we would just hop-to like good 'wooden soldiers.'"

The Corps was made up of companies of platoons broken down into squads. The ranks of colonel and captain were based on academic standing and military aptitude. The cadets were part of everyday life at Dunbar. They could be seen marching in formation in the armory, the open center of the first floor of the Dunbar building. Each year, Dunbar's Drill Team, with their rifles and military gear, would compete against other high school drill teams. At the time, a young Larry Chambers was most proud of being Colonel of the Cadet Corps. As Dunbar was the number-one ranked Black high school, Larry was given the privilege of leading the ROTC procession before President and Mrs. Roosevelt. But Larry was crushed when he learned that prestigious honor would occur the same day as his entrance exam for the Naval Academy. The most important day of his young life was snatched away, and "[my] deputy got all the glory that I was supposed to get, all because I had to take what I thought at that particular moment was a stupid exam."

During Larry's senior year of high school, the most difficult decision, unlike most high school students across the country, wasn't if he was going to go to college, but how the family would finance his education. Thanks to his stellar academic record and the discipline of the ROTC program, Chambers was accepted by the prestigious Ivy League college Harvard University and the Massachusetts Institute for Technology (MIT) in 1948. Unfortunately, he was only provided with partial financial scholarships for each school. As hard as his mother worked, Larry was extremely sensitive to the fact that she would not be able to afford the costs of the colleges in Boston, no matter how hard she would try.

However, the financial conditions of the Chambers family would have a profound effect on the eventual military careers of Rear Admiral Chambers and his brother Andrew who later became a Lieutenant General in the U.S. Army. Larry was a smart kid and knew how hard life was for his mother and the sacrifices she endured to take care of her parents and her five children. He knew his mother would work extra jobs if she had to. That's what Dunbar parents did, and the school had an alternative suggestion for the Chambers' family.

As Black congressmen and their supporters began the internal debate with the Roosevelt White House over desegregation of the armed forces, their civil rights argument was grounded in the success of African Americans in the military during World War II. The success of the Tuskegee Airmen was crucial evidence in debunking misconceptions about African American ability in combat roles, which further supported integration of the armed forces.

From World War I to after World War II, the United States Armed Forces was a reflection of American society, including the practice of a segregated, Jim Crow military. American society was predicated on the assumption that one race was superior and the other race was inferior, and the United States military was a window to these beliefs. Despite the need for African American men in the military, a series of reports were published supporting ill-conceived notions that African Americans "lacked courage and the mental capacity" to serve as soldiers. However, these claims were not supported by facts or any actual test results.[7] In fact, once the test results were made public, they showed a very different outcome.[8] African Americans in the North actually scored significantly higher than their white counterparts from the South, raising many issues as to why and how this could be possible.

Figure 1: Test Results of Black and White Soldiers, Army Results, 1918

Southern Whites		Northern Blacks	
Mississippi	41.25	Pennsylvania	42.00
Kentucky	41.50	New York	45.00
Arkansas	41.55	Illinois	47.35
Georgia	42.12	Ohio	49.50

Source: R. M. Yerkes, "Psychological Examining in the U.S. Army," National Academy of Sciences, Vol. 15 (1921), in Broadnax, *Blue Skies, Black Wings*.

Throughout World War I and early into World War II, as African Americans were recruited, they served in the most menial of tasks. During World War I, African American men served only as a cooks and laborers, and although many of them wanted to be pilots, they were rejected by the United States Army Air Corps. As African American political, business and religious leaders all across the country continued to address the racial injustices of Jim Crow laws, they knew the military was yet another obstacle to overcome before they could achieve racial equality.

In the late 1920s, African American aviation social clubs appeared and by 1936 "some thirty-seven African American flying clubs had been organized."[9] As African Americans became more interested in aviation, and as civil rights organizations became more interested in the role of African Americans in the military, it was inevitable that the two would merge into a coordinated voice advocating for integration of the United States Armed Forces, particularly the Army Air Corps. From its inception, the Army Air Corps was considered the most elite branch of the United States military. As the military's "most aristocratic unit," its advertising depicted a strikingly handsome white airman with a "trailing white silk scarf draped around the neck, highly polished boots, and the long-stemmed Prince Albert pipe." With this kind of glamour, "the Air Corps stood out as the ultimate branch of the Army."[10]

In 1939, German Chancellor Adolf Hitler marched across Europe and invaded the Czechoslovakian capital city of Prague. He also declared war against one of the United States' strongest allies, Great Britain. Although the United States had declared neutrality in Europe's affairs, it prepared its military apparatus as a precaution. As the war in Europe escalated, in the same year the United States Congress, under continued pressure from civil rights groups, established the Civil Pilot Training Program at six Black colleges, including Delaware State College, Hampton Institute, Howard College, North Carolina A&T College, Tuskegee Institute, West Virginia State College and the private Coffey School in Chicago. This would become "an important breakthrough in allowing African Americans to participate in federally funded flight training programs."[11] Despite the effort of Congress, the Army delayed the program.

The 1940 "presidential election created a heated context in which to demand the end of racism in the American military, and President Roosevelt, seeking an unprecedented third term, needed the black vote."[12] While the "civilians and military leadership of the army" were publically indicating that they were moving forward with the admittance of "black aviation mechanics" there was very little movement, if any, on the admittance of African Americans to the Army Air Corps. To combat this delay, "Walter White, executive Secretary of the National Association for the Advancement of Colored People (NAACP) prevailed on Mrs. Eleanor Roosevelt to arrange a meeting for him and A. Phillip Randolph, President of the Brotherhood of Sleeping Car Porters." White also arranged for "T. Arnold Hill, acting head of the National Urban League, to meet with President Roosevelt on September 27, 1940."[13]

After the meeting, President Roosevelt came forward with a number of mandates signaling that African American pilots and mechanics would be used, and on October 24, 1940, under much pressure, the "Air Corps was directed to abandon its long-standing refusal to admit Blacks and was obliged to develop a detailed plan for the establishment of the unit that would be ultimately known as the Ninety-ninth Pursuit Squadron."[14] Despite the President's best efforts, the military was not moving fast enough, and by December 1940, "The agitation over the Army Air Corps participation reached fever pitch ... when the NAACP's monthly magazine *The Crisis* showed a U.S. Army training airplane in flight over Randolph Field, Texas with the caption 'FOR WHITES ONLY.'"[15]

As civil rights groups continued to protest the military's lack of progress in admitting African Americans, they also discussed the insurmountable unemployment of African Americans as a result of the nation's economic depression. Civil rights groups pressed the President for reforms in the hiring process, particularly since the defense industry had expanded tremendously as a result of the growing wartime economy thanks in large part to federal support and dollars, and though the industry was hiring millions of Americans, very few were African American.

On June 25, 1941, President Franklin D. Roosevelt issued Executive Order 8802, which ended "racial discrimination in the hiring practices of the defense industries and the War Department, and decreed by Executive mandate that Blacks could be admitted to training in the Army Air Corps."[16] After many promises and a long delay, in July 1941, the U.S. Army Air Corps training program for African American pilots was formed. On March 7, 1942, five graduates completed the program at the Tuskegee Army Airfield Flying School and comprised the Class of 42 Colored.

On Sunday, December 7, 1941, the government of Japan attacked the United States Pacific Naval Fleet by bombing the naval base at Pearl Harbor. The United States government was now at war. The Japanese bombing had destroyed much of the United States naval fleet, except the aircraft carriers in the Pacific. The American defense industry went into expanded wartime production and built a number of amphibious assault ships, cruisers, destroyers, submarines, transport docks and aircraft carriers to transport fighter planes and bombers. The United States defense industry developed a series of new generation aviation fighters and bombers.

When the United States entered the war, training for cadets at the Tuskegee Institute was already underway. The original 99th Fighter Squadron was sent overseas in 1943. The 332nd Fighter Group, which initially only included three squadrons (the 100th, the 301st, and the 302nd) was deployed overseas in 1944. Young men took the rigorous U.S. Army Air Corps' psychological research unit's standardized test that reportedly measured a prospective candidate's dexterity, intelligence and potential leadership qualities. The tests were administered to all of the prospective candidates, white and Black. The Army Air Corps used the tests as an instrument to ensure that only the "most skilled and intelligent young men would be allowed into the program." Many were surprised that young African American men scored high on the test, rebutting any claims that they were ill prepared or lacked the intellectual skills to fly complicated aircraft.[17]

The graduates of the Tuskegee Army Airfield were the first African American military aviators in the United States. They flew in high performance military fighter planes in combat missions. In order to distinguish themselves from other fighter groups, the 332nd Fighter Group painted the tails of their P-51 Mustang airplanes a bright red. This enabled the pilots of the U.S. bombers to know that they were being accompanied by the fighters of the Tuskegee Institute training program and were in trusted hands. Because of their bravery, despite all the challenges they went through, this group of "Red Tail Pilots" was respected by white and Black Americans alike. During their service in World War II, the Tuskegee Airmen achieved an impressive military record:

932 pilots were trained for high performance combat pilots from 1941 to 1946

355 were deployed overseas and 80 lost their lives

1579 combat missions were flown by the 99th Squadron and the 339 Fighter Group

179 bomber escort missions

129 reconnaissance escorts

of the 312 combat mission with an excellent record of protection with only a loss of 26 bombers

409 enemy aircraft destroyed or damaged

112 enemy aircraft destroyed in air-to-air combat with only 12 Red Tail pilots were shot down (10-to-1 ratio)

950 rail cars, trucks and other motor vehicles destroyed

One destroyer put out of action

40 boats and barges destroyed

Despite their achievements, the Tuskegee Airman endured racial discrimination throughout most of their training by civilian and military members of the United States Armed Forces, both in the United States and while serving their country overseas. Despite the initial perception that the Tuskegee Airmen were not qualified to serve and did not fit the white Anglo-Saxon perception of what a U.S. Army Corps' pilot should look like, their military record as pilots was distinguished. The Red Tail pilots were awarded some of the nation's highest military honors.[18] The national recognition and awards of the Tuskegee Airmen are as follows:

Three Distinguished Unit Citations

99th Pursuit Squadron: 30 May–11 June 1943 for actions over Sicily

99th Fighter Squadron: 12–14 May 1944: for successful air strikes against Monte Cassino, Italy

332d Fighter Group (and its 99th, 100th, 301st, and 302nd Fighter Squadrons): March 24, 1945: for a bomber escort mission to Berlin, during which it destroyed 3 M262 enemy jets, probably destroyed two others and a M163 Rocket Plane, and damaged 3 jets.

At least one Silver Star

96 Distinguished Flying Crosses

14 Bronze Stars

744 Air Medals

8 Purple Hearts

The Red Tail Pilots had shown great heroism on the battlefield and earned the respect of their white peers and military commanders. However, once the war was over and the legendary Black pilots returned stateside, the racism they had endured prior to the war didn't end just because the war had. Despite the success of the U.S. Army Air Corps training program at Tuskegee Institute, and the caliber and military achievements of the Red Tail pilots, their treatment back home after the war, combined with the ill treatment of African Americans in general, caused civil rights organizations including the NAACP and the Urban League to pressure Congress and the President to address the issue of African Americans in the Armed Forces and segregation in society as a whole.[19]

Civil rights organizations prompted public discussion as to the merits of the United States Congress Civil Pilot Training Program at Tuskegee Institute and the other five Black colleges, and whether the intellectual abilities of African American high school students to enter and succeed in military academies could be replicated on a national level. African American Congressman William Levi Dawson of Illinois, along with other African American elected officials nationwide, argued that if an African American student were provided the same opportunity as a white student, he would be able to pass the military school exam and excel in these rigorous programs.

Congressman Dawson endorsed 35 candidates to take the Naval Academy entrance exam, a number of whom were African American. This endorsement came with his promise that if they passed, he would recommend them for admission to the United States Naval Academy. Of the 35 students who actually took the exam, Chambers, an African American from Washington, D.C.'s segregated Dunbar High School, was the only applicant to pass.

True to his word, Congressman Dawson nominated Chambers for entrance into the Naval Academy in Annapolis, Maryland. There he could be educated at no expense to his widowed mother. Although MIT had been Chambers' first choice, he realized that his decision to attend the Naval Academy would mean that his family could afford to send both of his younger brothers to Howard University. Chambers had been raised to put family first and he never hesitated in his acceptance of Congressman Dawson's nomination.

During Chambers' senior year at Dunbar High School, he was chosen as Colonel of the High School Cadet Corp. At his graduation in 1948 he was class valedictorian, an honor earned by the student with the highest grade point average, and he delivered the student graduation address. In July after graduation, Chambers prepared to join Wesley Brown and Reeves Taylor as the only three African American Midshipmen at the virtually all-white United States Naval Academy.

Chapter 3

The Annapolis Years

When President Franklin Delano Roosevelt died of a cerebral hemorrhage on April 12, 1945, and Harry S Truman became the President of the United States, one of his first orders of business was overseeing, along with England's Winston Churchill and the Soviet Union's Joseph Stalin, the May 8, 1945, Allied victory in Europe. While the Germans had surrendered, the Japanese Emperor refused to surrender, prompting President Truman to make one of the most difficult decisions of World War II, and the United States dropped two nuclear atomic bombs over the island of Japan. The first atomic bomb was dropped over the city of Hiroshima, and three days later, the second atomic bomb was dropped over the city of Nagasaki. On August 15, 1945, the Second World War came to an end with the surrender of the Japanese government. This was quickly followed by the formation of the United Nations:

> *In the aftermath of World War II, on October 24, 1945, an international body to be known as the United Nations was formed to maintain international peace and security, to develop friendly relations among nations and to promote social progress, better living standards and human rights.—United Nations*

In the war's aftermath, the United States changed drastically, and soldiers returned home to a booming post-war economy that swelled the ranks of the middle class. The nation, having endured two long and costly world wars, wanted a world at peace and became a founding member of the United Nations. African Americans, having gained new freedoms and economic opportunity, wanted parity in all aspects of American living. But what the nation and its new President did not realize was that in a few short years the desire for peace and prosperity would not coincide with geopolitical realities.

After World War II, civil rights groups pushed even harder toward full equality for African Americans across the country. As the nation grasped the full impact of the racial genocide and atrocities committed in Europe against

3. The Annapolis Years

the Jews, the Romani and homosexuals, many found the United States' attitude toward its African American citizens hypocritical. As African American veterans returned home only to be discriminated against, beaten and maimed, many Americans became concerned over the country's racism, including President Harry S Truman:

> "My very stomach turned," he told a friend shortly after the war, "when I learned that Negro soldiers just back from overseas were being dumped out of Army trucks in Mississippi and beaten." Referring to an incident in which a returning soldier ... had lost his sight. Truman continued: "When a mayor and a city marshal can take a Negro sergeant off a bus in South Carolina, beat him up and put out one of his eyes, and nothing is done by the state authorities, something is radically wrong with the system."[1]

On July 26, 1948, President Truman promulgated Executive Order 9981, which ended racial discrimination and segregation in all aspects of the United States armed services, including housing and training. With the signing of the Executive Order, for the first time in modern history, African Americans joined the armed forces hoping to advance far and successfully in an integrated military.

A month earlier on June 30, 1948, Larry Chambers packed his bags and entered the United States Naval Academy, a four-year federal service academy located in Annapolis, Maryland, as a midshipman.

The United States Naval Academy, commonly referred to as Annapolis, was established in 1845 under Secretary of the Navy George Bancroft. It is the second oldest of the United States' five service academies. The 330-acre campus serves as the training ground for officers commissioning into the United States Navy and Marine Corps.

As with the other service academies, the Naval Academy was steeped in tradition, challenges and obstacles, all of which helped Chambers become an effective and decisive leader in combat and life. However, like the other segregated military academies in 1948, Annapolis had a longstanding reputation of poor race relations, a reflection of the overall attitude of the Department of the Navy. For example, in April 1941, Superintendent Rear Admiral Russell Wilson refused to allow the school's all-white lacrosse team to play a visiting team from Harvard University because the Harvard team included Lucien Alexis, Jr., an African American player. According to Alexis' daughter, Lurita Alexis Doan, "The academy insisted that my father, the only black team member, be removed, declaring that no midshipman would take the field with a colored man."[2]

After the 1941 incident at Annapolis in which the school refused to play an athletic event if a visiting black athlete attended, A. Philip Randolph, President of the Brotherhood of Sleeping Car Porters, pulled together civil rights leaders across the nation with the objective to end segregation in the entire United States military and its academies.

African American members of Congress, including Congressman William Levi Dawson and Congressman Adam Clayton Powell, along with leaders of key civil rights organizations such as the NAACP, the Brotherhood of Sleeping Car Porters, the Urban League and the National Council of Negro Women put tremendous pressure on the White House and threatened to conduct a massive protest on Washington, D.C.

Of the military branches, the United States Navy stood out in its poor race relations and its opposition to desegregating its ranks. Morris J. MacGregor Jr., from the Department of Defense Center of Military History, in his book *Integration of the Armed Forces, 1940–1965*, said the period between World War I and World War II "marked the nadir of the Navy's relations with Black America. Although the exclusion of Negroes that began with a clause introduced in enlistment regulations in 1922 lasted but a decade, black participation in the Navy remained severely restricted." According to MacGregor, "in June 1940 the Navy had 4,007 black personnel, 2.3 percent of its nearly 170,000 man total. All were enlisted men, and with the exception of six regular rated seamen, lone survivors of the exclusion clause, all were steward's mates, labeled by the black press "seagoing bellhops."[3]

The Navy's policy makers believed that the close quarters in which seamen had to live and sleep in would be detrimental to white sailors if they had to interact or bunk with black seamen. The Navy's personnel office, the Bureau of Navigation, opposed any changes to its policy on race relations. The bureau "reasoned that since segregation was impractical exclusion was necessary. Experience had proved, the bureau claimed, that when given supervisory responsibility the Negro was unable to maintain discipline among white subordinates with the result that teamwork, harmony, and ship's efficiency suffered. The Negro, therefore, had to be segregated from the white sailor."[4]

It was the Navy's segregationist polices, embedded with Jim Crow attitudes and philosophies of the South, that not surprisingly caused civil rights organizations and their supporters in Congress to demand a change in overall military policy. On June 25, 1941, President Roosevelt signed Executive Order 8802, Prohibition of Discrimination in the Defense Industry, stating, "It is the policy of the United States to encourage full participation in the national defense program by all citizens of the United States, regardless of race, creed, color, or national origin." Through his executive powers, the President ordered, "All departments and agencies of the Government of the United States concerned with vocational and training programs for defense production shall take special measures appropriate to assure that such programs are administered without discrimination because of race, creed, color, or national origin."[5]

Seven years later, upon entering the Naval Academy in the summer of 1948, Chambers was immediately impressed with both the rigorous academics and physical programs of the institution. The curriculum at the Naval Academy was grounded in academic programs of science, technology, engineering and mathematics. The courses were designed to make the entering trainee class think critically and begin the process of developing leadership and professional skills needed to command as naval officers. The Naval Academy's curriculum was specifically designed to ensure "that graduates are able to think critically, solve increasingly technical problems in a dynamic, global environment, and express conclusions clearly."[6]

The Academy's curriculum was designed to be challenging for all of its midshipmen in order to "teach the leadership and professional skills required of Navy and Marine Corps officers."[7] Midshipman Larry Chambers' strong academic background, acquired at Dunbar High School, gave him the foundation he needed to compete with his classmates and succeed.

Six African American students entered the doors at Annapolis before Chambers. He was recruited by Colonel Henry O. Atwood, head of the Cadet Corps (the equivalent of today's Junior ROTC program) at Washington, D.C.'s, black high schools. According to Chambers, Colonel Atwood, a retired military man, was the instructor for the Cadet Board, and "was instrumental in encouraging all of the Cadets to go on to college, and particularly interested in getting Cadets into the military academies." Colonel Atwood "was not a tall man and he was even-tempered, but he seemed larger than life, and demonstrated a strength and a resolve that we appreciated and respected."

From the time a student entered Dunbar High School until the time they left, Atwood worked on them. Atwood had been working in conjunction with Black members of Congress since the 1930s to find exceptional African American candidates for West Point and Annapolis. In the 1940s, he truly believed that one day and one day soon the military was going to desegregate, and so it was his job as part of the staff at Dunbar to prepare the next generation's men to lead the battle and win the war. As a recruiter, Atwood focused on selecting the best and brightest young Black men from Washington's four segregated high schools for a future in a service academy.

In his definitive book on the racial attitudes at Annapolis, *Blue & Gold and Black: Racial Integration of the U.S. Naval Academy*, Robert J. Schneller states that Colonel Henry O. Atwood had encouraged Wesley Brown, who had been a Cadet Corps colonel, to take the entrance exam. Brown accepted New York Congressman Adam Clayton Powell's offer of a full scholarship to attend the Naval Academy. According to Schneller, while Brown knew he would face challenges, he also knew he had the opportunity to do something groundbreaking, so Wesley Brown "made a conscious decision to try to break the color barrier at the Naval Academy, to serve his country and serve his race."[8]

Chambers and Wes Brown, along with other young men who would break the color barriers at military schools, knew of the challenges and obstacles they would face. In an attempt to prepare the young recruits for the harassment they would encounter, Colonel Atwood shared with them over and over again the story of the degradation that Benjamin O. Davis Jr. (who eventually became a Four Star General) endured when he enrolled in the military academy at West Point before he became its fourth Black graduate in 1936, and the first since 1889.

Chambers could not imagine the hell that General Davis went through at West Point. "For four years," shares Chambers, "not a living soul would speak to [General Davis], would sit with him, would eat with him, or show him any kind of human decency." Because of the negative treatment General Davis had received, Chambers was adamant and decided that he didn't want to take the West Point exam.

Despite the ill treatment, Benjamin Davis drew strength from isolation, which was a lesson that Colonel Atwood made sure his cadets understood. Benjamin Davis said these obstacles were the inspiration he needed to graduate, and graduate he did. He achieved the unthinkable in 1936 by graduating 35th in a class of 278. At the time a Colonel, Davis became the Commander of the Tuskegee Airmen.

As a teenage cadet at Dunbar, Chambers thought of General Davis as a legend, a man who succeeded despite the thinly veiled racism he had endured. Once Chambers finally had the opportunity to meet him at the first of many meetings, he told General Davis that he was a hero for all he had accomplished.

After the graduation of Benjamin O. Davis Jr., in 1936 and Wes Brown's acceptance of the Naval Academy's scholarship, there was tremendous pressure on civil right groups to continue finding exceptional Black high school students to follow in these men's footsteps and ensure the color barrier stayed broken. Civil rights advocates did not want Wes Brown's acceptance to the Academy to be an isolated incident.

Several exceptional academic students in the Washington, D.C., school system were identified, including Chambers. Even at a young age, Chambers understood that he was being groomed for academic excellence and to play a pivotal role in breaking down the color barrier. Colonel Atwood, as a mentor to Chambers, encouraged him to follow a path similar to the rigorous academic direction taken by Wes Brown. According to Chambers, Colonel Atwood knew that Chambers had received partial academic scholarships to Harvard and MIT but was having challenges raising the rest of the funds to fully pay tuition. He pushed Chambers hard to apply to the Naval Academy.

Like Brown, Chambers became Cadet Corps Colonel during his senior year of high school. Chambers remarked that even though he loved sports, he was not big enough to be a star athlete and would never be captain of a sports team, so he figured that being the head of the Cadet Corps was the next best thing.

Colonel Atwood remained keen on sending Black students to the Naval Academy. With Wes Brown a first classman at the time about to break the color barrier and be the school's first African American graduate in 1949, it was crucial to get an African American into the plebe class to keep it from "refreezing," as Chambers phrased it. Colonel Atwood pushed hard, and because of the potential financial incentives, convinced Chambers during college entrance exams to also apply to West Point and Annapolis, hoping Chambers would follow in Wesley Brown's footsteps. Chambers never did take the exam to West Point, but he finally took the Naval Academy entrance exam. The exam was heavily weighted toward engineering, science and mathematics, areas in which Chambers excelled.

Atwood arranged an interview with Representative William Dawson for Chambers and several other seniors. In April 1948, Chambers took the Naval Academy entrance exam along with 35 other prospective candidates. Of the candidates who took the exam, Chambers was the only one to pass. When Congressman Dawson's principal nominee failed to meet the entrance requirements, the Congressman decided to nominate Chambers to the Naval Academy.

Chambers had no college experience before becoming a midshipman unlike some of his classmates, many of whom had two years of college experience prior to attending Annapolis. While he found class work demanding, he had no major academic difficulties thanks to the college preparatory classes he took at Dunbar High School. His hardest subject was German, and the easiest were science and math.

Chambers has positive memories of his college roommates, each having now passed away. According to Chambers, "the kids today would call us three nerds, and they would be right. My college roommates, Pason Sierer from New York and Hugh Benton from Virginia, were two of the best and most supportive roommates one could have asked for." With a laugh, Chambers adds, "We were nerds, and we actually enjoyed studying in our room and challenging each other over complicated math, science, and engineering formulas and calculations."

Chambers' college dorm room was his sanctuary. Although he interacted with other classmates, he was all too familiar with the challenges Wes Brown had faced while breaking through the racial barriers at the school. Prior to Wes Brown, no African American had completed the four-year program with a degree. According to Chambers, as the young man who broke the actual color barrier, "Wes had it damn hard. He was called names that no man should be called. He was treated in a manner that no man should have to endure, and was challenged to do things that were downright mean-spirited."

During his first semester as a plebe, on several occasions Chambers seriously considered quitting school. But on each occasion he thought of his grandfather, Clement Selden, who always made Chambers feel like he was 10 feet tall. He always told his grandson that there was no challenge that he could not overcome and that quitting was never an acceptable answer to a complex challenge or problem. Chambers knew his recently departed grandfather was right. He was no quitter, and his detractors would have to try a whole lot harder if they thought they were going to break him.

Author Robert Schneller interviewed a number of the first African American men who enrolled at the Academy, and they shared with him some of the many challenges they encountered in the early days of the desegregation of the school and that

> During this period the Academy's culture reflected the racial attitudes of the American South. Many black plebes soon noticed the fact that racism was built into that culture. Racial slurs figured into the standard questions upper-classmen fired at plebes. "What's playing at the Star?" (a movie theater in a black neighborhood) went one such question. The approved answer, recalled a 1961 alumnus, was, "I didn't know you were dragging this weekend, sir." The answer implied that the upperclassman was dating a black female and derided him for doing so. The Navy song "Bible Stories" included the word "darkies" in the chorus. Another Navy song declared that the solution to the "vexing Chinese question" was to send "a hundred negro reg'ments" to China to "start a Coon Republic." Generations of white midshipmen referred to the janitors in Bancroft Hall, all of whom were black, as "mokes," an old racist slang term for "monkey." The 1936 edition of *Reef Points* defined *moke* as a "colored corridor boy or mess attendant." Although the word had disappeared from *Reef Points* by Wes Brown's plebe year, midshipmen continued referring to black janitors as mokes for decades to come. Such institutionalized racism both reflected and reinforced negative attitudes and stereotypes that midshipmen and naval officers had grown up with.[9]

Chambers was well aware of the horrible treatment that Wes Brown endured during his plebe year and was personally aware of the vicious games that upper classmen still took pleasure in. All plebes expected to be hazed as a rite of passage in the Academy, but Chambers was hazed more than many of his classmates and believed that much of the excessive hazing was race related.

On a number of occasions he heard the upperclassmen refer to him in the third person as the "nigger," in an attempt to intimidate him or get him to respond in anger. However, as the "skinny nerd" back in the old neighborhood, he was harassed by some of the biggest and toughest Black kids on the block and thought the white upperclassmen at the Academy were more immature than they were tough, and he was not easily intimidated.

Chambers was tougher than he realized once he went to the Academy. He knew that he "was not going to get full recognition for whatever [he] had accomplished. The object of the game was to get through. Don't lose your cool, don't fight, and be tough enough to take the worst of the worst."

Chambers knew Atwood selected him because they wanted recruits who were not going to be challenged by academics and who had the fortitude and stamina to survive hazing and other mistreatment without letting it interfere with their work. For Chambers, it wasn't always easy, but he knew that what he was enduring was not nearly as bad as what Wes Brown went through.

Chambers never considered himself to be a "quitter" in life. And each time he recalled the challenges faced by Wes Brown and Benjamin O. Davis, Jr., he came back to the same resolution: "They were not going to force me out of here." His grandfather had taught him well, and that life lesson of doing what you needed to do to get through the day would enable Chambers to persevere although it was hard.

Each morning, the upperclassmen would require Chambers and the other plebes to do push-ups and other strenuous physical activities. While the plebes were doing push-ups, they were asked questions, and if they couldn't answer them, they had to do additional push-ups. Chambers understood the "cat and mouse game" that was being played. After all, these were the same strenuous drills that he endured at Dunbar. Chambers knew that he needed to moan and groan as if he was in tremendous pain because the more pain he appeared to be in, the sooner the hazing would end.

Academically, Chambers was a strong student, and while doing push-ups, there were very few test questions he didn't know the answer to. He knew some of the other white plebes were getting it a lot worse than he did. Chambers did suspect, however, that some of the seemingly normal plebe treatment he was receiving might have been racially motivated. To avoid unnecessary exposure to prejudiced and unfamiliar upperclassmen, he remained in his company area as much as he could.[10]

The African Americans who worked on campus were Chambers' best friends. They were sensitive to the challenges of being an African American on a predominantly white campus, particularly for an impressionable young man who was learning and living in a non-segregated environment for the first time. On many weekends, they would hide Chambers in the backseats of the cars covered by a blanket and take him outside of the school's compound so that he could at least meet and befriend other young Black men in the Annapolis/Baltimore area.

While Chambers was involved with his coursework at the Naval Academy, President Truman and his military leaders were attempting to contain communism from stretching across the Sea of Japan to the Korean peninsula. After the war, Germany lost approximately twenty-five percent of its prewar territories and Japan lost its possession of the Korean peninsula. At the end of World War II, the two most powerful allies in the war, the United States and the Soviet Union, began to disagree with one another on the best way to address the rebuilding and reunification of Germany and control over the Korean peninsula. These early political and philosophical differences between the two nations would set the stage for major disagreements over how to realign war-torn European territories and the Korean peninsula in the war's aftermath.

In 1894 after the Sino-Japanese War, China was removed as "overlord and protector of the peninsula nation of Korea" located between the Yellow Sea and the Sea of Japan. After the Russo-Japanese War with Russia, victorious Japan annexed the Korean peninsula from China.[11] The Japanese ruled Korea until the conclusion of World War II when the Japanese nation lost to the Allied Forces who divided the Korean peninsula nation into two sections at the 38th parallel in 1945, Soviet Union military forces established a communist government in the north and the United States and Great Britain military forces established a pro–Western nation in the south.

In 1946, the Soviet Union established the Provisional People's Committee, which held elections under the direction of Kim Il Sung. The Provisional People's Committee established a new Stalinist-style communist government known as the People's Assembly. Under the new "quasi-government," Kim Il Sung began to consolidate power under the direction of the Soviet Union.[12] By 1948, over two million refugees fled North Korea to the south, creating a fear that the peninsula was on the verge of a civil war.

The Korean War was the United Nation's first war. The international body's founding members consisted of the five allied partners in World War II: France, the Republic of China, the Soviet Union, the United Kingdom, and the United States. In an attempt to unify the split peninsula, the United Nations moved for a national vote to determine the form of government that the Korean people wanted under a unified nation. On May 10, 1948, under the auspices of the United Nations, South Korea held elections and formed the Republic of Korea, making its capital city in Seoul. This ended the United States' occupation of the southern portion of the peninsula. The Soviet Union–led government refused to allow people residing in the North to participate in free elections, and on September 9, 1948, it formed the Democratic People's Republic of Korea, ending the Soviet Union's occupation of the northern portion of the peninsula.[13] After the formation of the two new governments, border clashes erupted and tensions grew between the new nations.

Kim Il Sung, with the support of the Soviet Union's Joseph Stalin, invaded South Korea on June 25, 1950, in an attempt to unify all of Korea under the communist rule of the Democratic People's Republic of Korea. The North's invasion caught the Republic of Korea's government off-guard and totally demoralized the South's army, and the Republic's President fled to the port city of Pusan (also spelled Busan).

Pusan, the second largest city in South Korea, is on the southeasternmost point of the peninsula nation. As its nation was under attack, the Republic of Korea's President Syngman Rhee escaped to Pusan as the capital city of Seoul and most of his nation fell to the invasion of the North's Democratic People's Republic of Korea.[14] The Soviet communist invasion was a clear tactical maneuver to control the entire peninsula, but more importantly, it was the first step in a greater Asian conflict that would eventually impact Japan and its economy.[15] Under the vote of the United Nation's Security Council, the United Nations and the United States immediately came to the defense of South Korea as the country's army collapsed immediately after the invasion: "The quick and virtually complete collapse of resistance in the South energized the United States to enter the war in force ... which soon committed American air and ground forces to the fight."[16]

The United States entrance into the Korean conflict was consistent with President Truman's Doctrine as delivered before a joint session of Congress on March 12, 1947. The President believed that foreign governments, such as the Soviet Union, were invading weaker nations and imposing a communistic will on free people, and by doing so were an overall threat to international peace, specifically to the national security of the United States. The Truman Doctrine, later to be known as the "Containment Policy," was designed to contain the expansion of communism worldwide and avoid a possible domino effect with one country after another falling into the hands of the Soviet Union:

> With the Truman Doctrine, President Harry S. Truman established that the United States would provide political, military and economic assistance to all democratic nations under threat from external or internal authoritarian forces. The Truman Doctrine effectively reoriented U.S. foreign policy, away from its usual stance of withdrawal from regional conflicts not directly involving the United States, to one of possible intervention in faraway conflicts.... Truman argued that the United States

could no longer stand by and allow the forcible expansion of Soviet totalitarianism into free, independent nations, because American national security now depended upon more than just the physical security of American territory. Rather, in a sharp break with its traditional avoidance of extensive foreign commitments beyond the Western Hemisphere during peacetime, the Truman Doctrine committed the United States to actively offering assistance to preserve the political integrity of democratic nations when such an offer was deemed to be in the best interest of the United States.[17]

At the Academy, Chambers was instructed in the philosophy of the Truman Doctrine while President Harry S Truman was dealing with the aggressive advances of communism, particularly in Eastern Europe and Asia. The Truman Doctrine served as the foundation for six subsequent presidents in a Cold War with tensions between the United States and its western North Atlantic Treaty Organization (NATO) allies on one side against the aggression of the communist Eastern Bloc nations on the opposing side. While not a traditional war with clearly defined battles, the Cold War was the result of global tension on both sides. Each side feared perceived gains in territory and power for the other. Moreover, each feared the growing nuclear strengths of the other, as evidenced by their respective nuclear arsenals and stockpiles, and the entire world feared nuclear annihilation. The primary protagonists did not engage each other directly. Instead, they did so via proxy wars through their client states around the globe.

Between enrolling in the Naval Academy and retiring from the military, Chambers lived through seven United States presidents, each with their own military doctrine, and each impacting Chambers' military career differently. This impact began with the Truman Doctrine. The Truman Doctrine became the basis for American Cold War policy for the next fifty years and was predicated on supporting weaker nations around the world that were being threatened by stronger Soviet Bloc nations that promoted communist forms of governments.

But for Chambers, each of the world events that precipitated an international doctrine directly affected the advancement of his career and the impact that he made as a result of each phase of his career. As the presidential doctrines changed from administration to administration and domestic and international events unfolded, each helped to shape the man who became an outstanding African American hero and a true patriot.

Figure 2: United States Presidential Doctrines

President/ Term	Year	Doctrine
Harry S Truman 33rd President (1945–1953)	1947	Suppress communist insurgency in Eastern Europe.

President/ Term	Year	Doctrine
Dwight D. Eisenhower 34th President (1953–1961)	1957	Intervene militarily in the Middle East to protect legitimate governments from communist subversion.
John F. Kennedy 35th President (1961–1963)	1961	Contain communism and the reversal of communism in the Western hemisphere.
Lyndon B. Johnson 36th President (1963–1969)	1965	Contain communism and reverse communism in the Western hemisphere.
Richard M. Nixon 37th President (1969–1974)	1969	Asian governments to wean themselves off U.S. military aid in the war on communism.
Gerald R. Ford 38th President (1974–1977)	1975	Strengthen U.S. position in South-East Asia against communalist aggression.
Jimmy Carter 39th President (1977–1981)	1980	Protect countries of the Persian Gulf from outside interference.
Ronald W. Reagan 40th President (1981–1989)	1981	Provide military and economic support to countries opposed to global influence of the Soviet Union.

Although World War II was over, President Truman began to build an international military defense system to serve as a counterbalance to the global spread of communism, which he believed to be a threat to the national security of the United States. Chambers would soon become part of that military structure.

While at Annapolis, Chambers' Class of 1952 was the first Naval class to start under Truman's Executive Order 9981, which ended racial discrimination in the United States armed services and intended to stop the spread of communism worldwide by supporting countries under threat from the Soviet Union at the start of the Cold War.

Even as a young man, Chambers had strong political ideals and communication skills. In an interview on the day of his graduation, when pressed to respond to a question about his experiences as the second African American to graduate from the Naval Academy, he responded by stating, "My four years at the Naval Academy have been among the most satisfying of my life. I will always remember these years with appreciation of the fair, kindly, and impartial treatment received from the Superintendent, officers, instructors, midshipmen, and enlisted personnel stationed there."[18] However, in an interview with the *Baltimore Afro American* more than twenty years later, Chambers candidly expressed a very different sentiment of his experiences at the Naval Academy, explaining that it had been over two decades since he had set foot in Annapolis, and although he "had some good memories, [he] also had some tough memories."[19]

When questioned about the discrepancies between the two interviews, Chambers remarked that African Americans at Annapolis intentionally kept a low public profile and during the early years at the institution wanted as little attention directed toward them as possible out of fear of unnecessary reprisals by upper classmen.

Despite the challenges of his youth—growing up in rural Virginia, raised by a widowed mother, and attending a segregated high school—Ensign Chambers graduated 119th in his class of 783 students. As impressive as his class standing was, according to those close to him, his academic standing was actually much higher. He received a number of non-academic demotions that intentionally brought his class standing lower. At Annapolis, class standing was vital to advancement in the Navy after graduation, and it was their belief that the demotions were specifically designed to thwart any long-term ambitions Chambers might have had in the military. Nonetheless, Rear Admiral Chambers had a long and illustrious career in the Navy.

Upon his graduation on June 6, 1952, Chambers became part of the first graduating class of military leaders to begin their careers during the Cold War. As a result of his academic standing, Chambers was able to select the first ship on which he would serve.

Sensitive to the issues of race on various ships, the commandant called Chambers into his office and advised him that Chamber's chosen ship would not be a good fit and strongly suggested that the USS *Columbus* was a better vessel on which

Annapolis, Maryland, 1952. Midshipman Larry Chambers upon graduation from the United States Naval Academy (personal collection).

to make a maiden voyage. Furthermore, skipper Gordon Campbell was a good friend of the commandant, and on that ship, Chambers would be given a fair shake.

Following graduation, Chambers' orders were changed and the first ship he served on was the USS *Columbus* (CA-74). In reflection, Chambers believes that being assigned to the *Columbus* was one of the best moves of his early military career. Assigned to the ship were a number of former World War II aviators who passed on to Chambers invaluable information and insight. The more they shared, the more Chambers realized what he didn't know and needed to learn as an ensign and beyond.

Chambers reflected on the many nights he stayed up and listened to the old war stories from these battled-tested men. While others discounted them as stories by a bunch of old men who flew planes during a different time period, Chambers realized that what he learned in the classroom was no more valuable than the lessons these men shared from their experience in actual air combat.

The stories that the World War II veterans shared with a young Chambers provided him with insight about what makes a good leader in the Navy from their individual perspectives, especially in the time of a military crisis. As part of their oral history sharing, they provided practical examples of commanders that they served under during the war who demonstrated effective leadership skills, and how as effective leaders—even when they had to make tough decisions—were respected by their men. Chambers credited much of his own effective leadership and management style to the origins of these stories that connected him to some of the great commanders of World War II whom he would otherwise never have had a chance to know.

The veteran pilots also told him how to be a good aviator and how to stay alive under the most unexpected adverse conditions, and shared with him the lessons they learned from men who made dangerous mistakes and died as a result of the risks they took. The World War II veteran pilots were coming to the end of their careers and respected Chambers unlike the other young aviators who were too busy for them. It was for Chambers' respect towards them that they shared their unique perspectives of the Navy, how it works and what he needed to do if he wanted to move up in the system.

A little more than a year after Chambers graduated from the Naval Academy, the Korean War ended on July 27, 1953, with a truce signed by North Korea and its supporter China with the United Nations. The South's Republic of Korea did not sign the agreement, leaving the peninsula divided with a communist government to the north separated by a demilitarized zone at the 38th parallel and a non-communist government in the south. The truce was a viable solution for the North Koreans who were supported by the Chinese and Russians, both of which wanted to expand communism over the entire peninsula. The South Koreans, supported by the United Nations and the United States, were able to maintain an open government, thereby thwarting the efforts of North Korea and their communist allies to obtain total control of the Korean peninsula.

As men tested in war will often do during idle time, the events in Korea caused the veteran pilots to speculate on the rapidly changing geopolitical dynamics between the once Allied Nations in the West and their former Allied partners from the East. The division of the Korean peninsula with a communist government to the north separated by a demilitarized zone at the 38th parallel and a non-communist government in the south, along with the division of Germany and Eastern Europe after World War II, gave way to speculation of the rise of communism and long-term hostilities between the East and the West.

Although Chambers only spent a relatively short amount of time stationed with these pilots, he was always intrigued about their discussions and what the veteran pilots saw as the prelude to the Cold War between the United States and the communist nations of China and the Soviet Union.

Chapter 4

Cold War

Rear Admiral Larry Chambers' career was intrinsically tied to the events of the Cold War, and the progression of his career occurred partly around critical events of the war in Indochina and the Navy's Pacific Seventh Fleet. The genesis for the Cold War was grounded in economic events that took place in the aftermath of World War II, where the once allied nations became archrivals. In the aftermath of World War II distrust developed between the eastern and western nations of the former Allies and the United States and Soviet Union became archrivals. When Truman made the decision to drop the atomic bomb on Japan, he told Soviet Union leader Joseph Stalin at the very last moment, setting the stage for icy geopolitical relations for generations to come. When the war ended the United States benefited from not having its industrial base damaged by war whereas the Soviet Union and much of Europe's economy and industrial infrastructure were devastated.

The Cold War was not a traditional war with clearly defined battles but the result of global tensions between the East and the West, with each side fearing perceived gains in economics, territory and military power as defined by nuclear strength. As the U.S. entered into a robust post-war economy, the Soviet Union built a post-war military economy as it attempted to rebuild its damaged manufacturing base and industrial cities. "The tragedy, of course, is that the largest difference between Russia and America in 1945 was that the former's economy had been destroyed by the war against Hitler, while the latter's had been rescued by it."[1] Nevertheless, Soviet military forces following World War II outnumbered American military personnel:

> By December 31, 1945, almost 1,670,000 men and women had been released from the U.S. armed forces ahead of schedule, and it soon became apparent that Soviet ground forces dwarfed any possible American counterpart. While American military budgets were constrained under the tight bookkeeping of the Truman Administration, Soviet military expenditures increased by perhaps 30 percent between 1948 and 1949, and

American intelligence estimated that the Soviets could mobilize 470 divisions and 12 million men within six months, not to mention their 2.5 million-man standing army. Conventionally speaking, the West was outmatched.[2]

In the aftermath of World War II and in direct response to the threats of a new type of war predicated on nuclear superiority, many had postulated that the U.S. Navy would not be able to compete in a nuclear Cold War environment. However, by the time Ensign Chambers graduated from the United States Naval Academy in 1952, the U.S. Navy demonstrated its vital importance as a Cold War strategic mobile military base serving different parts of the world, fully capable of delivering nuclear arms on relatively short notice. With the advent of fighter jets, those who doubted the value of the Navy discovered the importance of a mobile military force:

> those who predicted the Navy's inevitable obsolescence soon realized that a sea-borne force possessed a tremendously valuable asset to modern warfare: mobility. In a defensive sense, mobility provides a military base with a greater degree of invulnerability to enemy attack. Dispersed at will anywhere on the millions of square miles of ocean, a moving naval task force is extremely difficult to locate.... With the intrinsic asset of mobility, the Navy has combined a man-made asset: flexibility. The deployed fleet consists of the attack carrier striking force, the amphibious landing force, the fleet marine force, and the mobile logistic support force.... Yet, in spite of the radically changed nature of modern warfare and the new responsibilities of the fleet, the Navy nonetheless continues to retain its age old mission: control of the seas.[3]

Upon Chambers' graduation from the Academy, the "new" Navy was not his father's navy anymore. It had developed into a mobile nuclear fighting force supported by well-trained fighter pilots, state of the art aircraft, and best in class aircraft carriers. After graduation, Ensign Chambers enrolled in a preflight training program for the Navy's attack carrier striking force at the Naval Air Station in Pensacola, Florida.

While waiting for his assignment to the training program, Chambers learned a lot during his four months on the USS *Columbus,* and after being "schooled" by the older pilots, he couldn't wait to start training so that he could get his Navy wings. As Chambers soon found out at preflight training, there is an abundance of ground school instruction before a student ever gets near an attack airplane.

As a prospective aviator, Chambers learned a lot in the preflight training program and came to realize that much knowledge had been acquired in the field of combat aviation in the aftermath of World War II and the Korean War, and that many of the stories shared by the World War II pilots on the USS *Columbus* were not that different than what he was now hearing at flight school. Throughout his entire life, Chambers felt fortunate that there were older and wiser men who took an interest in him, particularly in his youth, and provided him with sage advice that would benefit him in the present and future.

A specific lesson he credits as being beneficial to him occurred during one of Chambers' preflight training sessions when a flight surgeon joined the group and shared recent definitive information that noise from flying is extremely hazardous to an aviator's long-term hearing. The flight surgeon distributed small foam rubber earplugs and advised the group to always use them when around flight deck or engine room noise. At eighty-five years, Rear Admiral Chambers credits this advice, which he seriously took to heart, as the reason that today he is probably "the only retired aviator that he knows who doesn't need a hearing aid."

While at the Whiting Field for basic aviation flight training, Chambers and the other trainees were required to take 18 1.5-hour sessions of actual flight training before they were considered safe for a solo flight. Chambers absolutely enjoyed his time in flight training. However, he soon learned that despite the desegregation of the Naval Academy, the problems of bigotry, oppression and segregation were not truly behind him or the Navy.

On the day Chambers was to have his safe solo check, he and his check flight instructor became airborne just as the winds started to pick up. According to Chambers because of the weather, there was a general recall for all students and instructors to return to home field, and the other students received an incomplete grade.

Chambers' flight instructor, however, instructed him to stay in the air and fly the plane despite the strong winds and inclement weather. As Chambers sat in the front seat with the flight instructor behind him, it became clear what the instructor was doing—and why he was doing it. There was no way this instructor was going to let the only black person in the class pass the solo flight test. Once it was clear that Chambers could not handle the weather, he was told to land. Upon landing, he was given a down check ride, the only black mark on his record for his entire career.

Once the plane was on the ground and Chambers was given the down check ride, the senior instructor pilot who had witnessed the incident clearly understood why Chambers was singled out and treated differently from the rest of the student pilots. The check pilot was ordered to take the plane back up and ensure that all of the other flight school students and instructors had heard the general recall and returned to base.

In an ironic turn of events, on taxiing out to the runway, the flight instructor "ground looped" the airplane because of the strong crosswind on the taxi way. The same inclement weather that enabled him to flunk Chambers was a bit much for the flight instructor himself to handle. Upon return to base, the embarrassed flight instructor exited the plane and was well aware that he was now being watched by all of the prospective pilots and his boss, who clearly understood that his subordinate had flunked Chambers because of his race. Chambers should have never been sent up in the inclement weather if the flight instructor couldn't handle the same weather conditions. While Chambers was angry that he received the black mark, he knew that the flight instructor was angrier to have been publicly humiliated by his superior, and particularly in front of Chambers.

During this period of the Cold War, Chambers became tangentially aware of the tenets of a classified plan to address the growing threat of nuclear war in a period when political adversaries with growing stockpiles of nuclear weapons were poised to strike the United States. Although early in his military career, Chambers understood that naval aviators were a strategic component of the plan but at this juncture knew little more. But as Chambers would soon learn, this "secret plan" would have a sustain impact on his career, along with the Cold War threat of the world's superpowers using nuclear weapons in the event they were fired upon by their adversaries.

As Chambers was engaged in pilot training, President Dwight Eisenhower, a five-star general in World War II, was taking office. Eisenhower was briefed on the highly classified Single Integrated Operational Plan known as SIOP, "the blandly bureaucratic name for the U.S. scheme designed to destroy the Soviet Union, Red China, and the Soviet satellite states in a single cataclysmic blow if the United States were attacked."[4]

Although much of SIOP is still classified, some components have become declassified over time, and we are now learning that it was the most highly classified document during the Cold War period. The plan provided the Pentagon under the direction of the President, a number of integrated options that could be used to launch nuclear weapons from aircraft carriers, intercontinental ballistic missiles from fixed based land operations, or from sea based submarine-launched ballistic missiles. With each international incident, the threat of a nuclear event became a real possibility.

After the height of the Korean War, China "yearned for conflict elsewhere and aggressively challenged the … assumption that America's dominance in nuclear weapons would deter Communist aggression. In Indochina and in the straits that separated mainland China … [China] refused to submit to the nuclear threat."[5] Quemoy, Matsu, and several other outlying islands between the communist mainland People's Republic of China and the neighboring island of Taiwan (known as the Republic of China) remained in dispute after civil war hostilities ceased in 1950. Although tensions between the two governments had subsided, the situation in the Taiwan straits, a waterway that separated mainland China and Taiwan, remained tense:

4. Cold War

In the spring of 1954, China began massing forces on the mainland near the islands, escalating that provocation just as the McCarthy hearings were reaching their feverish peak. Eisenhower calculated the American response: Would an attack on the islands constitute an act of international aggression or a battle in the continuing Chinese Civil War; more important, would it be of sufficient gravity that it warranted a nuclear response? It seemed frightfully provocative to meet the shelling of lightly defended islands of questionable strategic value with a nuclear attack on China, but the theory of American deterrence rested on the idea that the U.S. nuclear arsenal existed precisely to discourage aggression by threatening devastation in reply. Eisenhower took counsel of the military and diplomatic stakes and ordered the U.S. Seventh Fleet to pay "friendly visits" to the embattled islands, initially with instructions not to fire even if fired upon.[6]

During the height of the Chinese amassing their forces on the coastal mainland, on June 6, 1954, Lieutenant Chambers completed his training at the Naval Air Training Command, received his Navy wings and became a naval aviator assigned to Anti-Submarine Squadron 37 aboard the USS *Princeton* (CVS-37) as part of the U.S. Seventh Fleet. As the Seventh Fleet was realigning its assets in the coastal waters of the Taiwan Straits, one of the first major tests of the Cold War superpowers' resolve was what became known as the First Taiwan Strait Crisis.

On September 3, 1954, mainland China began to take military action to control Quemoy, Matsu, and several other outlying islands. When Taiwan sent troops to defend the islands, the Republic of China began an aggressive bombing campaign on the islands and made outright threats to invade Taiwan. During the Korean War, Taiwan came under the protection of the United States. In response to mainland China's aggression, the United States diplomatically opposed the Chinese govern-

Barin Field, Foley, Alabama, 1954. Larry Chambers is one happy man, having just successfully achieved Carrier qualifications (personal collection).

ment's Cold War efforts and feared its ultimate desire was to control the South China Sea and most of Asia.

Lieutenant Chambers and other pilots assigned to *Princeton* conducted exercises around Taiwan and the outlying islands in an effort to provide a strong air and sea presence. In the event that there were any Chinese submarines with the ability to launch ballistic missiles, the squadron that Chambers was assigned to patrolled the Pacific Ocean looking for combatant submarines and sinking any they found. However, according to Chambers, "at that point in time, there were no combatant submarines found."

Tensions in the Taiwan Straits were high, and it probably just as well that there were no submarines. If one had been found and fired upon, it might have started an unfortunate chain reaction. In Washington, as China was "shelling Quemoy and Matsu ... Admiral Radford ... saw the chance for the long-awaited showdown with China. In the National Security Council, he argued that the United States should defend the islands from invasion by attacking Chinese airfields and other targets with nuclear weapons."[7]

While on the *Princeton,* Chambers was then ordered to join a Naval Avi-

NAS Pensacola, Florida, 1954. A very proud Larry Chambers, receiving his Wings of Gold, 1954 (personal collection).

ation Attack Squadron which he knew was an excellent opportunity to broaden his skills as an aviator. There he got to fly the Douglas Sky Raider, which at the time was a major career boost for a young aviator as it gave him valuable experience in offensive weaponry in an attack squadron. Once the government of Taiwan acquired state of the art aircraft from the United States government, the experienced members of the attack squadron conducted joint training exercises with the Taiwanese military. Chambers considered himself fortunate to have participated in the exercises. He learned from watching the more senior aviators in his squadron display their skills, but he also realized how much he had learned when he was also able to share his knowledge with the Taiwanese pilots, who he said were quick learners.

According to Chambers, the "mainland Chinese consistently engaged the Taiwanese pilots in aerial dogfights and usually flew away with their tails in between their legs." Chambers was thoroughly impressed with the ability of the Taiwanese pilots in mastering control of the American aircraft in short order, and in being able to fly with such precision against the mainland Chinese.

Chambers and the other pilots conducted, almost on a daily basis, a series of training and tactical maneuvers in the Taiwan Straits and the South China Sea, oftentimes with the Taiwanese Air Force. The Chinese pilots on occasion would approach and fly alongside the Americans; very seldom would they engage in an actual dogfight or display overly aggressive maneuvers with the Americans. However, Chambers and the other pilots began to notice that the mainland Chinese were becoming more aggressive in aerial dogfights with the Taiwanese after each encounter.

As the pilots reported their observations up the chain of command, the commanders of the Seventh Fleet reported to Washington the incremental aggressiveness of the Chinese in aerial dogfights as well as their aggressive behavior in several small naval engagements along the coastline. It was becoming clear that the Chinese were testing the fortitude of the Taiwanese people and their overall defense systems.

U.S. Secretary of State John Foster Dulles visited the Seventh Fleet and the leaders of Taiwan in late February 1955 to ascertain firsthand the challenges each faced with the Chinese government. In a March 8 speech to radio and TV audiences upon his return stateside, "Dulles had raised the specter of nuclear weapons" and sought to "rebut Beijing's propaganda that the United States was a 'paper tiger.' He proclaimed that U.S. naval and air forces were 'equipped with new and powerful weapons of precision, which can utterly destroy military targets without endangering civilian centers.'"[8]

On March 10, Dulles "reported to Eisenhower and his assembled National

Security Council. 'The situation out there in the Formosa Strait is far more serious than I thought.'" The Red Chinese, he said, were determined to capture Formosa. The only way to make Beijing back down was by threatening to use nuclear weapons. In his gravest churchman's tones, he concluded, "before this problem is solved, I believe that there is at least an even chance that the United States will have to go to war."[9]

As the Americans continued with their flight maneuvers and tensions escalated, Chambers recalls that pilots were instructed, "if fired upon by the Chinese, not to fire back." While the Eisenhower Administration publicly spoke definitively of the steps it would take in the event China invaded Taiwan, behind the scenes the administration was more restrained with their actions so as not to unnecessarily provoke the Chinese. A concern of Eisenhower and his Strategic Air Command (SAC) going back to the Korean War was that once an attack was made against China, particularly a nuclear attack, "war with the Soviet Union would shortly follow."[10]

With a real public threat of a U.S. nuclear attack, and having received as tepid response by the Soviet Union to come to their aid in such an event, the Chinese backed down. Once tension subsided the United States conducted training for special weapons at their training facilities in Yuma, Arizona, and El Centro, California. Chambers had the unique opportunity to practice gunnery, bombing and rocket training flights. It was clear even at this early point in his military career that he was being exposed to opportunities in the Navy that few before him had experienced, white or Black.

After tensions temporarily subsided in the Taiwan Straits and on the Korean Peninsula, the communist Chinese agitated another conflict by supporting dissidents on the Indochinese Peninsula who were engulfed in a revolutionary war with their colonial French government. The Indochinese Peninsula, a region in Southeast Asia bordering China to the north, the Gulf of Thailand and the South China Sea, was divided into four major nations following World War II: Cambodia, Laos, Thailand and Vietnam, an area to the east of the peninsula bordered by the South China Sea.

After World War II, a weakened France attempted to reclaim the colony only to be confronted by militant Vietnamese who wanted independence from their former colonial rulers and were now supported by communist powers in China and Russia. In 1945, under the direction of revolutionary leader Ho Chi Minh, the rebels declared an independent Democratic Republic of Vietnam. The French, not prepared to relinquish control, fought to retain their colonial power. By 1949, the communist powers of China and Russia provided aid to Ho Chi Minh and his militants.

The Vietnamese resistance against the French was strong and fierce. The rugged mountainous terrain of Vietnam, combined with the communist-supplied weapons, created favorable conditions for the rebels. As the war continued, the Chinese provided valuable military and necessary supplies, further emboldening the revolutionaries who safely hid in the mountains. Meanwhile, the consistently under-supplied and understaffed French army could only maintain a "static position."

In his speech before Congress on March 12, 1947, Truman established the Truman Doctrine, also known as the "Containment Policy," designed to limit the expansion of communism worldwide and to prevent one country after another from falling into the hands of the Soviet Union. President Truman believed that foreign governments such as China and the Soviet Union were entering weaker nations and imposing communist policies on free citizens, and by doing so were a threat to international peace, and specifically, a threat to the national security of the United States.

Truman sent military assistance to the French, including technical and logistical specialists to Indochina, a team that was later known as the Indochina Military Assistance and Advisory Group. The Advisory Group "served exclusively as inspectors, observing the distribution of American military equipment and supplies intended to help the French crush Vietnamese efforts to overthrow colonial rule."[11] By the time President Eisenhower took office, the liberation revolutionaries in Indochina, with direct support from China, had chipped away at the French defensive positions. By March 1954, the French were trapped for three months in the Battle of Dien Bien Phu. After a "fifty-five day siege," the French positions were overrun and defeated, and the French decided to pull out of Vietnam.[12]

At a news conference on April 7 in response to the Battle of Dien Bien Phu, President Eisenhower "invoked what he called the 'falling domino principle…' [implying that] if Indochina fell, Burma, Thailand, Malaya [now Malaysia], and Indonesia would [soon] follow."[13] Although Eisenhower's military advisors, as well as the French government, recommended the President intervene in Vietnam, "at the meeting of the National Security Council on April 29, 1954, Eisenhower laid down the law. There would be no intervention in Vietnam."[14]

In July at the Geneva Conference the diplomatic negotiators concluded with the decision that Vietnam would be temporarily divided into two separate zones divided at the 17th parallel, with the intent that elections would be held in 1956 to establish a stable, single unifying government. The events at the Geneva Conference and the Vietnam divide at the 17th parallel, would result in the Vietnam War and have a direct impact on Chambers' career as a naval aviator and commander in the U.S. Navy:

> [The] conference sponsored and attended by the United States, the Soviet Union, France, and Brittan had already convened on April 26 in Geneva, Switzerland, to discuss the problem of the two Koreas and also to find ways to end the war in Vietnam.... After seventy-four days of negotiations, a cease-fire agreement was signed on July 20. The principal clauses of the Geneva agreements provided for the temporary partition of Vietnam at the Seventeenth Parallel, with the forces of the Democratic Republic of Vietnam in the north and those of the French Union in the south....[15]

In fear that they were establishing another Korean-type peninsula conflict between interests in the north and south, the framers of the Geneva Agreement clearly intended that the "military demarcation line" was to be "provisional and should not in any way be interpreted as constituting a political or territorial boundary." The Geneva Agreement's final declaration, Article 6, elaborates on that objective:

> The Conference recognizes that the essential purpose of the Agreement relating to Vietnam is to settle military questions with a view to ending hostilities and that the military demarcation line is provisional and should not in any way be interpreted as constituting a political or territorial boundary. The Conference expresses its conviction that the execution of the provisions set out in the present Declaration and in the Agreement on the cessation of hostilities creates the necessary basis for the achievement in the near future of a political settlement in Vietnam.[16]

Although the Geneva Agreements were endorsed by members of the United Nations, the Democratic Republic of Vietnam in the North, which was supported by the communist Soviet delegation, rejected the Agreements, setting the stage for 20 years of internal strife on the peninsula. The communist sympathizers saw the Agreements as a continuation of French colonial influence and American dominance propping up the South Vietnamese government, known as the State of Vietnam.

Between 1954 and 1956, the communist North and the non-communist South began to sharply differ on regional issues of religion, economics and politics. By early 1955, it was clear that escalating tensions existed between the two regions. In 1956, elections took place only in the South as dissidents in both regions began to mobilize against each form of government.

Chambers, young and ambitious, wanted to fly with the Pacific Command. He correctly surmised that since the Atlantic command at that point was fairly peaceful, all of the action was going to take place in the Pacific. Korea was still fresh in everybody's minds. The United States still had patrols and carriers operating in the vicinity of Korea even though the North and South were not engaged in open warfare. There was now increasing focus on the Vietnamese peninsula in anticipation of the 1956 elections.

President Eisenhower had a unique perspective on the rise of communism having served as the first Supreme Commander of the North Atlantic Treaty

Organization (NATO), an international alliance between member states for mutual defense in the event of an attack. As a result of the Korean War and the threat of communist countries working together, Eisenhower knew that nations that were not part of NATO, such as Vietnam, were especially susceptible to communist encroachment. Consistent with the earlier support of the French against the Chinese-supported insurgents, several months after the insurgents defeated the French at Dien Bien Phu, the United States began assisting the South Vietnamese against incursions of the northern communists:

> Several months after Vietnamese insurgents ... defeated the French at Dien Bien Phu, the United States quietly changed its mission to training the new Army of the Republic of Vietnam (ARVN). This new Military Assistance and Advisory Group-Vietnam (MAAG-Vietnam) soon numbered more than 300 trainers, mostly career officers or veteran noncommissioned officers (NCOS) with combat service in World War II or Korea. In two- or three-man teams, they attempted to organize the new 150,000-man ARVN into the kind of army they understood best: a conventional force that could repel any North Vietnamese attack across the demilitarized zone (DMZ) that had come to serve as the border between North and South Vietnam.[17]

As the Cold War progressed, NATO nations began to standardize and unify their military procedures, protocols and operations. Although NATO's standards were generally based on American standards, the United States began to integrate the NATO standards into their training curriculum worldwide across all of its military branches. Aviators like Chambers adapted to the new techniques and protocols in accordance with the adoption of new unified standards.

On his second deployment, Chambers was aboard USS *Bon Homme Richard* (CV-31) in VA-215 Attack Squadron where he went out to the Western Pacific in the vicinity of Okinawa and the islands off the coast of the Philippines. On this cruise he got the opportunity to fly the Douglas AD-6 Skyraider, a new propeller aircraft that "was in many respects the most remarkable nuclear strike aircraft produced by any nation."[18] The Skyraider is a lightweight single seat aircraft with a maximum takeoff weight of 22,500 pounds with a top speed of more than 500 miles per hour and a thermal cockpit shield for nuclear weapons delivery.

The Skyraider, "despite its versatility and effectiveness as a conventional strike aircraft ... was considered primarily a nuclear strike aircraft by the U.S. Navy."[19] On tactical missions, Chambers was expected to launch within minutes armed with nuclear weapons, and if necessary, descend on Russian or Chinese targets. He often practiced the delivery of weapons on short notice to several abandoned islands in the Pacific.

On one mission, the squadron was launched with the intention of going to a target area and then returning to the aircraft carrier. Chambers believes that this exercise was the longest flight in his logbook, where he was airborne in a single-piloted airplane for over 14 hours. This flight was memorable not only because of its duration, but because it was launched during the middle of a typhoon around 2 a.m. No matter the weather, Chambers was expected to practice long flights and train for the delivery of special weapons.

During the practice flight, Chambers and the other pilots were required to return to *Bon Homme Richard* during the typhoon and in its accompanying rough seas. The young pilots were at a disadvantage because they were flying without all of the normal radar signaling devices. As part of the mission, the devices were turned off because the Chinese military at the time were sending homing signals on the same frequency as the aircraft carrier, and *Bon Homme Richard* did not want the Chinese to know their whereabouts and tactical maneuvers.

As the storm intensified in the vicinity of the ship, the admiral, concerned about the pilots already airborne, decided not to launch any more airplanes as he didn't want any additional loss of life or assets. According to Chambers, "the Commanding Officer of the Airborne Early Warning Squadron volunteered to go up to provide radar coverage to help the young pilots find their way back to the ship."

While most of his fellow pilots were challenged by the increased adverse weather conditions as they approached the ship, Chambers, already experienced with flying through severe weather thanks to the training he received on his previous cruise onboard USS *Princeton*, was able to get his homing needle pointed in the right direction. Instead of flying toward mainland China, Chambers began his approach back towards the USS *Bon Homme Richard*.

Because there were so many planes out in the storm, the Admiral and his staff kept contacting the pilots by radio to determine their coordinates. When the Admiral radioed Chambers, he informed the Admiral that he was in control, knew where he was, and was about to make a visual approach to the ship. Chambers shared that when he "got back to the ship, she was really rolling and pitching in the high seas. The strong winds and turbulence from the typhoon buffeted the aircraft. The aircraft bounced up and down in response to the turbulence."

As he approached, Chambers could only remember how defeated he had felt back in flight school, when after flying through bad conditions, he was failed by his instructor and given the only black mark of his career. Chambers had thought of that terrible moment a thousand times, trying to imagine what he could have done differently to prove to the biased flight instructor that he was indeed a superior and skilled aviator. But while he would never admit it to anyone else, he and his fellow pilots knew exactly why the instructor had failed him—it was because Chambers was Black, and that particular instructor did not want a Black man to succeed.

In the midst of the tumultuous western Pacific typhoon winds, Chambers knew one thing: that harrowing day with the flight instructor was then, and this was now, he was going to prevail. Now he knew exactly what he needed to do to land successfully on board *Bon Homme Richard*. Like all aviators Chambers knew that an aircraft carrier normally rolls and pitches in high seas. It goes through a steady phase of movement, and then it starts to move all over again. The inexperienced crews watched as Chambers timed his approach with the ship's movements and got aboard on his first pass at the ship.

Chambers smiled proudly as he recalled his successful landing, as if it happened only yesterday. It had taken the other returning pilots an average of twelve attempts before they successfully landed onboard. However, in reflection, although he wouldn't have told anyone this at the time, Chambers admitted that the ship's deck was probably the roughest deck he saw in his whole Navy career. While training and skill guided him through the severe storm, he admits that he "was damn lucky."

Even though Chambers was still a young aviator only two years past graduation, the skill and ease with which he landed his aircraft during the intensity of the typhoon on the first pass did not go unnoticed by his senior officers. When asked by his commanding officers how he was able to approach the flight deck and safely land on the first approach Chambers replied that it was "a piece of cake" and that he intuitively knew what he needed to do to land safely onboard. On July 1, 1956, Chambers was promoted to Lieutenant.

The storm that Chambers had flown through was echoed by the storm the United States government was now navigating, and no one could comprehend how dark the horizon was about to become. At the time, Chambers was aware that they were conducting special weapons training operations in the Far East. However, little did he know how close he was to being in the midst of a nuclear war.

With the fall of the French at Dien Bien Phu on May 7 and the provocation between mainland China and Taiwan, the Americans feared the worst. As the Cold War between the United States and the Soviet Union (both of which possessed nuclear weapons and threatened to use them if "forced") continued and the world became a more dangerous place, a new figure was about to enter the world stage.

Nikita Khrushchev served as First Secretary of the Central Committee of the Communist Party of the Soviet Union after the death of Joseph Stalin in March 1953. As commander in chief in 1955, Khrushchev started his first major international crisis over the Suez Canal, a manmade waterway in Egypt that connected the Mediterranean Sea and the Red Sea.

In response, President Dwight Eisenhower provided a "Special Message to Congress on the Situation in the Middle East" on January 5, 1957, in which he set forth a military outline as to when the United States would protect legitimate governments in the Middle East to defend the region from communist subversion. The speech, which is now referred to as the Eisenhower Doctrine, was in response to the Soviet Union's intention to use the Suez Canal Crisis as a ruse to occupy Egypt. Then the Soviets would control the vital link between the Mediterranean Sea and the Indian Ocean, a strategic move that would ensure Russian dominance in the region. In his message to Congress, President Eisenhower proposed a policy that would

> Authorize the United States to cooperate with and assist any nation or group of nations in the general area of the Middle East in the development of economic strength dedicated to the maintenance of national independence. It would ... authorize the Executive to undertake in the same region programs of military assistance and cooperation with any nation or group of nations which desires such aid. It would ... authorize such assistance and cooperation to include the employment of the armed forces of the United States to secure and protect the territorial integrity and political independence of such nations, requesting such aid, against overt armed aggression from any nation controlled by International Communism.[20]

As tensions escalated between the two world powers and their proxy nations, Chambers was at the end of his second cruise and received orders to attend the Navy Postgraduate School in Monterey, California. Between the end of his second cruise and the start of his postgraduate studies, he was sent to El Centro, California, to attend unmanned aerial vehicle school to learn how to fly drones. Chambers became fascinated with the new and emerging technologies that were being advanced by the Department of Defense.

The Cold War brought tremendous advancements in the field of technology and nuclear capabilities as the United States and Russia each sought a competitive edge. Although drones had been used with limited success in World War I and in World War II, as technology advanced, the United States Army and Navy each began to explore the usage of unmanned drone technology in reconnaissance and battlefield missions.

While Chambers was enrolled at the Naval Postgraduate School, his brother Andrew, who was attending Howard University, introduced him to Janet Murphy of Boston, Massachusetts. Chambers was smitten by the pretty coed. Chambers admits that Janet "was one tough lady, and she didn't take nonsense from anyone, including me." After what he refers to as a respectful courtship, the two married at Saint Cyprian's Church in Boston. The newlyweds moved to Monterey, California, while Chambers pursued a master's degree in aeronautical engineering from the Naval Postgraduate School with a third year of graduate studies at Stanford University.

Chambers describes his young bride, a graduate of Howard University, with the vivid detail than any groom still on his honeymoon would. Janet, he recalls, "was stronger than any man I knew. When we were dating, she was a summer playground manager, responsible for creating summer activities for neighborhood children. She was small and very pretty, and some of the more aggressive teenager boys would come by and try to harass her by picking on the smaller kids." Chambers continues, "Janet would not have any of it. She was a fairly good softball player and would play softball with the younger kids. What the bullies didn't realize until they made her mad enough was that she would use the bat on them—and she would only have to use it once!"

A natural beauty, Janet Chambers didn't have to concern herself with extravagant beauty routines or fashions. One evening the couple was attending an event at the Navy Postgraduate School. Janet kept asking Chambers if he liked her new shoes. Like any smart husband, he reassured his bride that everything about her was absolutely beautiful, including her shoes.

At the gathering, the ladies gravitated together as they often did at these events, and the men joined together for drinks and cigars. But the peaceful party was soon interrupted by a loud commotion coming from across the room. Chambers realized that Janet was giving one of the men, who was known as an obnoxious ladies man, a stern verbal lashing about putting his hands on her. "Apparently," Chambers recalls, "this jerk came up behind Janet and placed his hands inappropriately where he shouldn't have." Unbeknownst to Chambers, this "jackass" had tried the same tactic with several other women, but when he touched Janet, "she turned around and took the heel of her high heel and jammed it into his foot. The loud noise coming from the direction of the women was actually him screaming in pain." But Chambers knew he didn't need to intercede. "I'm not sure what hurt more, his foot or the tongue-lashing he took from Janet in the most proper of her Boston accents!"

The year of 1959 was initially filled with joy for Chambers and his wife of two years. Chambers had completed his studies and was recently assigned as part of the Attack Squadron to the USS *Midway* (CV 41), one of the premier flagships in the United States Navy and the ship he would command one day. On the home front, he and Janet were expecting their first child. In August 1959, Chambers received his master's degree in aeronautical engineering from the Naval Postgraduate School. But soon, the young couple's joy turned to sadness.

After the delivery of their daughter, Janet became ill, and after a series of tests, she was diagnosed with leukemia. Within a week, Janet unexpectedly passed away: "she never came home from the hospital." Chambers was devastated. He had found his soul mate, fallen deeply in love, and lost her in the blink of an eye. For all of his accomplishments on the job, all of his specialized training and impressive performance record, there wasn't anything he could do to help the woman he loved.

After Janet's death, Chambers immersed himself in work. Chambers had hoped that being with his second love, that of flight and being in the cockpit, would help him deal with the loss of his first love. Despite being an accomplished aviator who could fly for fourteen hours and land in a violent storm with ease, Chambers now found himself losing control and slipped into depression.

Upon Janet's death, Chambers placed his infant daughter in the care of her maternal grandmother and went back to sea aboard the USS *Midway*. As Chambers was mourning the death of his wife, both his subordinates and his superiors noticed Chambers' condition. In 1959, the military was a difficult organization for a newly widowed husband during a period of emotional stress, especially for a rising lieutenant with a long and promising career before him. At this point in time, the military frowned upon any type of emotional or psychological counseling, even if it was for bereavement.

As Chambers continued to mourn, his commanding officer was concerned that the aviator might become careless during routine flight operations, and initially confined Chambers to his stateroom. The order was intended to help Chambers, giving him privacy while he worked through his grief. He was then assigned to administrative duties, responsible for completing the other aviators' paperwork, normally done by an administrative aide. In short order, Chambers, tired of being confined to his stateroom and the tasks of completing paperwork, informed his commander that he was ready to get back to work.

As Chambers was facing his own personal crisis and the challenges of getting back to a sense of normalcy, the world and the United States military were facing a new challenge—becoming engulfed in the many facets of the Cold War between the United States and China. Chambers, who wanted to be in the Pacific, was assigned to the United States Navy's Seventh Fleet which was involved in all major operations in the Pacific, including the Korean War and tensions over the Quemoy and Matsu islands, the first event that almost brought the United States and China to the brink of nuclear war. The Seventh Fleet home ported in Yokosuka, Japan, and had more than 70 ships, over 400 aircraft and over 60,000 Navy and Marine Corps personnel.

Tension in the Pacific between China and the United States was not the only Cold War challenge faced by the Eisenhower administration. In November

1958, Eisenhower had to address another serious foreign policy issue: the division of Germany's capital city, Berlin, located in former Soviet-occupied East Germany. After World War II, the four major nations that comprised the Allied Forces, France, Great Britain, the Soviet Union and the United States, divided Germany into four quadrants, and the capital city Berlin was divided into the same four quadrants.

By 1958, as West Germany prospered and East Germany floundered, tensions escalated between the former Allied Forces. Because East Germany was struggling economically, many citizens fled the control and occupation of the Soviet Union, creating a huge population loss for the Soviet-occupied territory. The escalating tensions were officially referred to as the Berlin Crisis when the Soviet Union's Premier Nikita S. Khrushchev took steps to cut off the West's access to West Berlin and attempted to incorporate all of Berlin into East Germany. The Cold War maneuver brought the United States and the Soviet Union to the brink of war, with each side threatening the use of nuclear weapons. If Khrushchev closed Western access to West Berlin, the United States would retaliate, and if the West did not terminate their presence in West Berlin, the Soviets would do the same.

While the events of the Berlin Crisis evolved over a three-year period, Lieutenant Chambers slowly began to resume normalcy of life after his wife's passing, returning to sea on a new assignment aboard the USS *Midway* and back to the air as an aviator. In January 1960, *Midway* deployed to the Far East and changed operational control to Commander Seventh Fleet whose flag ship was stationed in Yokosuka, Japan. Although Chambers had only been away from his post for a short period of time, upon his return it was clear that the world around him was on the verge of dramatic changes, under a very real nuclear threat.

As Chambers was slowly rebuilding his personal life, he concentrated on his career and flying. During the same period, incumbent Republican Vice President Richard Nixon and Democratic United States Senator John F. Kennedy were running for president from their respective political parties. At the famous Kennedy-Nixon debates during the 1960 presidential election campaign, the issues of Berlin, Cuba, and the dispute between mainland China and Taiwan over the Quemoy and Matsu islands were major areas of disagreement between Nixon and Kennedy.

The phrase "Quemoy and Matsu" became part of the American political discourse when both candidates agreed to protect Taiwan from Chinese invasion, consistent with Cold War policies of the Truman and Eisenhower administrations. Both candidates pledged to use American forces if necessary. However, the two candidates disagreed as to the strategic importance of the two islands to Taiwan's national security. Kennedy argued that the islands were over 105 miles off the coast of Taiwan, and only 5 miles off the coast of mainland China; therefore, they were not vital to Taiwan's national security. Nixon took the position that the islands were not part of China's mainland and belonged to Taiwan and should be defended against the expansion of communism.

Assigned to the USS *Midway* as part of an attack squadron, Chambers patrolled the waters adjacent to the islands as the presidential candidates' political discourse had broader, more concrete geopolitical implications. The Cold War was becoming more narrowly defined as the Indochina domino principle was being expanded to all corners of the globe, and the implications would have far-reaching impact on Chambers' career while in the Navy.

While Chambers patrolled the Pacific waters, John F. Kennedy, a United States Senator from Massachusetts, took office as the nation's 35th President on January 20, 1961. Kennedy was a Lieutenant in the United States Navy during World War II when he survived a serious crash between his PT boat and a Japanese destroyer. After the war he entered politics and won the 11th Congressional district in Massachusetts in 1946. He served in the U.S. House of Representatives for six years, at which time he was elected the junior U.S. Senator from the state of Massachusetts.

During the transition period, the incoming President received briefings on Cold War activities on the Pacific, including issues around Quemoy and Matsu islands for which the Navy was the lead military agency, and on issues affecting Berlin for which the Army was the lead agency. The deciding factor for which agency would take point was based on the abutters of land mass—if a country abutted a major body of water, the Navy was in command, if there was no water, the Army was in command. As part of the military briefing, Kennedy was also made aware of challenges on the Indochinese peninsula, particularly in Vietnam.

Many on the transition team warned President Kennedy that the Soviet Union's Premier Khrushchev would likely try to test the resolve of the new president, particularly since he was young, untested and had won only by a narrow margin. The big question was where and when Khrushchev would decide to challenge Kennedy and his leadership—and might the first move be just a diversionary tactic? During the transition period, President Eisenhower made Kennedy aware of another Cold War challenge: the Central Intelligence Agency's (CIA) buildup of a Cuban anti–Castro force.

The island of Cuba, some 90 miles southwest of the United States, was in political turmoil throughout most of the 1950s until a young, brash Cuban revolutionary with communist beliefs named Fidel Castro overtook the government after the Cuban President, Fulgencio Batista, fled the country on January 1, 1959.

Castro, who had Marxist beliefs, entered into a number of trade agreements with the Soviet Union and nationalized a number of America-owned, placing them under state control. This prompted the Eisenhower Administration to develop a CIA plan to overthrow the newly formed revolutionist government. The plan included using Cuban exiles to reenter Cuba and attempt a coup.

The plan was approved by President Eisenhower who was briefed on every detail of the CIA's buildup of a Cuban anti–Castro force and fully approved of the intention. He insisted that no landing should take place until the Cuban exiles had produced a viable and popular government in exile and that while the landing or landings must be Cuban, the United States should be prepared to supply an effective air cover.[21] Because of Cuba's close proximity to the U.S. and the threat of its revolutionist government to national security, Kennedy approved the continuation of the CIA's plan (which came to be known as the Bay of Pigs Invasion).

Three months after President Kennedy took office, on April 17, 1961, the CIA moved to execute its plan, which ultimately failed. Within three days, the infiltrating Cuban exiles were overwhelmed by the Cuban military and retreated to the beaches. Rescue ships, including the USS *Conway*, USS *Eaton*, USS *Essex*, USS *Murray*, USS *Shangri-La* and USS *Threadfin* found the exiles.

The unsuccessful execution of the plan was a humiliating blow to the United States and its new president. It only emboldened the Soviet Union's Premier Khrushchev who believed that the young American President might have had a soft belly. The failure also hardened the resolve of Premier Castro that to prevent another invasion attempt from America, he needed to take sides in the rapidly escalating Cold War. He chose the Soviet Union.

On June 3, 1961, President Kennedy and Premier Khrushchev met for a two-day conference in Vienna where, in a test of Kennedy's resolve, Khrushchev informed the American president that he was renewing his intent to end the four-power agreements that allowed England, France, and the United States access to West Berlin. Confident that Kennedy was going to be a weak President, Khrushchev issued an ultimatum: on December 31, the Soviet Union "was eager to sign a peace treaty with East Germany that would automatically bring an end to all the institutions of the occupation, including the corridors to West Berlin."[22]

The Vienna Summit ended on a sour note on June 4 as Kennedy and Khrushchev each firmly stated their opposing positions on the matter. Kennedy informed the Soviet Premier that he would not tolerate the loss of rights of access to Berlin, but "Khrushchev was equally frank. He told Kennedy that if the United Sates tried to exercise these rights [to West Berlin] after a peace treaty had been signed, there would be a military response." Kennedy replied, "Then it will be a cold winter." The summit was over.[23]

On July 25, while Lieutenant Chambers was onboard the USS *Kearsarge* designated as the officer in charge of attack squadron 22, Detachment Romeo, United States attack squadrons all around the world were placed on high alert as a result of the events in Berlin. That evening in a televised address to the American public, President Kennedy revealed the seriousness of the Soviet Union's threat and his intention to request immediate funds to increase the resources of the military, along with steps he intended to take to increase its size as well.

Kennedy's response was not what Khrushchev had anticipated, and he believed that "Kennedy [had] declared preliminary war on the Soviet Union."[24] In anticipation of potential actions that might be deployed by the United States, the Soviet Union "drafted a proposal for countermeasures should the West impose an economic blockade on East Germany." The Soviet Union also devised a scheme to keep the West busy responding to Soviet crises around the world before they could develop and sustain a strategy in response to the Soviet's ultimatum.

On July 29, the KGB (Russian Military Security Force) chief Alexander Shelepin "proposed a series of measures around the world that 'would favor dispersion of attention and forces by the United States and its satellites, and would tie them down during the settlement of a German peace treaty and West Berlin.'" In particular, Shelepin advocated assisting

USS *Kearsarge*, 1963. LCDR L. C. Chambers, Officer in Charge, Virginia 22 DET "R" (personal collection).

the revolutionary movements in Latin America to distract Washington. These recommendations, if accepted, would mark a major shift in how Khrushchev would attempt to minimize U.S. power in the Third World.[25]

On August 13, 1961, East German soldiers launched Operation Rose by "stringing barbed wire and tearing up roads along West Berlin's twenty-seven-mile border with East Berlin and the remaining sixty-nine miles of border with East Germany."[26] The erection of the barbed wire was the first phase of East Germany walling itself off from the remainder of Germany. The construction of the 96 mile Berlin Wall further escalated tensions between the Soviet Union and the United States. As a demonstration of American resolve, on August 19, Vice President Lyndon B. Johnson and retired General Clay flew into West Berlin's Tempelhof Airport and conveyed to West Berlin citizens that they would not be isolated from the world.

The long, heartfelt battles of World War II in the air and on land and sea were fresh in the minds of Americans, especially for the men and women who fought battles on the Atlantic and Pacific fronts. While a third world war was not something any American wanted, they also wanted their government and its leaders to defend, protect and promote democracy in Europe. President Kennedy, a wounded World War II veteran himself, understood the importance of a free West Berlin and the long-term implications of a walled-in city:

> For the generation that fought World War II, Berlin symbolized the costly allied victory over the Nazis, the subsequent division of Germany, and the Cold War division of all Europe into two military camps. The rival Western and communist armies now stood toe to toe across the heart of Germany and also across the middle of Berlin, whose western half had become a democratic island a hundred miles inside Soviet-run eastern Germany. West Berlin would have slowly faded into its communist surroundings had Stalin not tried to strangle it with a blockade of ground traffic in 1948. Alarmed by other Soviet advances in Europe, the United States broke the blockade with an extraordinary airlift of an average six hundred flights a day, seven days a week, which kept the city supplied with food and fuel for nearly a year. When East Germany's hunger for trade with the West finally caused it to reopen the roads to truck traffic, West Berlin still stood free, all the more revered by Americans as a trophy of forceful, nonviolent resistance to Soviet expansion.[27]

On August 20, Soviet-backed East Germany began to erect a permanent 11-foot wall along the border with West Germany, replacing the temporary barbed wire erected seven days earlier. Three days later, East Germany imposed limitations on travel between East and West Berlin. By August 26, 1961, all crossing points for West Berlin citizens were closed to the outside world, creating a military standoff between U.S. and Soviet military personnel over the permanent walling of Berlin.

During the Cold War the world was becoming a gigantic chessboard where the United States and the Soviet Union jockeyed for every competitive advantage in the balance of power. The Soviet Union knew the United States had the capacity of a first nuclear strike, so they had to find a countermeasure that would neutralize and hopefully mitigate that competitive advantage.

Although the United States had superior nuclear capability, there was concern that the Soviet Union would attempt to strike first. In that event, the United States would implement its Single Integrated War Plan and attack by air, land and sea.

As Cold War tensions increased, Chambers was trained as an attack squadron pilot in every aspect of the Single Integrated War Plan (SIOP), where under certain clearly defined conditions, he would go out on practice runs where he carried "dummy blue ordinances to simulate an actual nuclear weapon and fly to his designated targeted area," then launch his simulated weapons. The only time Chambers would actually carry a nuclear weapon was when he participated in the Operational Readiness Inspections off of Hawaii, where he participated in the process of loading and plugging the bomb and checking the electrical circuits from the cockpit to the bomb.

In the event that the highly classified code was given to strike, each pilot had their own predetermined route to fly whether or not they had a map. Chambers, as with the other pilots, were expected to memorize his coordinates and be able to fly to the designated spot on a "minute's notice." The pilots were constantly taken into secure test areas and tested on their memory of their sites' coordinates and their ability to fly under the most extreme conditions. At the conclusion of the exercise, Chambers was required to provide a complete debriefing of his activities and explain the timing and justification of all of his coordinates.

As an aviator, Chambers understood from his SIOP training and debriefings that upon launching from his aircraft carrier, if he had to actually drop nuclear weapons at his designated targets, there was no guarantee that the ship would be there upon his return. The training that Chambers and other military personnel received could not come soon enough. While Khrushchev's primary objective was the situation in Berlin, he moved forward with distracting the United States by creating turmoil closer to the American home.

As a diversionary tactic, Khrushchev took strategic steps to create turmoil in Latin America, including developing a closer relationship with Cuba's Fidel Castro. Castro, who feared another attempt by the Kennedy administration to invade Cuba, warmly received the overture. Castro looked to the Soviet Union for support, trade, defense and weapons.

Castro sent his brother "to Moscow in July to negotiate a treaty of 'mutual defense.' As finally written, it pledged both countries to 'take all necessary measures to repel' aggression against Cuba."²⁸ The agreement, although initially secret, was what Castro needed to protect his island from American aggression or invasion and what Khrushchev needed to distract the Americans from his more serious designs for Berlin and Eastern Europe. On September 8, 1962, the Soviet Union began to secretly deploy strategic nuclear missiles to Cuba in an attempt to have their own first strike capability to hit American cities.

Khrushchev would now have the desired competitive advantage that he wanted over the United States. By October 15, the CIA discovered what some had suspected and feared. The Soviet Union had taken steps to build medium-range nuclear missiles on the Caribbean island, and U.S. spy planes identified four clearly defined operational sites in Cuba when

> On October 14 a pair of U-2s flown by SAC ... pilots took extensive aerial photographs of western Cuba. By Monday evening, October 15, CIA photographic analysts had studied the U-2 pictures and informed McGeorge Bundy, President Kennedy's national security advisor, that the Soviet Union was in the process of building launching sites for both 1,000 mile-medium-range missiles (MRBM) and 2,200-mile intermediate-range missiles (IRBM).²⁹

While stationed in the Pacific, as the officer in charge of attack squadron 22, Detachment Romeo, aboard the aircraft carrier USS *Kearsarge* to ensure their attack readiness in the event of a provoked incident, Chambers and other military personnel were receiving constant debriefings on ever-changing events in the Pacific as well as events in the Atlantic. On October 22, President Kennedy delivered a televised speech to the nation announcing the discovery of Soviet medium-range missiles pointed toward American cities.

During the speech, the President informed the nation that he ordered the Soviet Union to remove the missiles and ordered the U.S. Navy to conduct a "quarantine" of the Cuban island. The next six days were crucial in averting a third world war or a nuclear catastrophe on American soil, and

> The Cuban missile crisis marked the closest the world has yet come to nuclear destruction. For six harrowing days in 1962, from the time President John F. Kennedy informed the nation of the Soviet missile buildup in Cuba until Nikita Khrushchev agreed to pull back, the American people lived under the threat of disaster. The armed forces went from Defense Condition Five (peacetime alert) to Defcon 3 (war alert), and the Strategic Air Command was ordered to Defcon 2 (full war footing), only one step away from actual hostiles.³⁰

U.S. Naval Captains in the Caribbean Sea and the Straits of Florida notified Washington that they believed the Russians were intercepting their communications. This occurred around the same time that the Kennedy administration was trying to ascertain what technological capabilities the Russians really had. While the Russians were off the coast of Cuba shadowing U.S.

ships, Admiral Isaac Kidd, Jr., of the Atlantic Fleet believed the Russians were intercepting communications from ships in the Atlantic Ocean off the coast of Cuba. According to Chambers, "The Staffs at the Pentagon were so arrogant that they didn't believe, or at least didn't want to believe Admiral Kidd and his belief that the Russians had the capacity to listen electronically into our systems."

In order to prove his point, Admiral Kidd brought all of the commanding officers over to his flagship where they decided that there would be no transmissions on any frequency. The moment they resumed transmitting, the Russians showed up. Kidd then wrote to Washington and told them that his mail was being read. The Navy was instructed to have the Pacific Fleet immediately conduct reconnaissance on the Russians in the Sea of Japan and determine their capabilities.

While Chambers was onboard, the *Kearsarge* clandestinely went through the narrow Tsugaru Strait between the Japanese territorial islands of Honshu and Hokkaido at night into the Sea of Japan without any running lights or electronic emissions. Although the Japanese government knew that the *Kearsarge* was passing through their waters, everything was done in the dark of night.

For three days in the Sea of Japan, *Kearsarge* operated with no electronic transmissions of any kind, not even from aircraft, in an attempt to determine the full capabilities of the Russians and find out what they could and could not detect electronically. At a specified time, the admiral ordered the captain of Kearsarge to turn on the radio and other electronic emissions. The moment *Kearsarge* began radiating on various frequencies and lit off its radar, it apparently caught the Russians off-guard, but in about an hour, they sent about 25 large Russian Tupolev aircraft (also known as Russian Badgers) to the waters around the aircraft carrier.

The Soviet Tupolev Tu-16 aircraft was initially "developed as a strategic bomber [and] ... carried up to 19,841 pounds of free-fall bombs or two large nuclear bombs internally." Subsequent models were "configured for long-range maritime reconnaissance and for targeting anti-ship missiles...." The Russian "Badger" aircraft normally "operated only from Soviet bases during the Cold War, beginning in April 1970 pairs of Bear-D aircraft took off from the Russian Kola Peninsula, flew around North Cape and down the Norwegian Sea and North Atlantic to land in Cuba...." After a few days in Cuba, the Bears flew more than 5,000 non-stop miles on their return flight home while conducting "surveillance operations along the coast of North America, generally flying 200–250 miles off shore."[31]

Once the Russian Badgers appeared, no one knew what to expect, so the Captain of *Kearsarge* sent four fighter planes up in the air to provide cover for the aircraft carrier. Chambers was on the first intercept and had two sidewinder missiles and a full load of 20-millimeter ammunition onboard. As the Russians approached, they started to take pictures of *Kearsarge* and of the fighter jets. Chambers and the other naval aviators took pictures of the Russian Badgers. Not easily intimidated by their number and the enormous size of the planes, Chambers did not take any chances and had his master arm switch at the ready in the event he was fired upon.

Once the incident was over and the A-4s landed back onboard, each of the four pilots debriefed *Kearsarge*'s commanding officers on what took place in the air. When the Admiral was made aware that Chambers had his master arm switch on, he was not happy. But as Chambers recalls, his feelings at the time was that "if the Russians started shooting at me, I was going to at least bring down two of them, and as a young man I felt that the worst thing that would happen, I would just have to eject."

On October 23, 1962, in an attempt to reduce tensions at least on a temporary basis, Soviet President Nikita Khrushchev stopped Soviet ships en route to Cuba 750 miles offshore. This temporarily prevented a direct confrontation with U.S. ships that surrounded Cuba, although Soviet submarines trailed behind U.S. ships as they moved into place.

On October 24, Khrushchev informed the White House that its quarantine around Cuba put the world at risk of a nuclear war and that he would not remove the missiles from Cuba. The next day, Kennedy increased the number of flights over Cuba from once to twice per day, including night flights, in an attempt to monitor missile activity on the island.

On October 26, in anticipation that the Soviets might not back down on their threats, Kennedy's newly formed group of political and military advisors known as Ex-Comm began to develop contingency plans—including the real possibility of invading Cuba, taking control of the government and dismantling the missiles. Such an action would absolutely be considered an aggressive act against a sovereign nation and would certainly result in war between the Soviet Union and the United States.

Considered by some as a surprise move, on October 27 Khrushchev indicated that Soviet missiles would be removed if Kennedy provided assurances that the Cuban island would not be invaded and if the Americans agreed to remove missiles in Turkey that were aimed at the Russians. The next day, on October 28, Khrushchev delivered a radio speech in which he agreed with President Kennedy's secret offer to remove the 1954 missiles placed in Turkey by NATO as a deterrent to any Soviet aggression in Eastern Europe, and the Cuban Missile Crisis came to an end.

Chapter 5

Vietnam War

On March 28, 1975, when Captain Chambers took command of the USS *Midway* in Yokosuka, Japan, U.S. involvement in Vietnam was coming to an end after a tumultuous 20 years. As the first African American to take command of a U.S. aircraft carrier, the span and depth of Chambers' military career reflected the requirements needed to succeed in a Cold War military. As the Navy reengineered its operations to meet the ever-changing geopolitical challenges of the Cold War, Chambers was afforded unique opportunities and took advantage of the continuous training exercises and command posts that allowed him to manage one of the mightiest ships at the time.

The events in Vietnam unfolded during different phases of Chambers' career. In 1958, the turmoil in Vietnam began to escalate as he was completing his studies at the Naval Postgraduate School. Ho Chi Minh, the North's Democratic Republic of Vietnam's President, increased his efforts to unify the two Vietnams under communist control. He sent communist insurgents south over the 17th parallel to launch "small-scale raids against government strongholds. Under the slogan 'Extermination of Traitors,' they also accelerated their assassination campaign, targeting especially those South Vietnamese officials who damaged the communist cause...."[1]

In his inaugural address to the nation on January 20, 1961, President John F. Kennedy reaffirmed his commitment to the Cold War foreign policy initiatives and doctrines of his predecessors, Presidents Harry S Truman and Dwight D. Eisenhower. While Truman had focused on containing communism by providing technical assistance and military support to foreign countries, and Eisenhower provided economic and military assistance and support to prevent the spread of communism in the Middle East. President Kennedy intended to reverse communism in the entire Western hemisphere.

After the events in Cuba and Berlin, the conflict between North and South Vietnam brought into question Kennedy's commitment to the "survival and

5. Vietnam War

March, North Pacific Ocean, 1975. Captain Lawrence Chambers takes command of the USS *Midway* (courtesy Naval History & Heritage Command Photo Archive, Naval Subject Collection).

the success of liberty," particularly for President Ngo Dinh Diem's government in South Vietnam.

Communist North Vietnam began to covertly supply communist sympathizers in the South, primarily in rural areas, with supplies and manpower. So as to go undetected, the supplies and materials were shipped through the rough mountainous terrain from North Vietnam through neighboring Cambodia and Laos, then back into South Vietnam through a series of mountainous roads commonly referred to as the Ho Chi Minh trail.

The initial shipments were by primitive means, reflecting the narrow oxen paths of generations going between the North and South transporting products and supplies. As the roads became more widely used and cleared, the ability to transport supplies and weaponry to North Vietnamese infiltrating the South increased tremendously during periods of good weather, generally from October to March. Ho Chi Minh and his communist sympathizers, supported by

China and the Soviet Union, concerned the Kennedy Administration. On May 9, 1961, then Vice President Lyndon Johnson conducted a tour of Southeast countries where he met South Vietnam's President Ngo Dinh Diem, and Johnson assured Diem of the United States' continued support against the Russian-supported North Vietnamese:

> Returning home, Johnson echoed the domino theorists in a message that foreshadowed his later contention that the loss of Vietnam would compel America to fight "on the beaches of Waikiki." "The battle against Communism must be joined in Southeast Asia with strength and determination ... or the United States, inevitably, must surrender the Pacific and take up our defenses on our own shores."[2]

During Johnson's visit, President Diem requested American personnel to train South Vietnamese soldiers. However, Diem also made an unusual and controversial request of the United States. The thick forest vegetation of the Ho Chi Minh trail made the North Vietnamese supply trucks heavy with weapons and manpower difficult to find and neutralize. Diem asked that the United States conduct aerial spraying of defoliant and herbicide agents over the thick forest so as to expose the North Vietnamese trucks.

As the United States debated the request and its possible effects, the U.S. Air Force and Navy conducted joint reconnaissance flights over Laos. Pilots assigned to the Navy's attack squadron aboard the USS *Ranger* were among the naval aviators who made initial flights over Laos. Once the U.S. decided to honor Diem's request, the Navy's attack squadron would often commence the aerial spraying and take out any enemy posts before the chemical ordinances were dropped on the Ho Chi Minh trail and its distribution centers. Chambers commented that during these flights, pilots would see a portion of the trail that was taken out, but these sections of the trail would be quickly repaired wider and stronger than before. Likewise, when a distribution center was taken out, two more would spring up in its place.

As Vietnam became the next proxy war between the United States and the Soviet Union, in May 1961, President Kennedy decided to send 400 Special Forces to Vietnam to help train South Vietnamese soldiers. Although the administration sent advisors to South Vietnam, the President was concerned about mission creep (a change from the original objectives of a military mission), and was conflicted over the number of additional resources being sent to support Diem. Kennedy believed that the South Vietnamese had to address the issue of insurgents internally and not rely on American resources. As revolutionists from the North, aided by rural insurgents from the South, attacked key outposts in South Vietnam, military reports came back to the White House of corruption within the Diem regime and questions were continually raised about the capacity, readiness, quality and strength of the South Vietnamese Army.

South Vietnam's problems were not limited to aggression from the North. Internal class warfare and religious strife contributed to the conflict between Diem and his urban supporters, as well as the opposition from rural and peasant populations. As Americans became more involved with the Diem regime, they began to question his motives and, more importantly, his ability to bridge the various factions within his own country, let alone defend his country against the North's aggression.

The events between North and South Vietnam caused tremendous concern for the Kennedy Administration. The conflict was brought up as an agenda item at the June 3, 1961, Vienna Summit meeting between President Kennedy and Soviet Premier Khrushchev, at which point Vietnam and other Cold War issues including disarmament were discussed. Despite the Kennedy Administration's concern over Vietnam, its attention was focused on the Berlin Crisis and the escalation of events in Cuba. However, Kennedy knew that Vietnam was the place where the United States would have to take a stand.

As world tensions escalated, the United States needed to demonstrate American strength worldwide. The military needed to expand its ranks and the United States Navy took steps to expand its internal capacity. It established a list of qualified candidates for the position of Lieutenant Commander. Based on his merit and qualifications, Lieutenant Chambers was promoted on September 1, 1961, to the rank of Lieutenant Commander.

The promotion was historic in that it came at a time when an insignificant number of African American men were officers in the United States Navy. As illustrated in Figure 3, less than 0.2 percent of African American men were officers in the Navy, and of the remaining three branches of the military, the Marine Corps fared no better. The dismal record of the United States military in race relations would set the stage for political and community activism for the better part of the 1960s.

Figure 32: African American Strength in the Armed Forces for Selected Years[3] **(In Percentages)**

Year	Army		Navy		Marine Corps		Air Force	
	Enlisted Men	Officers	Enlisted Men	Officers	Enlisted Men	Officers	Enlisted Men	Officers
1949	12.4	1.8	4.7	0.0	2.1	0.0	5.1	0.6
1954	13.7	3.0	3.6	0.1	6.5	0.1	8.6	1.1
1962	12.2	3.2	5.2	0.2	7.6	0.2	9.2	1.2

As Cold War events in Berlin, Cuba and Vietnam escalated, Lieutenant Commander Chambers was assigned to the VA 22 Detachment Romeo on board the USS *Kearsarge* (CV-33) as part of its attack squadron on April 19, 1962. Chambers was now being trained to deal with international conflicts with an emphasis on the Navy and its evolving role with fighter pilots. Based on his academic credentials while at Annapolis and being proficient in several languages, Chambers was being trained to become a scholar on issues related to Russian and Chinese military culture, their interference with the waters and the events on the Indochinese peninsula.

Russia and China were intimately involved with the conflict in Vietnam, and for most of 1962 and the early part of 1963, the United States questioned the ability of President Ngo Dinh Diem. According to Vietnam historian Stanley Karnow in his acclaimed book, *Vietnam, a History: the First Complete Account of Vietnam at War*, the general belief was that the South Vietnamese president didn't have the capacity to effectively lead his people and bring the war to a successful conclusion:

> Diem, though dedicated, was doomed by his inflexible pride.... Ruling like an ancient emperor, he could not deal effectively with either the mounting Communist threat to his regime or the opposition of South Vietnam's turbulent factions alienated by his autocracy. His generals—some greedy for power, others antagonized by his style—turned against him.... His collapse would have been impossible without American complicity. President Kennedy, frustrated by Diem's inability to conciliate dissident groups in the face of the growing Communist challenge, conceded that the war could not be won under his aegis.[4]

Many within South Vietnam shared the same concerns that the Kennedy Administration had in Washington. On November 2, 1963, South Vietnamese President Diem was assassinated during a coup, one that was implicitly supported by President Kennedy:

> South Vietnam, he insisted, was too important to lose because of one man's bigotry and lust for power. Although Kennedy did not publically call for a coup, he hinted in a televised interview that it might be a good thing. Privately, he indicated that America would support those who overthrew Diem. Thus, by encouraging the plotters, he shared responsibility for their actions.[5]

A mere three weeks after Diem was executed by his own military, Lee Harvey Oswald, a former U.S. Marine and a communist sympathizer, assassinated President Kennedy on November 22, 1963, in Dallas, Texas. His assassination placed the legacy and the challenges of Vietnam in the hands of Kennedy's Vice President, Lyndon B. Johnson. As the nation mourned the loss of President Kennedy, the newly sworn in President Johnson met with members of his inherited cabinet and national security advisors, many of whom he had little-to-no trust in.

Upon review of President Kennedy's October 11, 1963, National Security Administration Memorandum 263 in which Kennedy intended to slowly disengage American involvement in Vietnam by reducing the number of troops by 1,000 by the end of the year, President Johnson reversed course. He issued his own National Security Administration Memorandum 263 on November 26, 1963, to the Secretaries of State and Defense and to the Chairman of the Joint Chiefs of Staff in which he directed an expanded war effort in Vietnam, as he believed this was the necessary tactic in order to bring the war to an end.

As American involvement was increasing under President Johnson, on the evening of July 31, 1964, North Vietnamese islands located in the Gulf of Tonkin were attacked by South Vietnamese gunboats. On August 2, "the destroyer USS *Maddox* appeared nearby in international waters. The North Vietnamese, believing that the gunboats and the destroyer were acting together, sent three torpedo boats after the *Maddox*." Following a brief, fierce fight, "the *Maddox* sank one torpedo boat and drove off the others. LBJ personally ordered another destroyer, the USSC *Turner Joy*, to join the *Maddox* without delay."[6]

Tension in the Gulf resulted in a second incident on August 4 when sailors aboard the *Maddox* mistakenly believed that the North Vietnamese were firing upon them for a second time. Together, the incidents became known as the Gulf of Tonkin Incident. On August 7, 1964, the United States Congress passed the Gulf of Tonkin Resolution in response: "By a House vote of 416–0 and a Senate vote of 88–2, Congress authorized the President to take 'all necessary measures to repel any armed attack against the forces of the United States and to prevent further aggression' … including the use of the armed force."[7]

On February 7, 1965, while U.S. Security Advisor McGeorge Bundy was on tour in South Vietnam, the Viet Cong attacked the South Vietnamese Army Base at Pleiku and killed eight Americans. On March 2, 1965, the U.S. and South Vietnamese Air Force retaliated in a joint operation known as Operation Flaming Dart, striking military bases in North Vietnam and bombing Viet Cong encampments. The Viet Cong quickly "responded by killing twenty-three U.S. soldiers when they blew up a hotel in Qui Nhon."[8] In order to protect American interests in South Vietnam, the first U.S. combat troops arrived on March 8, 1965.

Johnson dispatched over 20,000 troops to the Dominican Republic on April 28, 1965, to protect resident Americans during a civil war on the island. Johnson used the protection of American citizens as a pretense to ensure a civil war in the Dominican Republic did not provide the Soviet Union and Cuba the opportunity to establish another Communist government in the Western hemisphere. In response to the events in the Dominican Republic, President Johnson enacted the Johnson Doctrine on May 2, 1965, an extension of the

Eisenhower and Kennedy Doctrines, to continue the containment and ultimate reversal of communism in the Western hemisphere and worldwide.

The Johnson Doctrine intended to not only address communism in the Western hemisphere, but also in Vietnam. Johnson, always the strategic politician, understood the concerns of members of Congress over the events in the Dominican Republic and the implications for the hemisphere. Johnson submitted to Congress "a request for $700 million to pay for American efforts in both Vietnam and the Dominican Republic."[9]

On July 28, after the Johnson Administration had debated "about options in the Indochina Theater ... [it] announced the dispatch of 125,000 more troops to South Vietnam."[10] Unlike the military buildup of the U.S. Army and Air Force, the naval branch of the military's involvement prior to 1965 was somewhat limited:

> In early 1965, the U.S. Navy activity was limited to support functions in the Saigon area, construction and medical activities, and advising the Vietnamese Navy and Marine Corps. In March of 1965, the first operational U.S. Navy units commenced counter-infiltration patrols. Late 1965 saw planning for the second major influx of operational U.S. Navy units. Operation GAME WARDEN, designed to supplement Vietnamese units in patrol if the Mekong Delta and Rung Sat Special Zone waterways, was to come into operation during 1966, with high speed River Patrol Boats as the principal units.[11]

On June 7, 1965, General William Westmoreland, the U.S. Commander of all military operations in Vietnam, informed President Johnson that the North Vietnamese supported by China, Russia, and the rebel Viet Cong "had at last declared [their] intentions in classical military terms." Westmoreland told the President that "North Vietnam's army had already crossed over into the south, and more were on the way." In Hanoi, jet fighters and light bombers dispatched from Russia and China arrived, "presumably to prepare for the onslaught." Finally, "Captured documents and prisoner interrogations ... confirmed other intelligence that a 'campaign [was] now underway to destroy government [U.S. and South Vietnamese] forces ... [and] The Communists believed final victory was within their grasp."[12]

According to Vietnam historian Karnow, General Westmoreland had developed a three-prong strategy in winning the war. His first tactic was to "deploy the American troops to protect the U.S. air and supply bases along the South Vietnamese coast and around Saigon." Then, he intended to "send units into the central highlands in order to block any attempt by the North Vietnamese and Vietcong to sweep across to the sea and slice the country in two." Finally, he would "launch a series of search-and-destroy operations in which the American forces, with their vastly superior mobility and firepower, would relentlessly grind down the enemy."[13] Westmoreland believed that his approach would win the war within three years.

Living in the shadow of the assassinated John F. Kennedy, President Johnson introduced legislation to address national poverty and leverage federal funds to combat poverty at the state and local levels on January 8, 1964. Johnson had several domestic policies he wanted to initiate that he hoped to leave as his legacy. President Kennedy had addressed the nation about escalating racial tensions in the South and the need to advance Civil Rights legislation to protect the rights of African Americans, but he was unable to get the legislation passed before his assassination. After President Kennedy's death, Lyndon Johnson went to the American people and Congress on November 27, 1963, and insisted that "No memorial oration or eulogy could more eloquently honor President Kennedy's memory than the earliest possible passage of the civil rights bill for which he fought so long."[14]

On July 2, President Johnson signed the landmark Civil Rights Act of 1964. Johnson wanted his legacy to be the elimination of poverty and racial injustice, creating what was to be known as Johnson's Great Society. He believed that the Vietnam conflict was diverting Congress and his own full attention from the fulfillment of his legacy. Intending to bring the Vietnam conflict to a successful end, on July 21, 1965, President Johnson made the difficult decision to commit the United States to a full-scale war in Vietnam. He ordered that the conscription be raised to 35,000 per month with the intent to increase the number of troops as needed.

As part of his Great Society programs, President Johnson signed the Voting Rights Act on August 6, 1965. For the following 12 months, communities all across the nation were being challenged with the question of the status quo of racial inequalities within their communities. Within these same communities, the question about why the United States was in Vietnam began to take hold.

On November 14, 1965, after an additional 100,000 American troops were sent to Vietnam, the Battle of Ia Drang occurred, the first American battle of the war with the North Vietnamese. American strength overwhelmed the North Vietnamese, and "More than two thousand enemy soldiers were killed during the fighting while 'only' two hundred Americans died. Westmoreland's new army had routed the enemy in their first encounter."[15]

In early 1966, the American public began to question the increasing casualties of war in a part of the world of which they had very little understanding, and questioned the vast sums of money used to support the war's effort. On February 4, 1966, Senator J. William Fulbright, Chairman of the powerful U.S. Senate Foreign Relations Committee, began to hold televised hearings on the

Vietnam War. Two days later, President Johnson convened a conference in Honolulu regarding the war.

While Americans were beginning to question the war back in the United States, political and religious dissidents in Vietnam, primarily Vietnamese Buddhists and students, began to protest against the Saigon government. On May 15, 1966, the South Vietnamese government fought with Buddhists, and over 80 dissidents were killed during demonstrations against the government. To draw further attention to the May 15 killings, on May 26, 1966, a Buddhist monk drenched himself in gasoline and set himself on fire in front of the United States consulate in Hue, South Vietnam, a moment that was captured by an American photographer.

While the strategic value of the war was being questioned, particularly in the aftermath Buddhists monks setting themselves ablaze, General Westmoreland was making plans to expand the military footprint in Vietnam. In the fall of 1965, Chambers was promoted to Commander.

In late summer and early fall of 1966 and throughout much of 1967, General Westmoreland planned for a major offensive into areas controlled by the Viet Cong, also known as the National Liberation Front (NLF), particularly in the areas around the South Vietnamese capital city of Saigon:

> During 1966 and 1967, Westmoreland repeatedly sent large forces to destroy NLF bases near Saigon.... U.S. and South Vietnamese troops killed thousands of enemy soldiers and seized tons of weapons, while razing hostile villages and wide swaths of jungle. Through it all, aircraft and artillery pulverized the area to assure that nothing remained of the communist strongholds. And yet none of these stunning displays of mobility and firepower succeeded in uprooting communist forces permanently.[16]

Initial assessments of the various operations were favorable to American objectives, and "major U.S. operations inflicted severe casualties and kept the communists off balance. But American forces could never seem to destroy the ability of the North Vietnamese to carry on the war."[17]

As a result of new technology applications learned from space programs and the constant fear of Russia having a competitive edge in the field of technology, during 1967 naval technology was changing rapidly, and the ability to transfer critical intelligence to the commanding officer was vital to a ship's coordinates and surroundings. The Navy, with an abundance of qualified candidates on the command screen lists, suddenly assigned Chambers and other men on the command list to the Combat Information Center (CIC) aboard the ships at sea.

After completing his two years on staff at the Naval Postgraduate School at Monterey, Commander Chambers hoped he would go back to a fighter squadron, but he was assigned as a Combat Information Center Officer aboard the USS *Ranger* (CV-61). The Combat Information Center is the aircraft carrier's centralized hub for the ship's air and surface radar equipment and serves as the ship's central point for its air and sea defense system. As the CIC Officer, Chambers was responsible for all of the tactical information that came into and/or left the ship's command. The USS *Ranger* was actively engaged in a number of diverse combat operations against North Vietnam. *Ranger* struck strategic military targets in North Vietnam with supporting air strikes by the ship's air wing.

The Navy had now introduced the A-7 attack aircraft into its carrier air wings, and these aircrafts were equipped with highly sophisticated digital avionics. The A-7 Corsair was a single-seat carrier based attack airplane used by the Navy as a replacement for the Douglas A-4 Skyhawk. First introduced during the Vietnam War, the aircraft went through several technical changes and with the A-7E model became one of the world's first aircraft to be equipped with a digital computer to aid pilots with onboard navigation and enhanced capability for attacking ground targets.

As an experience fighter pilot and now the CIC Officer, Chambers oversaw and coordinated the flight operations of *Ranger*'s aviators who supported the war effort in Vietnam. With the A-7's cutting edge mapping software, Chambers and the pilots could communicate bombing coordinates with higher precision rates, reducing losses with a higher target kill rate. The new technology also allowed for an increased sortie rate aboard the carriers by allowing turn around and relaunch in a shorter time span.

On September 29, 1967, President Johnson delivered a speech in his home state of Texas in which he offered to halt the continuous bombing of North Vietnam if Ho Chi Minh, President of North Vietnam, would engage in a negotiated peace settlement. The overture came with the condition that North Vietnam would not use the offer as a pretense to build up troops and supplies to the Viet Cong in South Vietnam. North Vietnam never acknowledged the offer.

The speech angered some and delighted others. The A-7 aircraft, built by aerospace-defense company Chance Vought Corporation (LTV), was built in Dallas, Texas, and employed over 30,000 people. Texans were angered that Johnson would take a step that could be costly to the jobs in his home state. However, during the fall of 1967 once college classes were back in session, college campus protest rallies began to develop nationwide. During the week of October 16, 1967, less than a month after Johnson's speech coordinated antiwar activities and demonstrations were held throughout the United States.

While Chambers was in *Ranger* as the Combat Information Control Officer, the USS *Pueblo* was boarded and captured by the North Korean government. On January 23, 1968, North Korea stated that the *Pueblo*, a highly classified electronic intelligence and signals intelligence ship, had strayed into their territorial waters. Although *Ranger* and *Pueblo* served different purposes within the Navy, the intelligence equipment aboard *Pueblo* was the same equipment Chambers used to receive and transmit information aboard *Ranger* as the CIC Officer.

Ranger was diverted to go and assist *Pueblo* but did not arrive in time to be of assistance. Had *Ranger* arrived, Chambers believes that it could have provided the necessary fire support to the *Pueblo*. (It should be noted that to this day, the USS *Pueblo* is in the hands of the North Koreans and is used as a museum in North Korea). As the incident progressed and additional United States assets moved to provide operational support to *Pueblo*, the Russians also began to move their assets into the area. A collision occurred between a Russian man-o'-war and a U.S. Navy destroyer. Chambers and the commanding officer of the destroyer were well known to each other, and on several occasions the commander had used racial epithets toward Chambers when he could not get his way on matters.

As *Ranger*'s CIC Officer, Chambers' tracking system was able to track the incident as the two vessels approached each other, and in looking at the ship's data Chambers could clearly see that it was the Russians' fault. The Russian commander did not follow international rules of the road and was playing a sophomoric game of chicken that caused the incident.

Chambers knew what the commanding officer of the destroyer thought about him—and how little he thought of him—but Chambers came forward with documentation that proved the collision was the Russians' fault. The commander came forward and thanked Chambers for his professionalism, relieved that his previous bigotry hadn't worked against him. But Chambers was an honest man, and he called things as he saw them. That was why his men relied on and trusted him. When Chambers was growing up, the issues of race were very easy to understand, since everything was segregated—it was either black or white. "If you were black, you lived in your end of town, you attended your own schools, drank out of your own water fountains, and used your own restrooms. If you were white you didn't have the same social limitations simply defined by race." But things were different now. Chambers was not defined by just being Black, but now as a man who was responsible for other men's lives, and they relied on him to return them safely back to the ship each time and every time they took to the air.

While they might have still cared that he was Black, what they really cared about more was that he was the most competent man on board and was calling the complex maneuvers that ensured their safe return aboard ship. Chambers' men knew he was good, he thought things through carefully, he didn't shoot from the hip, he excelled under the most demanding pressures and most importantly, he never made the wrong call.

Chambers' impressive success aboard the USS *Ranger* as the CIC Officer almost didn't happen. Once he was promoted to Lieutenant Commander on September 1, 1961, Chambers began to sense a change in the interactions he had with both his colleagues and some of his commanders. Prior to that moment, he had never really felt a threat to anyone since he was a low man on the "totem pole."

By the time he was deployed as an officer-in-charge of VA 22 in Detachment "R" on board USS *Kearsarge*, he began to notice a "sea of change" as he commanded his men. It was clear to his superiors and his subordinates that he was gifted and talented, exactly what the Navy looks for within its ranks for "tracked" promotions. Chambers was a young, extremely articulate, highly intelligent Black man, and his competitors and detractors knew he could easily be on an impressive career path that could cause problems for those who believed he was getting too close to the "glass ceiling."

In the military, if the "powers that be" wanted to kill a career, a military man would be sent to an assignment that would effectively become the end of his career. Once Lieutenant Commander Chambers was assigned to the Naval Postgraduate School in Monterey, California, as the Assistant Curriculum Officer for aeronautical engineering programs on December 1, 1963, he believed that his career was being shortchanged and coming to an end because of his race.

However, while working at the Postgraduate School, Chambers took advantage of having access to information technology courses and programs, which in fact became one of the best career moves for him. Once Chambers was sent as *Ranger*'s CIC Officer, he made his ship and his captain look good, and the commanders in the Seventh Fleet took notice. As Chambers endured subtle forms of racism in the Navy, and as more African American men entered service and slowly made their way up the ranks, issues of race were getting more complicated in the service and were beginning to reflect the racial atmosphere and animosity in American society as a whole.

Chapter 6

Civil Unrest

Upon his graduation from the Naval Academy, the White House and the Pentagon were very concerned about Chambers' initial success and wanted to make sure that his first experience on a ship was in a controlled environment where he would not be subjected to bigoted shipmates and commanding officers. The Commandant of Midshipmen, who was sensitive to the issues of race and race relations on the various ships, called Chambers into his office and advised Chambers that his chosen ship would not be a good fit, strongly suggesting that the USS *Columbus* was a better vessel on which to make a maiden voyage. The Commandant placed significant emphasis that the skipper, Captain Gordon Campbell, was a good friend who would ensure that Chambers would be given a fair shake onboard ship.

Throughout his entire naval career, including at the Naval Academy, Chambers witnessed firsthand how insidious racism in the military could be and how the system could "do a man in" if it didn't want to advance his career. He had witnessed how a man would be promoted with the expectation that he would fail so his career would be permanently derailed.

At each stage of his career, Chambers always heard his grandfather in the back of his mind: he was more than qualified for the position, but now he would have to work twice as hard to keep it so that he could advance in his career and avoid detractors, no matter where they lurked. His grandfather also taught him that if you get knocked down, get back up and continue to put one foot in front of the other. Chambers knew, thanks to his grandfather, that he should never become angry, since that would mean his opponents and enemies had won. In order to be a man who walked 10 feet tall, Chambers had to be smarter, run faster, and be better than his biggest critic.

In the early part of his career, this was hard because there were so few African American men to fall back on as a support group and sounding board. In 1962 when Chambers was a Lieutenant Commander, less than 0.2 percent of the officers in the United States Navy and Marine Corps were African American, and the percentage of African American enlisted men was 5.2 and 7.6 percent respectively, substantially lower than their representation in the general population as a whole. While representation in the Army and Air Force were slightly better, political and civil rights groups, similar to activism during World War II, called for better representation in the nation's Armed Forces.[1]

By 1967, as civil unrest across the country began to spread, African Americans were becoming part of the military in unprecedented numbers, primarily as a direct result of an outreach program initiated by Secretary of Defense Robert McNamara. Once President Johnson made the decision to commit the United States to a major war effort in Vietnam, the United States draft was mandated to raise a minimum of 35,000 troops per month, and had the capacity to raise an additional 50,000 men per month if needed.

McNamara, a political holdover from the Kennedy administration, and his new boss President Lyndon Johnson agreed on little, but the Secretary embraced wholeheartedly the President's War on Poverty. In August of 1966, before the less-than-friendly audience of the Veterans of Foreign Wars, Secretary McNamara addressed the devastating effects of poverty in the context of the "law that required that all boys turning eighteen take the Armed Forces Qualification Test, … [and how] each year about a third, or 600,000 of the 1.8 million who took it failed because, McNamara said, 'they [were] victims of faulty education or inadequate health services.'"[2]

At the veteran's annual conference, Secretary McNamara made a startling announcement about a bold new program titled *Project 100,000*. McNamara wanted to leverage the opportunity of the military with a program that would "uplift the 'subterranean poor' by taking into the military each year 100,000 young men who would normally be rejected." He informed the audience "that the approximately 100,000 of those who failed the test could be accepted and, through 'the application of advanced educational and medical techniques,' be 'salvaged,' first for 'productive military careers and later for productive roles in society.'"[3]

The basis for the program as illustrated in Figure 4[4] was the fact that the military needed to rapidly increase its numbers, juxtaposed with the data showing that a disproportionate number of those disqualified for military service were racial minorities.

Figure 4: Rate of Men Disqualified for Service in 1962 (In Percentages)

Cause	White	Nonwhite
Medical and other	21.8	10.1
Mental test failure	8.4	50.6
Total	30.2	60.7

In short order, civil rights advocates questioned if McNamara and his "fellow social engineers knew that the majority of project men would be assigned to the Army," and that eventually African American men would endure a "higher risk of becoming casualties in Vietnam than other entering servicemen who qualified, usually on the basis of higher scores, for noncombat jobs." The idea behind Project 100,000 was that

> low-aptitude men could be "fully satisfactory soldiers" by keeping their commanders ignorant of which men they were. Project 100,000 would be a blind experiment run on a 1.5 million-member organization.... Draft boards and recruiting centers were instructed to have 22.3 percent of all recruits be "Cat Fours," men who scored in Category Four of five on the AFQT. The boards and centers were told to single out, within the Cat Fours, a certain number of men with specific characteristics that marked them as victims of poverty. These project men were to be identified as part of the experiment only by a secret code in their file.[5]

A number of the Project 100,000 men assigned to the Navy eventually came under the command of Lieutenant Commander Chambers. Chambers initially embraced the project for its potential to provide access to military training, discipline, and employment skills to the large numbers of African American men who had been previously denied access to the military.

Having grown up in the segregated south, Chambers empathized with these men, many of whom had grown up in similar situations. Many had been raised by a single parent or by grandparents and had grown up poor, needing direction, guidance and a path forward, much like Chambers did at their age. He recalled his high school mentor, Colonel Henry O. Atwood, head of Dunbar High School's Cadet Program and the role he had played in Chambers' development in high school. The self-discipline he learned from Atwood as a young man certainly helped him at Annapolis and in his early military career.

In the early days of the program, Chambers heard the criticisms and deliberate, racially-coded, derogatory "dog whistle" words in reference to the men. He heard the underhanded remarks about their qualifications and readiness of the large number of Black men entering the Navy. He chalked these comments up to the same narrow-minded rhetoric and bigotry that he had heard about himself when he first entered the Naval Academy and during the earlier years of his career, and the disparate treatment of Wes Brown at the Naval Academy and Benjamin O. Davis at West Point.

But Chambers soon learned that even though he was barely 15 years older than many of the men who comprised "McNamara's 100,000," these men had not been afforded the same strong academic foundation that he had gained at Dunbar High School. Military recruiters, who were paid commissions, unfairly targeted men from rural and urban communities, particularly if they lived in certain designated poverty areas where Jim Crow practices fostered low aptitudes and marginal skill sets, and men who could be victimized by the "system" and would not have qualified for service under any other circumstances. As an African American Naval Lieutenant Commander who was literally only one of a handful, he wanted to give his men opportunities that the generation before had denied to his own father in World War I. But the Navy had now become a different organization than when his father served.

In 1967 when "McNamara's 100,000" were slowly being transitioned into the Navy, as the Combat Information Center Officer aboard the USS *Ranger*, Chambers was responsible for the ship's combat defense systems and managed sophisticated technology and nuclear weaponry. He and his crew conducted sophisticated maneuvers in hostile waters on classified missions, often under the cover of darkness. Reflecting upon his relationship with Colonel Atwood and drawing from his own life experience, Chambers discovered how to best mentor these young men without appearing to show encouragement or favoritism.

The lives and wellbeing of all of his men were entrusted to his command. Perhaps more importantly, Chambers was a straight shooter and made every effort to ensure that under his command, none of his men were treated poorly simply because of their race. However, the criticisms made stateside by Black elected officials and the African American press he believed to be justified, in that many young men in the program were specifically selected and intentionally set-up to fail.

In reflection, Chambers admits that if the program was well intended, it missed the mark; many of the men with whom he came into contact only had elementary school reading abilities and had limited skills sets upon arriving onboard ship. And, he speculated, few had any meaningful employable skills or trade after they left the service. "At the time," he says, "I just couldn't bring myself to admit that these young men weren't ready for the war that they were thrust into." He is all too familiar with the disproportionate number of poor young men, Black and white, who were drafted into the Vietnam War and served in the Marines who were subsequently maimed, exposed to the long-term effects of Agent Orange, or killed on the battlefield—simply because they couldn't afford to go to college and defer military conscription.

Chambers recalls reading articles sent to him while at sea of speeches given by the Rev. Dr. Martin Luther King, Jr., and how he "rallied against the Vietnam War and drew parallels to the war to Nazi Concentration Camps. As an African American," he adds, "I agreed with all of Dr. King's principles of the non-violent movement to end segregation and discrimination, and in his overall desire to improve race relations. That was the South that I grew up in, and Dr.

King was right, the time had come for change." However, as a Navy man, Chambers didn't necessarily agree with King's "strong rhetoric on the military and on the war."

Secretary McNamara continued to address systemic barriers that adversely impacted African Americans in the service ranks. He provided the opportunity for African American men in the service who otherwise may not have had the opportunity to serve. Moreover, once these men left the service, McNamara acknowledged that they continued to be discriminated against as veterans returning from Vietnam. He was concerned that the African American "serviceman [had] been loyal and responsible to his country. But the people of his country [had] failed in their loyalty and responsibility to him." McNamara instructed his staff to meet with off-base housing realtors, and warn them that "unless they stopped discriminating, the base commander would declare their businesses off-limits to *all* servicemen, black and white—a potentially devastating blow. The Realtors were given a schedule for compliance, and black servicemen were instructed to report if they had any problems." The desegregation of military housing had a significant effect on how Black servicemen lived:

> McNamara followed the launch of Project 100,000 in 1966 with an April 1967 announcement that Realtors in communities around military bases in Maryland would be required to rent to black soldiers and their families. Neighborhoods near military bases were usually prosperous and white; black servicemen were forced to live in poorer housing, far from the base, in black neighborhoods.... McNamara next turned his desegregation system on other military bases, in California and elsewhere.[6]

By 1967, Chambers had remarried and he and his family were living in Yokosuka, Japan, in military housing. McNamara's real estate announcement had no effect on Chambers in Japan, but eventually Chambers heard about it and began to realize that there were substantive changes taking place back in the states in which he was not involved. The military newspapers were printing more and more stories about marches protesting the Vietnam War. He understood that there was racial tension in the urban cites in the North and civil rights marches in the South to end racial segregation. As unemployment rose, particularly in Black neighborhoods all across the country, Chambers was aware of the mass demonstrations to create more educational, housing and employment opportunities for Black people.

As a newly appointed Lieutenant Commander in the Navy, Chambers was intimately involved on a daily basis with the execution of the war and had trouble understanding how former war veterans from Korea and the world wars could participate in protest rallies, burning their separation papers and sometimes even their duly deserved war medals.

An avid sports enthusiast who enjoyed boxing with his younger brothers as kids, Chambers loved watching the satellite feeds of the boxing matches of Muhammad Ali on board ship. Chambers would joke around with his men when describing their assignments, and would often use the phrase "Float like a butterfly and sting like a bee," referring to how Ali would often describe his graceful moves but powerful punch. But for all that Chambers admired Ali, he couldn't understand how the "world's greatest athlete" could become a conscientious objector and not serve in the military.

Chambers was a Washingtonian; however, having lived a good part of his adult life overseas, he slowly felt detached from what was going on stateside. On a personal level, one of the most iconic moments in history as far as Chambers was concerned was the March on Washington on August 28, 1963. Although Chambers was not at the March, this was one of the few things he felt connected to in a very personal way. Especially significant to him was the renowned keynote address in which Dr. Martin Luther King passionately stated, "I have a dream that my four little children will one day live in a nation where they will not be judged by the color of their skin, but by the content of their character."[7]

Chambers could visualize the neighbors from the old neighborhood walking down to the mall and cheering on Dr. King in the sweltering D.C. summer heat. He could almost see Boo Pop, his beloved grandfather, walking down the street drenched in perspiration, coming up on the porch and summoning his grandkids to share with them all he heard Dr. King say. He knew that his grandfather would have turned to him and said, "You're going to be judged by your character because Dr. King said you were ten feet tall." Chambers learned the lessons from his grandfather well and made sure that his life was predicated on being judged by his aptitude and intellect, never allowing anyone to judge him based on his race. Chambers was comfortable in his own skin and proud of who he was as an African American man descended from slaves.

Despite his support and admiration for Dr. King's positions on racial equality, Chambers was perplexed by King's criticism of the war. As with many in the military, Chambers was aware of the antiwar speech that Dr. King gave on April 4, 1967, to the Clergy and Laity Concerned about Vietnam group. In an effort to discredit King's advocating for civil rights, his views on Vietnam were used as an attempt to diminish his trustworthiness.

While Chambers understood and agreed with Dr. King's views on race and civil rights, he was also able to examine the war objectively and disagree with King's views on Vietnam. While King "reprised almost all of the themes of the leftist myth of the Vietnam War," Chambers believed that the themes were wrong and without merit.[8]

Dr. King spoke of how "Ho Chi Minh's communists saw the United States as a model," but Chambers knew firsthand of the brutality of the North Vietnamese. They did not model themselves after the Americans. Chambers, like many others in the military, knew that either wittingly or unwittingly, "King claimed falsely that North Vietnam 'did not begin to send in any large number of supplies or men until American forces had moved into the tens of thousands.'"[9]

Nonetheless, Chambers knew American support for the war was diminishing. While he knew the media was sensationalizing what was going on stateside, all anyone had to do was read military papers or catch a glimpse of the Japanese television news of the mass protests in the American streets to fully understand the growing American sentiment.

Civil rights groups in America, particularly under the direction of Dr. King, were quickly becoming active participants in the debate over Vietnam. In light of McNamara's *Project 100,000*, many civil rights leaders began to argue that the war placed a disproportionately heavier burden on racial minorities than on white Americans, and the monies spent on the war could have supported and sustained civil rights legislation and social service programs at home. Civil rights leaders now aligned themselves with antiwar activists and joined in the call to end the war:

> Unequal treatment for many African Americans started with their induction into the armed forces. One of the most contentious aspects of the Vietnam War was the use of the draft to supply much of the manpower needed for the conflict. Because of inequities in the draft, eligible men from the middle and upper classes could normally find ways of avoiding service, or at least service in Vietnam, meaning the burden of the draft fell on working-class whites and minorities. Consequently, African Americans were drafted in disproportionately higher numbers than were whites. African Americans of draft age made up about 11 percent of the general population, but from 1965 to 1970, approximately 14 percent of all draftees were black. To illustrate the problem another way, in 1967 nearly one-third of eligible whites were drafted, but for African Americans it was nearly 64 percent.[10]

As an officer in the Navy, Chambers could see firsthand that African American men were entering the service in staggering numbers. The Navy had very few fatalities in the war, but for African American men on the front lines in the Army or the Marines, casualties were unusually high, with some attributing the large number to men recruited under McNamara's *Project 100,000*:

> As more Americans poured into Vietnam, casualties mounted, and black casualties early in the war were unusually high ... one out of every four American deaths in Vietnam was black. By late July 1966, African Americans were 15 percent of American forces in Vietnam but represented 22 percent of the total casualties. The alarmingly high death rate for blacks in Vietnam declined after 1967, and by the end of U.S. involvement in 1973, the 7,257 African Americans killed in Vietnam constituted 12.6 percent of all U.S. deaths in the war.[11]

Despite protests at home, by the end of 1967, Secretary McNamara had deployed close to 485,000 troops to Vietnam. During the same period, McNamara believed that the reduced fighting with the North Vietnamese, the South Vietnamese insurgents and the Viet Cong was directly attributed to the buildup and strength of American forces. In Washington, it was conveyed to the White House and Capitol Hill that the U.S. strategy was working. According to Albert Marrin in his book *America and Vietnam: The Elephant and the Tiger*, General Westmoreland "was so sure of victory that he dared Hanoi's leaders to make an all-out attack." Westmoreland was quoted as saying, "'I hope they try something, because we are looking for a fight.'" Unbeknownst to the Secretary, so were the Viet Cong.[12]

During the fall of 1967, the North Vietnamese and the Viet Cong plotted a major offensive against the Americans where they wanted to take the war directly to urban centers and designated strongholds in South Vietnam. The communists and their sympathizers knew that they were strong enough to overthrow the South Vietnamese government, but they were no match for the American strength and firepower:

> South Vietnam was not the obstacle; left to itself, it would have toppled like a house of cards in a tornado. Everything ultimately depended on Saigon's ally. American aid, however misused, was still enough to keep the country going. The misused, was still enough to keep the country going. The ARVN, inferior as it was, could still count on the grunts to come to the rescue. American firepower could never be defeated on the battlefield. If the Americans held firm, the war would drag on indefinitely. Hanoi decided to force the issue with a massive offensive.[13]

In an attempt to distract the Americans, the North Vietnamese launched several minor battles away from the intended targets of their attacks and "prepared for the urban attacks scheduled to coincide with Tet, a holiday for which both sides had observed a cease-fire in previous years." At the start of 1968, the North Vietnamese attacks known as the Tet Offensive commenced in the early hours of January 30 "... with a monumental burst of fighting. Within hours, communist forces had struck five of six major cities, thirty-six of forty-four provincial capitals, and sixty-four district capitals. In Saigon, nineteen NLF soldiers blew a hole in the wall surrounding the U.S. embassy...." Following the blast, there was "a six-hour firefight with Marine guards before being killed or wounded. Other NLF units attacked the Saigon airport, President Thiev's palace, and the national radio station."[14]

Despite the impressive buildup of American forces, the North Vietnamese Tet Offensive initially surprised Secretary McNamara and General Westmoreland. In short order, American and South Vietnamese troops took control over most of the cities and provinces that were initially in the control of the North Vietnamese.

After the North Vietnamese offensive, General Westmoreland unleashed the full power and might of the United States military. He "was determined to root out the Viet Cong at all costs. Day after day, gunships hovered over the rooftops, spraying bullets and rockets into the houses below. Tanks rumbled through the streets, firing their canon point-blank at enemy strongholds. Entire streets went up in flames, and civilians died alongside their Viet Cong captors."[15]

From 1968 to 1970, Chambers was aboard the USS *Franklin D. Roosevelt* as commanding officer of an attack squadron and was slated to be part of Operation Rolling Thunder. According to Chambers, "the campaign's intent was to interdict the Viet Cong supply chain from North Vietnam, through the Ho Chi Ming Trail into South Vietnam." The aerial bombardment campaign was conducted by the United States Air Force and Navy, supported by the South Vietnamese Air Force.

Prior to Operation Rolling Thunder, Chambers was stationed on board USS *Ranger*, whose air wing flew combat missions into North Vietnamese and Laos airspace. According to Chambers, our objective was to destroy the North Vietnamese's transportation system, their air defenses and industrial bases. We were also responsible for stopping the flow of insurgent men and supplies to the Viet Cong in South Vietnam. Prior to the actual bombing of Operation Rolling Thunder, on February 1, Chambers was transferred to the USS *Oriskany* as the Air Boss.

Meanwhile stateside, on February 20, 1968, the Senate Foreign Relations Committee began to conduct hearings on the 1964 Gulf of Tonkin incident as a result of tremendous public pressure and Congressional concerns about Operation Rolling Thunder's bombing. Two weeks later on February 28, President Johnson was informed that General Westmoreland needed an additional 206,000 troops in Vietnam.

Unbeknownst to the American public, on March 16, 1968, U.S. soldiers killed hundreds of unarmed Vietnamese civilians in the town of My Lai, later known as the My Lai Massacre. Most now believe this massacre was in retaliation for the Tet Offensive. The war was not going well. American casualties were increasing and young men were avoiding the draft by going to Canada. The cost of the war was escalating, and public support was shrinking. The public discourse about the war forced Johnson to constrain further increases of troops to Vietnam.

Whenever a presidential administration is faced with a disjointed and fractured mission, as well as dwindling staff support, the time comes for a "shakeup." Tension began to build between President Johnson and his Secretary of Defense. McNamara recommended that the troop strength be frozen and the bombings of Hanoi be halted. Although the President never acknowledged his recommendations, McNamara also advocated the need for the South Vietnamese army to take a leadership role in the ground fighting. Secretary McNamara announced his intention to resign in November 1967, "after a conversation with Johnson ... at a hastily convened press conference in the Pentagon...."[16] On February 29, 1968, Robert McNamara, the longest serving Secretary of Defense in U.S. history, left his position.

On March 31, 1968, a stoic Johnson announced a unilateral halt to all U.S. bombing north of the 20th Parallel and that he would seek negotiations with North Vietnam for a peace settlement. Johnson, who had wanted his legacy to be the Great Society and progressive social programs that fought against racism and poverty, reluctantly accepted the fact that his legacy would forever be tied to the failures of Vietnam. At the conclusion of his speech, a frustrated Johnson startled the audience when he announced that he would not seek reelection to the presidency.

The rest of the world was equally surprised at Johnson's announcement, and "in Washington ... officials professed to be flabbergasted that Hanoi had accepted" Johnson's offer to enter into the peace negotiations. On April 4, 1968, Johnson had been talking "about prospects for peace negotiations when a wire service bulletin was passed across his desk. Martin Luther King had been assassinated on the balcony of his motel room in Memphis, Tennessee."[17] In the aftermath of Dr. King's assassination, over 100 major cities across the country, particularly those with large African American communities, erupted in racially fueled violence and unrest.

The city in which Chambers grew up, Washington, D.C., was plagued by riots following Dr. King's assassination. Blocks from where Chambers lived, residential homes, department stores and public buildings burned for six violent nights of racial riots. The U Street corridor where he had walked to the movies and shopped for his grandmother lay in ruins. The neighborhood's main business corridor, 14th Street, looked more like Berlin after World War II than it did the nation's capital.

As causalities mounted, particularly among African American sailors and soldiers, they began to question the rationale of fighting a war to free the South Vietnamese from communist control when African Americans themselves were being treated as second-class citizens by America's supposed "democracy." Many felt that they would rather be back in the States fighting for African American civil rights instead of fighting for the rights of a people they didn't even know. Racial tension after the death of Dr. King was not limited to just urban centers around the country. Chambers recalls that the military was also faced with racial tension on bases all around the world, including in the Navy, and

That summer riots with racial overtones erupted at both the Navy brig at Da Nang and the sprawling Long Binh Stockade outside Saigon. Sporadic racial violence continued throughout the military establishment that year, and more than 160 racial assaults were recorded at Camp Lejeune in North Carolina alone. On July 20, 1969, the sporadic violence plaguing that installation erupted into a major racial gang fight, leaving one white dead, dozens of Marines injured, and 44 blacks and Puerto Ricans arrested and charged with complicity in the riot. The "rumble at Camp Lejeune" marked the beginning of one of the worst periods of racial violence in the history of the armed forces. Ten days later a large racial gang fight occurred at Millington Naval Air Station near Memphis, Tennessee, followed by fights at the naval installation at Cam Ranh Bay and Kaneohe Marine Corps Air Station in Hawaii. Over the next three years major racial confrontations took place throughout the military establishment from Fort McClellan, Alabama, to Machinato, Okinawa, and on board naval vessels, including the aircraft carriers *Constellation* and *Kitty Hawk*.[18]

A year later when Chambers came home on leave, although he had read the stories in military newspapers and received constant letters from his mother and sisters, nothing had prepared him for what he saw as he walked down the U Street corridor towards 14th Street.

Upon graduating from Washington's Dunbar High School, Chambers went to college in nearby Annapolis, Maryland, to go to the United States Naval Academy. He had always considered Washington, D.C., as his home, but for the first time he realized that the city he had always called "his anchor in turbulent seas" had changed dramatically from the sleepy southern town in which he had grown up to a city boiling over with racial animosity and urban blight. Being stationed overseas, he had no idea of the pent-up emotions that were brewing back at home.

In the aftermath of an aerial bombing Chambers had seen the remnants of villages and the thick-forested countryside of Vietnam that was bombed. However, he could not fathom the destruction of the burned out neighborhoods where he once grew up. He drove block after block in disbelief as to what he was seeing. While others compared the total devastation to what Berlin must have looked like in the aftermath of the Berlin air raids of World War II, Chambers was not mentally or emotionally prepared for what he observed. He could not understand how people in the neighborhood could destroy their own community. A faraway enemy had not caused this destruction during the height of war, but instead was caused by residents who had now moved into the neighborhood where Chambers once lived.

In a short period of time, the segregated schools and neighborhoods that had once encouraged Chambers and his peers to achieve success were now holding back young Black talent. Chambers began to realize that the new generation of young Washingtonians didn't have a Colonel Atwood to help pave a path to opportunities.

As Dunbar, like greater Washington, had been slowly integrated, the overly qualified teachers now found higher paying jobs in the Federal government and elsewhere, and younger and less experienced teachers didn't have the same capabilities as their predecessors. The neighborhoods where Chambers had grown up were no longer working class communities, but becoming poor and blighted areas with little hope. After serving in the military and living overseas, the sight of his ruined city helped Chambers better understand the antiwar fervor and the increasing racial animosity he had been reading about.

On May 12, 1968, in Paris, the Johnson Administration began peace negotiations between the United States and North Vietnam. While negotiations were taking place on June 10, 1968, an exiled South Vietnamese government was formed, called the Provisional Revolutionary Government of the Republic of South Vietnam. The exiled government was supported by communists and was in direct opposition to the American-supported South Vietnamese government.

Johnson, frustrated with how the war was bogging down the final days of his administration, continued to conduct a series of additional personnel changes within the Defense Department. General Westmoreland, who had been the public face of the war and was in charge of U.S. troops in Vietnam, was replaced by General Creighton Abrams. As key architects of the war were being replaced, the American public's antiwar sentiment only grew stronger.

From August 26 through the 29, 1968, during the Democratic National Convention in Chicago, antiwar demonstrators rioted at the convention site and violently clashed with Chicago police in an attempt to bring their grievances to public attention on the television screen. As Americans were going to vote in the 1968 presidential election, Vietnam was at the forefront of the minds of voters. After the successful riots at the convention, antiwar momentum grew across the country and on October 15, 1968, the largest coordinated antiwar demonstrations took place all across America.

A week before the presidential election, on October 31, 1968, Johnson announced a complete bombing halt over North Vietnam, effectively ending his much-opposed Operation Rolling Thunder. The week after Richard Nixon was elected president, a massive march took place in Washington, D.C., where over 500,000 antiwar demonstrators protested, marching from the White House along the Mall to the Capitol Building. By the end of 1968, the U.S. troop strength in Vietnam reached 540,000.

According to Nixon biographer Conrad Black in his book *Richard M. Nixon: A Life in Full*, upon being sworn in as President, Richard Nixon believed that his "greatest immediate issue was Vietnam. Nixon was also concerned about reconstructing the Western Alliance, pursuing arms control, exploring a possible relationship with China, activating a peace process in the Middle East...." Nixon's primary concerns in domestic affairs were "adopting anti-crime measures ... [and] accelerating desegregation by sensible means...."[19] According to Black, Nixon knew that "the world waited to see ... [what he] proposed to do about Vietnam. The American Army in that country was suffering about three hundred dead a week—a total of thirty-one thousand dead by inauguration day, 1969."[20]

On March 15, 1969, Nixon conducted a series of covert operations, including ordering aerial bombing of North Vietnamese possessions in Cambodia along the South Vietnamese border. The secret bombing of communist bases in Cambodia, known as Operation Menu, took place over a 15-month span where over "109,000 tons of bombs would be dropped on Cambodian targets...."[21]

On June 8, 1969, President Nixon announced that 25,000 U.S. troops would be withdrawn by the end of August, the beginning of his "Vietnamization" policy, the gradual withdrawal of American involvement and troops in Vietnam, coupled with the expansion of South Vietnam's combat role. Although the policy had its antiwar detractors, it was widely applauded.

According to Chambers, Vietnamization was designed not only to reduce the military footprint in Vietnam, but was also to improve South Vietnam's military infrastructure and readiness. Chambers recalls when he first went to Vietnam he was amazed at the weakness of the South Vietnamese military and its inability to defend its own country. While there were some joint operations early on, the South Vietnamese military remained weak, due primarily to political appointments to the military command, nepotism, and a vague understanding of military command and control.

Although public perception of Nixon's Vietnamization policy was favorable, the reality of the situation was more covert and aggressive. While Nixon was publicly withdrawing troops from South Vietnam, he was secretly conducting Operation Menu:

> Nixon understood that for political reasons he had to begin to withdraw troops from Vietnam. The result was a contradictory policy. To try to placate critics of the war, Nixon would gradually withdraw U.S. troops from Vietnam, their responsibilities turned over to the South Vietnamese; at the same time, Kissinger would conduct secret negotiations with the North Vietnamese government, bypassing the South Vietnamese regime.[22]

While a presidential candidate, Richard Nixon campaigned on ending the war in Vietnam. Once elected, President Nixon took public steps to reduce the American footprint in Vietnam. Although many Americans believed that Nixon was winning the war, antiwar protest continued.

On October 15, 1969, the largest antiwar demonstration called the "Moratorium," referred to as a "teach-in," took place across the country, primarily on college campuses. As the American public was beginning to fully grasp the number of troops in Vietnam, and as the number of casualties escalated from the war, American sentiment rapidly changed to full opposition against the war.

As college and university campuses all across the country became centers for student discontent, they also became epicenters for civil disobedience, including shutting down campus buildings. College protests became so frequent that schools' security budgets became overextended and local governments requested state and federal support to curb the protests. After much consultation, on November 3, 1969, President Nixon spoke before the nation on television in what has been referred to as the "Silent Majority Speech," where he outlined and defended his Vietnam War policies.

On November 13, 1969, the American public became aware of the startling news of atrocities committed against hundreds of Vietnamese civilians during the My Lai Massacre. Once the previously hidden news was revealed to the public, Americans were outraged. The national antiwar sentiment only intensified. On November 15, 1969, over 250,000 antiwar demonstrators converged on Washington, D.C., in their continued opposition to the Vietnam War.

In his memoir, Nixon rationalized the need to call out the National Guard on college campuses because of mass student protests across the nation as "fear was increasingly generated throughout the country. It was accompanied by demands for effective government action." According to Nixon, J. Edgar Hoover, Director of the Federal Bureau of Investigation, "informed me that FBI agents had begun to pick up rumors of a calculated nationwide terrorist offensive by radial student groups using arson, bombing, and kidnapping of university and government officials."[23]

On April 30, 1970, Nixon went on television and informed Congress that United States troops would attack enemy locations in the Fishhook region of Cambodia. Nixon spoke with "the aid of a map of Cambodia and reassured his viewers that this was not an invasion, it was an operation to get rid of the North Vietnamese and Viet Cong in Cambodia, following which the U.S. and South Vietnamese forces would withdraw."[24] Although Nixon did not share with the public the United States' covert involvement in bombing targets in Cambodia was part of Operation Menu, his pronouncement still only further incited antiwar demonstrators.

One such campus was Kent State University in Ohio where a major protest was scheduled for May 4, 1970: "There, as elsewhere, antiwar students had attacked the reserve officers training building.... Governor James Rhodes ...

ordered national guardsmen onto the campus to impose order ... nettled by the demonstrators, they shot a volley of rifle fire into the crowd, killing four youths."[25]

Congressional hearings were conducted on January 1, 1971, resulting in Congress' forbidding the use of U.S. ground troops in Laos or Cambodia.

Chapter 7

Fall of Saigon

On January 28, 1973, U.S. military involvement in the conflict between North and South Vietnam came to an end with the signing of the Paris Peace Accords and finally provided for a cease-fire between the two factions. The signing of the Accords set the stage for the historic events that took place during the evacuation of Saigon on the morning of April 30, 1975, and for the amazing 30 days that took place after Captain Chambers took command of the USS *Midway*.

The signing of the Accords came after a series of turbulent political negotiations for both sides in the conflict; the time had come for both interests to favor bringing closure to the war. The genesis of the peace settlement started on July 25, 1969, while Nixon was giving his "Vietnamization" speech in Guam. According to Nixon's memoirs, the "trip provided the perfect camouflage for Kissinger's first secret meeting with the North Vietnamese." It was arranged that Kissinger would go to Paris, ostensibly to brief French officials on the result of Nixon's trip to Guam, but he actually "would meet secretly with [Xuan] Thuy," North Vietnamese Chief Negotiator during the Paris Peace talks.[1]

On August 4, 1969, Henry Kissinger began secret negotiations in Paris to end the war with North Vietnam's Xuan Thuy. "By April 1970, Nixon, frustrated by the lack of more progress in the war and the deadlock in the Paris peace talks, was determined to make a show of strength…. Nixon decided to, in his own words, 'go for broke,'" intending to invade Cambodia and destroy North Vietnamese supply lines and outposts. In May of that year, in a newspaper article that infuriated Nixon and Kissinger, "William Beecher of the *New York Times* revealed the bombing" of Cambodia.[2] Anti-war demonstrators, as well as many in Congress, believed that Nixon's actions in Cambodia were illegal, and

> William Beecher's disclosure of the bombing of Cambodia so enraged Nixon and Kissinger that Kissinger approved the wiretapping, without a court order and in the

name of "national security," of some of his own aides, whom Nixon had been suspicious of almost from the outset because of their "dovish" leanings. In time, the wiretapping was expanded to include some journalists with access to high officials.... The Nixon administration's defense of the warrantless wiretaps in the name of national security was later overturned by the Supreme Court.[3]

On February 8, 1971, the South Vietnamese launched an offensive cross-border campaign in Laos in order to disrupt North Vietnam's activities along the Ho Chi Minh Trail. In his book *Interdiction in Southern Laos, 1960–1968*, military historian Jacob Van Staaveren stated that U.S. intelligence estimated 6,295 enemy infiltrators routinely moved south on the trail in 1961, and that the number had more than doubled to 12,857 by 1962.[4] By 1965, U.S. intelligence believed that

> there was no abatement of enemy infiltration and that in October, as monsoon weather was ending, an estimated 1,500 enemy personnel passed through Laos on their way to South Vietnam. The figure was expected to soar to 4,500 monthly during the dry season. The briefers offered no estimate of enemy supply tonnage entering the South but believed it was substantial. The DRV's capability, they said, was about 234 tons per day with about 195 tons moving on Laotian routes, 25 tons through Cambodia, and 14 tons by sea.[5]

The South Vietnamese Operation Lam Son was supported by the U.S. Air Force and Navy in the Gulf of Tonkin. Ground forces were prohibited from participating in the ground offensive in accordance with the December 22, 1970, Cooper-Church Amendment to the Supplementary Foreign Assistance Act of 1970 that banned ground troops in Cambodia and Laos after January 5, 1971.

While Nixon's covert activities were taking place in Cambodia, Commander Chambers became the Air Boss aboard the USS *Oriskany* (CV-34) from 1970 to 1971. At the time he believed the best career move would have been becoming an Air Wing Commander, but he did not make the cut. He soon learned that the assignment to Air Boss was the best career move for him because it gave him tremendous practical experience and enabled him to advance his career in a direction he had not anticipated.

As the Air Boss aboard *Oriskany*, he was involved in the diversionary ploy by the U.S. Navy to intentionally have the North Vietnamese believe that they were watching tactical maneuvers off the coast of Vinh, North Vietnam. The tactical maneuvers were designed to get the North Vietnamese to believe that the Navy was about to invade the city.

While the war continued in Vietnam, on March 5, 1971, Nixon brought the U.S. 5th Special Forces Group, the first American unit deployed to South Vietnam, back to the United States in an attempt to appease his critics. By March 24, 1971, the ill-prepared South Vietnamese had experienced heavy casualties and were driven out of Laos by communist counterattacks. According to Chambers, although the United States had been training, equipping and preparing the South Vietnamese Army for 10 years, they were no match for the well-organized and deeply entrenched North Vietnamese whose strength was derived from its sponsor states, the Soviet Union and China.

Chambers' view was supported by Vietnam historian Stanley Karnow who wrote that from the onset of the war, in order for the North Vietnamese to succeed, they "needed Soviet surface-to-air missiles, radar, communications equipment, and other sophisticated military material to counter the American bombing." And, the North Vietnamese would have to depend heavily on Chinese rice to feed their population.[6]

But according to Chambers, a crack in the armor between North Vietnam's two sponsor states was beginning to have a complicated effect, and the growing rift between the Soviet Union and China was slowly having a chilling consequence on these aid programs. The differences between the two countries were further agitated through their client states, e.g., North Vietnam and North Korea, where the Soviet Union and China exerted their political and ideological differences.

On August 20, 1968, the animosity between China and the Soviet Union became more apparent "when Soviet and Warsaw Pact forces invaded Czechoslovakia…. The Soviet Communist party … issued a 'doctrine' warning that the Soviet Union might intervene in any Communist country whose policies deviated from its standards." In 1970, China's Chairman Mao Zedong, "to whom any relationship with the Americans had once represented a breach of the Communist faith, now contemplated a reconciliation with the United States in order to offset the Soviet menace."[7]

In an attempt to thaw relations between the two nations, Chairman Mao Zedong extended an invitation to President Nixon to visit China. Nixon accepted, and on February 21, 1972, he made an historic visit to China. The visit served many purposes, primarily to normalize diplomatic relations between the two nations, but also to send certain signals to the North Vietnamese: their relationship with one of their key communist allies might be in jeopardy.

As Nixon took the bold initiative to meet with the Chinese for diplomatic reasons, it also helped his political objectives for his reelection campaign. The campaign was in full swing and took several steps to appease the American public, including a drawdown of troops from Vietnam. In his memoir, President Nixon stated:

> I approved the withdrawal of 70,000 more American troops from Vietnam over the next three months. Coming on the eve of a new session of Congress and just before the beginning of the presidential primaries, I felt that the number had to be significant

in order to underscore the downward direction of my withdrawal policy. By May 1, less than four months away, there would be only 69,000 Americans remaining in Vietnam, and they too would be getting ready to leave. Even as I made this announcement, however, I was facing the unsettling prospect that a successful Communist invasion of South Vietnam might seriously jeopardize the safety of those decreasing numbers of Americans still there.[8]

As the administration anticipated, after Nixon visited China, the North Vietnamese believed they needed to strategically restore their bargaining power and influence by conducting a three-pronged attack north and west of Saigon. They believed a successful campaign would provide them with tremendous leverage at the Paris Peace talks, particularity since this was an election year in the United States. They hoped that since Nixon was having his own political problems back at home, they could affect American public opinion and provide the necessary leverage needed at the peace table. They also needed to make sure that the U.S. opened up a dialogue with the Russians. The North Vietnamese felt emboldened after their South Vietnamese opponents had failed miserably during Operation Lam Son and began to plan for an offensive attack across the demilitarized zone into South Vietnam.

On March 30, 1972, the North Vietnamese and Viet Cong conducted what is now referred to as the Easter Offensive. According to all accounts, the U.S. was expecting some type of major attack before the presidential elections in the United States, but the size and magnitude of the attack caught the military intelligence and commanders by surprise. With each attack, the South Vietnamese were unable to hold the line:

> The long awaited North Vietnamese–Viet Cong offensive to try to crush the Saigon government and drive the U.S. forces into the sea, after an 85 percent reduction in their levels, began on March 30. An entire North Vietnamese Army (NVA) armored division, with two hundred new Soviet tanks, attacked directly across the DMZ. A whole army attacked from Laos and northern Cambodia eastwards into South Vietnam, and the enemy concentrated a large force in the South and attacked toward Saigon, surrounding the provincial capital of An Loc, sixty miles from Saigon.... The U.S. Air Force and Naval Force said the weather was too cloudy and stormy to support the ground forces with any precision.[9]

Nixon was furious and feared that the U.S. military was turning on him. He became more agitated when his advisors believed that the Easter Offensive was conducted by the North Vietnamese in order to force the Americans to attack, then force the Russians to cancel the May 8 Summit in order to defend the North Vietnamese against the Americans.

According to his memoirs, Nixon believed he had no choice but to retaliate, and forcibly. On May 8, 1972, President Nixon ordered Operation Linebacker, a fitting title for the bombing of strategic assets and the mining of all

North Vietnamese ports. Nixon "ordered a massive air and sea buildup, [which] increased the number of B-52s in theater from forty-five to a hundred and thirty…." In addition, he had two aircraft carrier battle groups "deployed offshore; and the number of air force and navy combat aircraft was increased in the first ten days of April from nearly six hundred to almost a thousand."[10]

Nixon wanted the North Vietnamese, his critics and his adversaries to understand that he intended to release the full power of the U.S. military and that each day would be worse than the day before. According to former Secretary of the Navy John Lehman, "after all American ground forces had been withdrawn from Vietnam, Hanoi launched an all-out invasion of South Vietnam." To retaliate, Nixon rejected former President Johnson's bombing restrictions, and "ordered the mining of the North Vietnamese ports. Morale in the Navy and Air Force soared as jets cheerfully pulverized the NVA military establishment that had been off-limits for a decade." At the end of summer 1973, "the communists were totally defeated in both North and South and secretly offered terms that after the final 'Christmas bombing' of Hanoi resulted in the Peace Agreement of 1973."[11]

Operation Linebacker was a success. However, Nixon was now unsure if there would be a Moscow visit. In his memoirs, Richard Nixon shared that it was "often said that the key to a Vietnam settlement lay in Moscow and Peking rather than in Hanoi." Had the communist countries not given regular, massive aid to the leaders of North Vietnam, the war would not have lasted beyond a few months.[12] Nixon now needed to thwart any offensive moves that the Russians might take, so he sent a carefully written, personally drafted message to the Soviet Union:

> We expect you to help your allies, and you cannot expect us to do other than to continue to help our allies, but let us, and let all great powers, help our allies only for the purpose of their defense, not for the purpose of launching invasions against their neighbors…. Our two nations have made significant progress in our negotiations in recent months. We are near major agreements on nuclear arms limitation, on trade, on a host of other issues. Let us not slide back toward the dark shadows of a previous age. We do not ask you to sacrifice your principles, or your friends, but neither should you permit Hanoi's intransigence to blot out the prospects we together have so patiently prepared.[13]

The sincerity of the letter worked. On May 22, 1972, Richard Nixon met Nikita Khrushchev's successor, General Secretary of the Communist Party Leonid Brezhnev, in Moscow for the summit conference. While the visit was intended to negotiate trade agreements and nuclear pacts, it achieved another objective. Up to this point, the North Vietnamese were able to leverage differences between China and Russia to their own advantages. However, the Russian response to move forward with the visit provided the necessary leverage that the United States needed at the bargaining table with the North Vietnamese, who were beginning to understand that the "Communist giants had developed priorities more important to them than Vietnam."[14] As President Nixon stated:

> I had long believed that an indispensable element of any successful peace initiative in Vietnam was to enlist, if possible, the help of the Soviets and the Chinese. Though rapprochement with China and détente with the Soviet Union were ends in themselves, I also considered them possible means to hasten the end of the war. At worst, Hanoi was bound to feel less confident if Washington was dealing with Moscow and Beijing. At best, if the two major Communist powers decided that they had bigger fish to fry, Hanoi would be pressured into negotiating a settlement we could accept.[15]

As the events unfolded between the United States, the Soviet Union and China, the U.S. Department of the Navy was finalizing a list of potential candidates for the position of Naval Captain. On July 1, 1972, Commander Chambers was promoted to captain. During a phone interview in which he was informed of his promotion, he was advised that because his name was so far down on the list he would probably not go through the screening until the following year. The moment he got off the phone, Chambers took out a postcard and wrote on it so that he would not forget once the phone call came through, "accept only a deep draft, command at sea, anyplace, and anywhere." Chambers was then assigned to the Naval Air Systems Command (NavAir) as Program Manager of the highly classified A-7E Aircraft Procurement Program (PMA-235).

The A-7 Corsair aircraft was a single-seat, carrier-based attack airplane used by the U.S. Navy as a replacement to the Douglas A-4 Skyhawk and was introduced during the Vietnam War. The aircraft went through several technical changes and with the A-7D and A-7E models became two of the world's first aircraft to be equipped with digital computers to aid the pilot with onboard navigation and enhanced capability for attacking ground targets.

As an experienced fighter pilot flying the A-7 aircraft, and with his extensive experience as the Combat Information Center Officer aboard the USS *Ranger* and advanced engineering degrees and understanding of the system's architecture, Chambers' management support and technical knowledge became instrumental in assisting development of modifications for the A-7E system's architecture by enhancing the systems integration and updating the cockpit displays. This enabled Navy pilots to deliver ordnance with better precision.

The navigational equipment and software modeled by Chambers and his team was "cutting edge" technology, and Captain Chambers felt that if he couldn't be in a cockpit, then this was what he wanted to be involved in and that he would be able to advance the accuracy of weapon delivery and overall safety of Naval aviation.

By the autumn of 1972, all parties were tiring of the long protracted war. On September 26, 1972, there was finally a breakthrough, though not a full peace settlement. Henry Kissinger was able to establish the construct for a peace talk with the North Vietnamese. However, the South Vietnamese were against the talks, fearing the U.S. would sell them out although Nixon adamantly told them he would not. Without the South Vietnamese at the table, Kissinger continued discussions with the North Vietnamese.

On October 8, 1972, secret discussions with the North Vietnamese between Henry Kissinger and North Vietnam's Le Duc Tho in Paris produced a tentative settlement of the war. Nixon was skeptical at first, but warmed to the initial terms: "There would be a stand-still cease fire in place, followed sixty days later by full American withdrawal and an exchange of prisoners ... [and] Thieu's government would remain." Although Nixon was open to the tentative settlement of the war, he knew that the "North Vietnamese would violate the agreement and Thieu would object to it...."[16]

As expected, on October 22, 1972, South Vietnam's President Thieu was angry, feeling betrayed by the secret talks, and rejected the proposed settlement. He wanted 69 amendments to the proposed agreement, most importantly that the North Vietnamese withdraw all forces north of the demilitarized zone line. Kissinger tried to help President Thieu understand that although Nixon was his ardent ally, support for the Vietnamese government in America was quickly waning.

Kissinger tried in vain to get the North Vietnamese to agree to amended terms of the proposed settlement, but North Vietnam went public with the "secret peace talks" then demanded changes in the discussions, forcing a deadlock at the negotiation table. Nixon recalled, "on December 13, Le Duc Tho made it clear that he had no intention of reaching an agreement" ... and returned to Hanoi."[17] Nixon was not pleased and on December 14, 1972, ordered a second phase of Operation Linebacker, with the desired effect to get the North Vietnamese back to the negotiating table.

While the Nixon Administration was working to bring President Thieu back to the bargaining table once the North Vietnamese were ready, it was also necessary to make sure that Hanoi would come willingly. Nixon began Operation Linebacker II on December 18, 1972, and destroyed everything that wasn't destroyed during the first offensive. Taking a page out of the Berlin bombings of World War II, Nixon had North Vietnam's industrial infrastructure bombed.

Within ten days the beleaguered North Vietnamese agreed to resume negotiations, provided that the Nixon Administration stopped bombing above the 20th parallel. Nixon was clear with Kissinger: the discussions would only start from where they ended on October 8 in Paris, when a tentative settlement of the war was made.

By January 18, 1973, Henry Kissinger and Le Duc Tho reached an agreement similar to the one achieved the previous October. To prevent the agreement from being undone once again by the North Vietnamese, Nixon announced the signing of the Paris Peace Accords, taking effect on January 27, 1973.

Anti-war demonstrators didn't trust Nixon and continued to protest across the country, insisting the Nixon Administration not only fulfill its promise to withdraw troops and end the war, but also honor a second campaign promise that Nixon made. Nixon had pledged to end military conscription, commonly known as the draft. As political pressure continued to mount over the war and over Watergate, Nixon thought it was best to stem the tide that was turning against him and, hoping to improve the public's opinion of him, ended the military draft on January 27, 1973.

After the Accords were signed on February 1, 1973, Richard Nixon sent a secret letter to North Vietnam's Pham Van Dong promising postwar reconstruction aid.

On February 12, 1973, American families all across the nation patiently waited for the long-awaited release of U.S. prisoners from the onset of the war. By March 29, the last of U.S. troops and the last-known prisoners of war left South Vietnam.

In the late spring of 1973, Chambers received an unexpected phone call from his detailer who identified himself. Chambers, without hesitation and while trying to find the note he had once written to himself in the event he ever got the call for an assignment, said, "I'll take it, but only if it's a command at sea." The detailer was skeptical of Chambers' initial quick acceptance as he had called approximately 15 previous prospective commanding officers and each had turned down the offer to command the ship in question.

The detailer carefully explained to Chambers that the ship was the USS *White Plains* (AFS-4), a Combat Stores Ship with a less-than-stellar reputation. The assignment was out of the U.S. Navy base in Sasebo, Japan. Still not convinced that Chambers understood what he was in for, the detailer explained that the assignment would require Chambers and his family to relocate to Sasebo, Japan. Sasebo, an industrial city with some of Japan's largest industries, was not a particularly glamorous assignment like being stationed in Honolulu, Hawaii, or in the city of Yokosuka, Japan, the home port of the Navy's Seventh Fleet. To the continued surprise of the detailer, Chambers said, "If it's a command at sea, I'll take it."

On July 1, 1973, Captain Chambers was assigned to the USS *White Plains*

South China Sea, 1974. The USS *White Plains*, while under the command of Captain Larry Chambers (courtesy Naval History & Heritage Command Photo Archive, Naval Subject Collection).

as the Commanding Officer as part of the Seventh Fleet's logistic support force. *White Plains* was a combat replenishment ship responsible for "supporting six carriers that were on the line in Vietnam, with approximately 5,000 nineteen-year olds per CVA, or approximately 30,000 sailors to feed each day, along with another 20,000 support personnel." Chambers was now responsible for providing food, mail, electronics and spare parts, as well as hauling jet engines around and transferring them as needed to the aircraft carriers at sea.

Former Secretary John Lehman said that, "the effects of the war on the Navy were far reaching. The policy of the Johnson Administration to avoid appearing to be actually at war … meant that normal research, maintenance, training and replacement accounts were used to fund the war, and when it was over, the entire Navy was worn-out and obsolete."[18] As his new assignment began, Chambers agreed. He conducted an initial visual inspection of the vessel where he found a ship that was in "tough condition and needed a lot of help." What Chambers found was a ship that was a workhorse and pretty good at operating, but "physically dirty."

South China Sea, 1974. Larry Chambers (left) becomes Commanding Officer of the USS *White Plains* (courtesy National Archives).

White Plains had an automatic throttle control system that could be operated from the bridge so that the captain could dial up whatever RPM he wanted the engines to make. The engineers below would monitor the system. If working properly the ship's propellers would turn at the ordered speed. During Chambers' first day on the job a most embarrassing moment occurred: *White Plains* automated hydraulic control system didn't work. The ship went dead in the water at the pier.

Chambers called the chief engineer to his stateroom to ascertain when it would be fixed so that the ship could get underway. He was informed that the systems worked only intermittently. In order to set the tone for the management changes that were going to be implemented on the ship, Chambers informed the engineer that, "we weren't going to live this way, and once we had cleared the sea wall, I was going to order the ship all ahead forward and followed by crash back until the engineers adjusted the automatic controls so that the main engine could be controlled from the bridge."

Chambers could tell that the engineer and his staff didn't believe him so he went on the bridge and proceeded to ring up "full bells followed by crash backs." This maneuver was continued until the engineers calibrated and adjusted the automatic controls. Chambers repeated the process until the ship's

7. *Fall of Saigon* 111

South China Sea, 1974. Under the command of Captain Larry Chambers, a ton of needed supplies is lifted off of the USS *White Plains* for the USS *Tripoli* (courtesy Naval History & Heritage Command Photo Archive, Naval Subject Collection).

South China Sea, 1974. USS *White Plains* (center) conducts underway replenishment with the USS *Tuscaloosa* and the USS *Schenectady* (courtesy Naval History & Heritage Command Photo Archive, Naval Subject Collection).

automatic controls worked properly from the bridge. He clearly was making his point: it was easier to fix the system so that it worked properly than for the engineering staff to have this new captain embarrass them for failure to maintain the ship's automatic control systems.

But the awkwardness of a very short "honeymoon" period with the *White Plains*' new captain paid off. While in the Philippine Sea, *White Plains* was on a full belt at 22 knots and there was a lot of small fishing boats with bright lights creating a hazardous environment since they were often unaware of other vessels around them in the channels. As *White Plains* approached the area, there was a group of fishing boats ahead, so Chambers blew the whistle four blasts, indicating that the ship was in danger. The smaller fishing boats froze like deer looking into headlights. Chambers realized what was about to happen so he rang up a crash-back and reversed the ship, avoiding a collision.

Chambers believes that had he not confronted the chief engineer that first day and insisted the throttle system be repaired, the ship would not have been able to maneuver quickly and there would have been a catastrophe of some sort at sea. Once the ship was out of immediate danger, he proceeded full steam ahead and once again called on the chief engineer, personally thanking him for fixing the hydraulic control system.

In order to institutionalize the needed changes aboard ship, Chambers met with the executive officer and the senior chief petty officer of the command and informed them that under his watch the ship had to be cleaned up. The chiefs, who in part were responsible for quality control, were the men who inspected everyone else aboard the ship. However, when Chambers inspected their mess area—their private dining area—it was in a deplorable and dirty condition.

He informed them that unless the area was immediately cleaned, he would shut it down. The chief executive officer and the chief petty officer of the command informed Chambers that he could not do that, to which the Captain replied, "You're wrong. I just did." He closed off their mess area without hesitation, but assured them it would be reopened once cleaned.

Sensitive to the fact that chief officers needed privacy when they ate, Chambers "walled off an area in the crew's mess," creating a section of the crew's mess area for the chief petty officers so that they could eat their meals—but the message was clear and reverberated throughout the ship. The chief petty officers were mortified. The new captain on board meant business, and the ship was going to be cleaned up from top to bottom.

In just two days, the executive officer and the master chief petty officer of the command came back to Chambers and informed him that their mess area was now ready for him to inspect. Chambers waited for three or four days before he went down there to conduct the inspection because he wanted to send a strong message. As Captain Chambers went into the area, he didn't bother to hide his smirk as he walked into the dining room. The walls had been newly painted, the floors and corner crevices had been washed clean—the area was immaculate.

Chambers congratulated them for a job well done and then informed the entire crew that it was time to shape up. To ensure that the message was clear, he then informed the master chief petty officer of the command that every month there would be a zone inspection aboard ship, including the chief petty officers' quarters, the exclusive berthing space for the most senior enlisted men aboard the ship.

Everyone in the Navy understands the concept that "water flows downhill." It didn't take long for the petty officers to command their men to clean up their own spaces, thereby cleaning up the rest of the ship. For the next thirty or so days, the men worked tirelessly, and by the time Chambers got back to port, the USS *White Plains* that had left port side was not the same *White Plains* that returned. Prior to docking at home port, Chambers sent a helicopter out to pick up the admiral to show off what his men had accomplished. Once aboard, the admiral could not get over the ship's transformation. In no time, *White Plains* and Captain Chambers were the talk of the Seventh Fleet.

The cleanliness of *White Plains* was not the only challenge for Chambers. As with any manager in any organization, corrective change came hard for some subordinates. Chambers had a disruptive and divisive chief petty officer on board who attempted to undermine Chambers' directives. But as the men began to gain respect for Chambers and his management style, particularly as he cleaned up the ship and improved overall morale, some men came forward with information about this particular chief. Chambers realized that he had more than just a disgruntled subordinate—he had a major problem on his hands.

Based on the information received, Chambers was made aware that the divisive chief petty officer was gambling with the Japanese, a major infraction of the Uniform Code of Military. When Captain Chambers was about to leave port he informed the chief petty officer in question that he was now assigned to his shore detachment.

Shortly after being placed on the shore duty detail, the chief participated in a poker game with the Japanese, and the Japanese Police caught him during a raid engaged in an illegal poker game. Once the Japanese police caught the chief, he was no longer under the control of the Captain of *White Plains*. Chambers in turn shipped the chief back to the states because he was now unfit for overseas deployment. Once this chief was off the ship, morale onboard improved tremendously. The men aboard *White Plains* knew that Captain Chambers was a man of strong conviction and that change aboard ship would be permanent.

White Plains was tasked to participate in a joint exercise with the South Korean Navy en route to the South China Seas. As Korean ships began to come up alongside for underway replenishment, Chambers noticed that the Korean sailors were "ramrod straight, their uniforms were pristine and starched well." Before the two ships pulled fully alongside each other, Chambers called his executive officer and the master chief petty officer of command and expressed his embarrassment at the way his men looked compared to the Koreans. He pointed out the demeanor and attire of the South Korean sailors, and told his men that any time they were going to go alongside another ship, they needed to look their best, and better than any other Navy's men because they were representing the United States Navy.

From that point forward, Chambers made sure his men looked professional every time *White Plains* went alongside, including replenishment of aircraft carriers. He made sure that his colleagues on the other ships took notice of his men, and in short order, *White Plains* and her men were no longer the brunt of jokes in the Seventh Fleet, but a supply ship and crew that the Navy could be proud of. As a direct result of Chambers' management of the ship and his leadership skills, the ship began to receive accolades for on-time delivery of every commodity item that was ordered by the ships and aircraft carriers of the Seventh Fleet.

The time came for annual inspection for the Ney Award for food service excellence. A distinction separate from the larger cruisers and aircraft carriers, the USS *White Plains* won the prestigious *Captain Edward F. Ney Memorial Award for the Best Small Ship Afloat* in the entire Navy, thanks to Chambers' command. The award was a testament to Chambers' leadership, for this was a major accomplishment for the men of the USS *White Plains*. In the past the ship had always been at the bottom of the pile.

With a war-weary American public, a cynical United States Congress took a series of measures to restrain the Office of the President. Its first step was to force "Nixon to agree to end all military operations in Indochina by August 15, 1973." Following that, Congress "passed the War Powers Act, which created barriers to future use of American forces." That measure required the president to "inform Congress within forty-eight hours of any deployment of American troops anywhere in the world and to withdraw them from hostilities within sixty days unless Congress approved."[19]

Chapter 8

Operation Frequent Wind

On October 10, 1973, the troubled Nixon Administration was rocked by another major scandal when Vice President Spiro Agnew was forced to resign from office for "having taken bribes and kickbacks—over one hundred thousand dollars—from Maryland contractors for public works contracts when he was governor" and throughout his vice presidency.[1]

However, during the previous eight months, the Vietnam War had provided some ray of hope for the administration. On January 15, 1973, Richard Nixon believed that Secretary of State Henry Kissinger's negotiations in Paris with the North Vietnamese would offer the first real sign of peace in the troubled region. As part of the negotiations, Nixon ordered the ceasefire of aerial bombings over North Vietnam. After eleven years that were costly for both sides, combat operations across South Vietnam ended within eight days, and the United States and North Vietnam agreed to a major breakthrough on January 23, 1973—a ceasefire.

While the Nixon Administration was working through the terms of the ceasefire in Vietnam and accepting the facts surrounding the resignation of Vice President Spiro Agnew, President Nixon needed to select a new vice president, a man whom he could trust and had the respect of the U.S. Congress. Nixon selected Republican Minority Leader Gerald R. Ford who had served as a congressman from the state of Michigan for 25 years. With his appointment by Nixon on November 23, 1973, Ford became the first vice president to be appointed under the terms of the 25th Amendment.

As Nixon was being challenged by the Watergate investigation and Gerald Ford was adjusting to his new role as vice president, the U.S. Congress was taking advantage of the vacuum within the Nixon White House. Congress took steps to reign in U.S. spending on South Vietnam. In August 1974, legislators approved just $750 million in military and economic assistance, half of the $1.5 billion desired by the White House and less than a third of the $2.3 billion

Washington had spent on military aid alone in 1973. The cutback dealt a psychological blow to Saigon and hampered South Vietnamese military operations by creating shortages of fuel and equipment. But declining American support was hardly the only problem confronting Saigon. The government's gravest weakness remained what had always been an inability to build effective national institutions supported by its citizens. Despite Vietnamization the South Vietnamese Army continued to suffer from rampant desertion and poor morale. Meanwhile, Saigon's economic failings became more glaring than ever. For years the United States had sustained South Vietnam by flooding the country with consumer goods and directly or indirectly employing hundreds of thousands of Vietnamese as everything from clerks to taxi drivers to prostitutes.[2]

However, within nine short months, on August 9, 1974, Richard Nixon was forced to resign as a result of his involvement in the Watergate scandal, and Vice President Gerald Ford became the 38th President of the United States as per the succession guidelines of the 25th Amendment.

As the United States sat on the verge of a constitutional crisis with the resignation of Richard Nixon and the resulting ascension of Vice President Gerald Ford to the presidency, Ford became the first President in United States history to serve as Vice President and President without being duly elected by the Electoral College. With the political tumult in the White House, the North Vietnamese felt emboldened to attack vulnerable posts north of Saigon:

> All these problems coalesced to bring about the collapse of South Vietnam. The final phase began on August 9, 1974, when Nixon resigned the presidency. Overnight, Hanoi no longer had to worry about the American leader who had done most to assure Saigon of U.S. support. To test the intentions of the new president, Gerald Ford, North Vietnam launched a major attack northeast of Saigon in December. The operation brought doubly good news for the communist. The entire province of Phuoc Long fell to the communists, while Ford, hemmed in by Congress and wary of embroiling his presidency in Vietnam, did nothing.[3]

By December 12, 1974, events in South Vietnam had worsened. Congress had constrained funding to the American military, and whether or not they would honor former President Nixon's commitment against the North Vietnamese hung in the balance.

According to presidential biographer Douglas Brinkley, after Nixon's resignation, the President was to be held "on a much shorter leash. As passed by Congress over Nixon's veto in November 1973, the War Powers Act held the president's authority to commit U.S. troops to combat abroad without congressional approval for only sixty days." This meant that although there was increasing pressure on South Vietnam from aggressive communist powers,

"Ford could do little but keep negotiating—and begging for aid money from Congress."[4]

The discord and disconnect in Washington gave the North Vietnamese the opening that they believed they needed. The North Vietnamese decided to "double down" as they believed victory was in sight, and planned for bold offensives in 1975. Communist leaders in Hanoi were emboldened by the political restraints on the U.S. president ... continued stepping up military action on the ground"[5] in what they hoped to be followed in 1976 by a "victorious conclusion of the war."

The Battle of Phuoc Long demonstrated to the North Vietnamese that, as they hoped, American support was over for the South Vietnamese. The war was going badly for South Vietnam, and from the American perspective, "there was mounting concern in the Embassy ... the signs kept mounting and the intelligence kept getting harder and harder that the North Vietnamese would start a major offensive in early 1975, which they did."[6]

By March 1975, conditions in Cambodia and Vietnam were even more unstable and getting worse. In Vietnam, the North Vietnamese's resolve to end the war had hardened, and "total victory came much more quickly than anticipated. In mid–March, communist troops captured the strategically important city of Ban Me Thuot in the Central Highlands." As the communists advanced, President Thieu ordered "ARVN forces to evacuate the Central Highlands altogether. The chaotic withdrawal left six provinces in communist hands and obliterated any remaining confidence in Thieu's leadership." As of April 1, the skirmish had reached the coast, and "Hue, Da Nang, and other cities fell to the communists, sometimes without a fight. Astonished by the rapidity of their advance, North Vietnamese Commanders hurriedly turned their attention to capturing Saigon."[7]

Believing South Vietnam to be in serious peril, "President Ford asked Congress for $722 million in emergency military aid. But most Americans—Ford included—saw no hope of rescuing the country." The Ford administration feared "damaging American credibility if it did nothing," but Ford knew Congress would likely reject the request, as it was "unwilling to pump more money into a losing cause [Congress] quickly blocked the proposal, approving instead $300 million to pay for humanitarian relief and the evacuation of Americans from South Vietnam." Frustrated and left with no other choice, "Ford declared on April 23rd that the Vietnam War was 'finished as far as America [was] concerned.'"[8]

In winter 1974, with the expected fall of Saigon soon to come, the Navy brass was looking for a new commander for the USS *Midway*. They needed a commander who was a strong and bold manager, tested in his ability and could

8. Operation Frequent Wind

lead by example in taking command over a troubled ship. While *Midway* was one of the prized jewels of the Seventh Fleet, it needed someone experienced at the helm.

Midway was at the time perceived as a troubled vessel. Within a 47-year period, it had 40 commanding officers and lacked the leadership stability needed for its next possible mission, the possible evacuation of Saigon of U.S. citizens and foreign nationals. It had a reputation of problems and very few wanted to take command for fear that they couldn't get the ship under their control. The Navy chose the captain who was able to turnaround the troubled USS *White Plains*; it chose Captain Chambers to take command.

Upon his appointment in mid–January 1975, Chambers was sent to Hawaii for a series of debriefings with CINCPAC and staff. Chambers then flew to San Diego to meet with the Commander Naval Air Forces Pacific's engineer who shared responsibility for the overall condition of *Midway*, including the status of needed repairs of the vessel, maintenance issues he needed to look out for and items that would need his attention but were not yet funded.

By early February, Chambers flew to Washington to have meetings with

South China Sea, December 1974. Commanding Officer Chambers (right) receives a "Job well done" as he departs from the USS *White Plains* (courtesy Naval History & Heritage Command Photo Archive, Naval Subject Collection).

Washington, D.C., 1975. President Gerald Ford Meeting with Graham Martin, General Frederick Weyand and Henry Kissinger in the Oval Office to discuss the precarious situation in Vietnam (courtesy National Archives).

staff at the Pentagon for additional briefings and consultations where he was shared intelligence reports that events in Vietnam were not going to come to a favorable or honorable conclusion. While in Washington he went "up on the hill" to apprise key members of Congress on the condition of various funding requests necessary to keep Midway at peak performance.

While Chambers was in Washington meeting with members of Congress, the U.S. Ambassador to South Vietnam, Graham Martin, was also in Washington meeting with some of the same members of Congress. In his book *Tears Before The Rain: An Oral History of the Fall of South Vietnam*, Larry Engelmann provides interesting insight into American Ambassador Graham Martin where he explores the final months and weeks before the evacuation of Saigon and how the Ambassador became a crucial figure during the final days of the fall of Saigon.

Engelmann explores how Martin implored members of Congress and the White House for assistance during his visit to Washington in an effort to get aid for the South Vietnamese. He warned them that an inevitable flood of people seeking aid was about to befall them: "you'd better prepare for refugees, you'd better prepare the setup, you better get the authority" that they may need for an evacuation and the resources necessary to protect Americans during an evacuation.[9]

Upon his return from stateside, on March 26, 1975, Captain Chambers took command of the aircraft carrier USS *Midway* (CV-41). One of the largest warships in the world at the time, *Midway* was a 75,000 ton vessel. It was almost 1,000 feet in length at the water line and supported by a crew of 4,500 men.[10] Its impressive flight deck is 1,001 feet long, the equivalent of three football fields and 258 feet wide spanning an area of 4.02 acres.[11] The enormousness and operational requirements of *Midway* caused many to refer to it as a "hotel," while still others referred to it as a "city" for the number of compartments, light fixtures, food preparation and "guests" on board.

Figure 5: USS *Midway* by the Numbers

Ship
- 240,000 gallons of freshwater produced daily
- 212,000 horsepower
- 190,000 pieces in the flight deck
- 43,000 pounds of laundry
- 30,000 light fixtures
- 2,000 compartments
- 1,500 telephones
- 1,800 feet of anchor chain aboard
- 156 pounds: each anchor chain's link
- 1,001 feet long: More than 3 football fields
- 258 feet wide
- 18 decks, equivalent of a 20 story building

Fuel
- 3.5 million gallons of ship & aviation fuel
- 100,000 gallons consumed daily in the ship's boilers
- Fuel economy: approximately 260 gallons to the mile (or about 20 feet per gallon)

Crew
- 200 aviators
- 4,300 others worked so 200 could fly
- Approx. 650 men in engineering
- Approx. 225 cooks
- Approx. 30 corpsmen
- 40 commanding officers in 47 years
- 3 chaplains

Logistics
- 10 tons of food per day
- 13,500 meals a day
- 10,500 cups of coffee at a time
- 4,500 pounds of beef per meal when served
- 3,000 pounds of potatoes per day
- 1,000 loaves of bread a day
- 500 pies when served
- 198 pounds of dry laundry for each of 6 washing machines
- 4,752 pounds of laundry could be washed every 12 hours
- Food storage
  ◊ 1 butcher shop
  ◊ 2 bakeries
  ◊ 1 vegetable prep room
  ◊ 15 storerooms
  ◊ 5 freezers
  ◊ 4 chill boxes
  ◊ Capacity
    + 70 tons of food
    + 10–11 tons consumed daily
    + 14,000 pounds of chicken
    + 14,400 pounds of grill steaks
    + 16,000 pounds of coffee
    + Daily cost of feeding crew in 1976: $10,000

The enormity of the vessel and the tasks at hand made Chambers the right man for the job at the right time. When asked what was going through his mind upon taking command, Chambers replied, "I had finally gotten a job that all young tail hook aviators aspired to. I was elated. However," he added,

"I was also concerned that the Admiral and staff on board *Midway* at the time would be second-guessing every move I made because the Admiral was a former skipper of *Midway*. At that very moment, I was glad that I had a good engineering background."

Upon taking command of the USS *Midway*, Chambers brought tremendous experience to his command. He brought impeccable academic credentials, having graduated in the top 20 percentile at the U.S. Naval Academy and having received a master's degree in aeronautical engineering from the Naval Postgraduate School at Monterey, California. Compared to his contemporary classmates, Chambers likely had more at-sea experience, as well.

Chambers' at-sea experience included serving as the air officer (Air Boss) on the aircraft carrier the USS *Oriskany* (CV-34) from February 1970 to December 1971, which gave him tremendous experience in commanding the USS *Midway*. As the Air Boss, he was responsible for the flight deck and hanger deck aircraft handling crews, the catapults and arresting gear maintenance and operating crews and the aircraft fueling crews (storage, purification and delivery of aviation fuel). The aircraft directors, crash crews, the aircraft handling officer and aircraft catapult officers all reported to Chambers. As the Air Boss, Cham-

South China Sea, 1971. The dashing Captain Chambers aboard the USS *Oriskany* sporting a mustache and a regulation style Afro (courtesy National Archives).

bers ran the control tower and either he or his assistant was in the control tower twenty-four hours a day, seven days a week while on Yankee Station (off the coast of Vietnam). The Air Boss or his assistant slept in the tower when they were on station, and they had fighters on five-minute alerts when they were at sea in the warzone.

Prior to becoming the Air Boss, Chambers was the Combat Information Control Officer (CIC) on the USS *Ranger* (CV-61), one of four Forrestal class super aircraft carriers from April 1967 to August 1968. As the CIC, Chambers was the number-two man in the Operations Department. The radar operators, air intercept controllers and Naval Tactical Data System (NTDS) operators reported to him. He was responsible for maintaining the big status boards, the ones that are often seen in the movies. Chambers and his team controlled the aircraft arrival and departures. As the CIC, he provided radar guidance for departing and returning aircraft and tracked all aircraft within 200 miles of the ship.

Chambers' previous stint on the USS *Midway* and his extensive experience on *Oriskany* and *Ranger* were invaluable, and now, having commanded and turned around the USS *White Plains* to an award-winning ship, Chambers was exceptionally qualified to take command of the USS *Midway*—and the first African American to command an aircraft carrier.

According to Vernon Jumper, the Air Boss of the USS *Midway*, he knew very little about Captain Chambers when he initially heard that Chambers was coming aboard. Jumper had initial instinctive concerns when he learned that the new captain had previously been the Air Boss on the USS *Orkiskany*. Jumper explained that "a lot of Commanding Officers get in the way of any ship's Air Boss, and make getting the job done difficult." However, after his initial meeting with Chambers, Jumper was very impressed with the new Captain: "having been a former Air Boss, Chambers had firsthand knowledge of what my job was. We discussed our management and leadership philosophies, and it was apparent that we were both on the same page."[12]

During the debriefings on *Midway*, Chambers was made aware of the challenges that made *Midway* a problem vessel, including the lethal combination of drugs and racial problems onboard ship and a backlog of over 300 disciplinary cases awaiting adjudication by the captain. Chambers had an opportunity to set a precedent of cleaning house and to conduct necessary investigations around the clock, day and night, up on the bridge. He needed to resolve these matters expeditiously so that he and his men could meet the anticipated challenges ahead of them: the possible evacuation of Saigon in the event the North Vietnamese invaded the city, which they presumed would be in short order.

One of Chambers' first orders of business was to reduce the enormous backlog of disciplinary actions. New to the ship and not emotionally involved with the men or the incidents at that point in time, he handed out discipline to the men who were found to be in violation of the Navy's Uniform Code of Military Justice; it was done by the book. Depending on the severity of the offense, some men were sent to the brig for a couple of days with just bread and water, some were demoted in military grade, others had a reduction in pay and each disciplinary action was handled swiftly and fairly.

Chambers also immediately took steps to stem the flow and usage of drugs aboard ship by instituting a random drug search policy. One afternoon the ship's chaplain asked to meet with Chambers. As captain, Chambers knew that when one of his men asked to meet with him there was something they needed to share or discuss. The chaplain proceeded to inform his captain that his number was drawn and wanted to share his indignation as Chaplain to having to be strip searched. Chambers, who treated everyone the same, lowered his voice as if to share an important secret and informed the Chaplain that his own number had come up the week before. He then shared with the chaplain that the search was a little embarrassing, but his was only a couple of inches so it needn't be worried about embarrassment. The chaplain smiled at the humor and went below for the search. Chambers, who was comfortable with himself, always tried to set his men at ease with humor that they could enjoy.

During one of his early inspections, Chambers and some of his senior staff, along with the chief engineer, climbed down the many ship's decks on each tier's ladders to inspect the ship's reduction gears which had been opened for inspection in anticipation of Operation Frequent Wind. Upon arriving at the engine room, Chambers was the only one in the inspection party who did not have his proper identification card with him. When the marine who was posted at the entrance and unfamiliar with the new captain asked Chambers for his identification, the chief engineer proceeded to explain to the guard on duty who Chambers was and that he did not need identification.

Always the straight shooter and believing that the process was as important as policy, Chambers, now in command of an aircraft carrier with nuclear capability, commended the marine for his actions and reminded the chief engineer that his specific order was not to let anyone in the engine room without proper authorization. Chambers then turned to the marine, thanked him for following orders, and said that he was within his duty and had the right and responsibility to question Chambers' access to the controlled space.

To make the point even clearer, Chambers climbed back up all those ladders of the many flight decks and back down so that he could provide proper identification to the marine. Chambers explains that *Midway* had classified sensitive areas of the ship, including its engine room, and ordered them protected by a 24/7 marine guard that was authorized to use deadly force in order to prevent sabotage. Upon his inspection of the engine room, as he left, Chambers turned and once again thanked the marine and told him that *Midway*'s respect of them started at the top, with him.

While Chambers' experience provided him with the solid foundation to succeed as captain of *Midway*, he did have concerns about Rear Admiral William (Bill) Harris and staff (CTG 77.4) being assigned to *Midway*. Chambers believed, or at least hoped, that since the admiral's experience mirrored his own—the admiral had been an air wing commander, a tough task master and a skipper of a deep draft vessel before he also became commanding officer of *Midway*—that Chambers' background would prove his capacity to manage the USS *Midway* under any adverse conditions and that the two men could coexist.

Despite Chamber's stellar background, academic credentials and his ability to manage under extreme pressure, nothing had prepared him for what was about to unfold within the next 60 days. His hopes of a peaceful coexistence on board *Midway* were dashed as Admiral Harris attempted to second guess and intimidate Captain Chambers whenever an opportunity presented itself. He would often accuse his own chief of staff and Chambers of working together to undermine his requests. Although Chambers was well aware of the admiral's reputation, he had more important matters to attend.

On March 31, five days after taking command, the ship and her crew got underway from their homeport in Yokosuka, Japan, on what was supposed to be a routine cruise, with visits scheduled for Hong Kong and Subic Bay in the Philippines. Chambers directed *Midway* to proceed to the operations area, the restricted area off the coast of Japan, and started conducting carrier qualifications: bringing the airplanes out, letting them land and run them to the catapult, then launching them again. These exercises ensured that the pilots were up to speed for routine carrier operations.

During these routine exercises, a *Midway* signalman reported visual contact with a surface combatant on a relative bearing of 340°. The lookout's visual contact correlated with a "Skunk" that had been previously reported by Combat Information Center (CIC). CIC had picked up this contact at over 30,000 yards and had been tracking it on a collision course with *Midway*. The pulse quickened on the navigation bridge when the signal bridge reported an ID for our "Skunk" as a Russian warship.

In an attempt to test the fortitude and leadership of new COs, Chambers firmly believed that the Russians kept a book on U.S. ships and their commanding officers. Ever since their trawlers had been harassing American ships on the high seas, Chambers had observed that those CO's who gave way were continually harassed while the Russians seldom confronted those who held firm.

Chambers ordered the signal bridge to inform the contact that his ship was a U.S. Navy aircraft carrier conducting flight operations and that she should remain clear. Under international law, since a vessel that is launching and recovering aircraft is restricted in maneuvering, all other vessels should remain clear. Because of light surface winds, *Midway* was steaming at 28 knots to get wind over the deck for flight operations. Needless to say, the Russian warship did not acknowledge Chambers' signal, but she appeared to pick up speed and the bearing started to drift to the right. At a range of 10,000 yards, the officer of the deck computed that the contact had a new closest point of approach of 1,500 yards. At 7,000 yards range from *Midway*, when it appeared that the warship would cross *Midway*'s bow safely, she commenced a hard turn to her starboard. After completing a 180° turn, she appeared to go dead in the water just as she was re-crossing the bow.

The Russian ship then ran up the international signal, which indicated that she had experienced a breakdown and was not under command. Under international law, other vessels are required to remain clear of a vessel not under

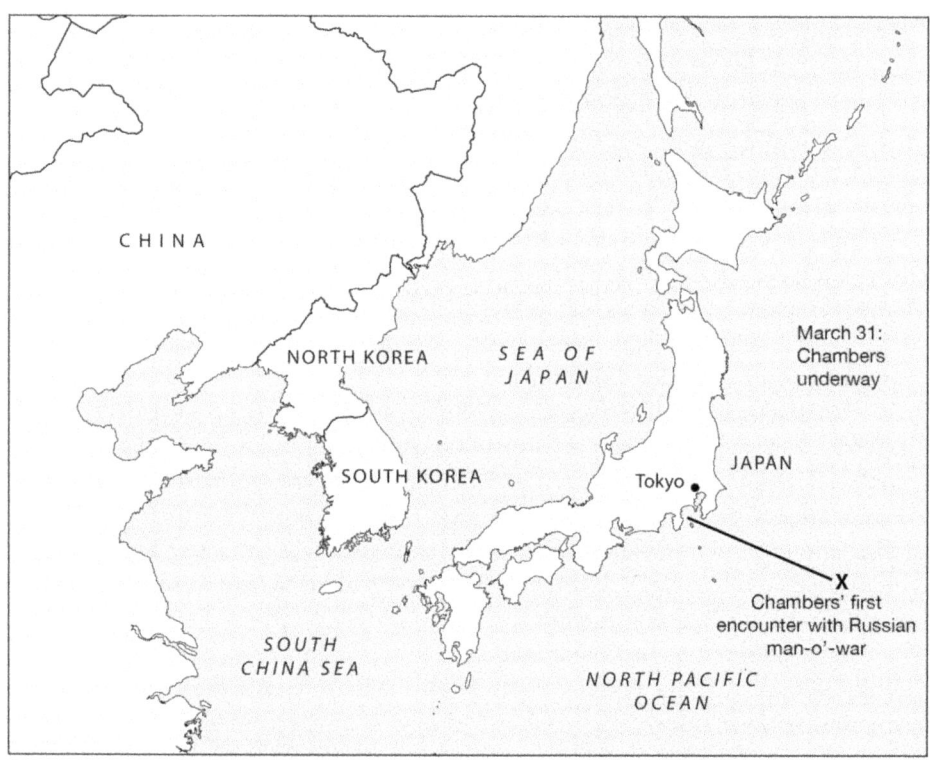

Map 2: USS *Midway* launches March 26, 1995, Yokosuka, Japan.

command. Chambers believed that the Russian warship somehow knew the *Midway* was under new command, and the crew was "playing possum" in order to test his fortitude. According to Chambers, he instinctively knew what the Russians were up to and thought to himself, "Those S.O.B.s are out to test me, and I'd cut him in two before I gave way."

As the Russian vessel went supposedly dead in the water off the port bow at 1,500 yards, the Air Boss informed Chambers that one of their F-4 Phantom jets was in trouble and wanted to land immediately. The recovery of the Phantom jet became Chambers' first priority. The Air Boss alerted the flight deck crew that they had an emergency in progress. Midway had no time to play games with a Russian warship. The tension on the bridge continued to build, but there was a sigh of relief when Chambers informed the officer of the deck that he was taking control of the ship.

This relief, however, was short lived. The tension returned instantly when Chambers ordered the helmsman to steer nothing to the right of 135 degrees and proceeded to bear down on the Russian ship, which was now dead ahead. According to Chambers, "When it became obvious to the Russians that I was not intimidated and had no intentions of altering course, she immediately hauled down her breakdown signal and cleared my bow." He described the retreating ship as, "making a wise decision, as she immediately began emitting black smoke with screws churning amid a big swath of foam and green water. As the Russian war ship was passing abeam to port at less than 300 yards from *Midway*, the F-4 Phantom with the hydraulic system failure landed on board."

As the Russian ship fell astern, and as Chambers returned the control of the ship to the officer of the deck, he was asked, "Skipper, at what point were you going to maneuver to avoid the Russians?" While Chambers did not answer this question, he believed that his actions spoke volumes. The truth was that he never intended to alter course or give way to the Russian warship. The one thing the Navy does when they put a man in charge of a ship is expect him to obey the rules and make sound decisions. The Navy does not expect him to play chicken.

The Russian commander knew that he was in violation of international rules, and when he realized that Chambers wasn't going to "chicken out," he decided that discretion was a better part of valor, and got out of Chambers' way.

Had the Russians had the opportunity to meet Chambers in advance, he could have avoided a potential international incident. Chambers, who talks in a soft tone, learned on the streets of Seventh and T in Northwest Washington, D.C., to always carry a big stick. After all, he was commanding a 70–75 ton vessel bearing down on a 1,500-ton Russian vessel, and he knew that the Russian commander knew better. If this was a test of the new commanding officer, the Russians soon learned that the "new kid in town" was made of the same sturdy steel as the *Midway*.

By early April 1975, the situation in Cambodia and Vietnam had gotten even worse. Violations of the cease-fire agreement increased in frequency and the South Vietnamese government was on the verge of collapse. Unfortunately, unlike today, there was no CNN broadcast from these capital cities via satellite with up-to-the-minute live pictures. The bad news, however, was all over the intelligence reports from that area.[13]

The U.S. Embassy in Saigon, reviewing internal and external intelligence reports, realized that if the war went badly for them they would have to evacuate not only their own staff, but all other Americans in Saigon, some of whom were married to Vietnamese, as well as foreign nationals from countries allied to the United States such as Australians, French, New Zealanders, South Koreans, and Thais. In addition, the U.S. embassy and administration felt duty-bound to evacuate all its South Vietnamese allies, many of whom were government officials, army leaders and South Vietnamese and their families who had worked for the Americans. According to Chambers, various briefings estimated that this could amount to as many as 200,000 people.[14]

Although the ambassador refused to plan for the evacuation, his military staff at the American Embassy drew up an evacuation plan without his knowledge, referred to as the Standard Instruction and Advice to Civilians in an Emergency. The plan instructed American citizens where to gather in the event that an evacuation was necessary, and if that time came, the code words "the temperature in Saigon is 112 degrees and rising" would be aired on the Armed Forces Radio, to be followed by the out-of-season song, "White Christmas." The writing was on the wall. Americans all across South Vietnam began to migrate toward Saigon, many with their Vietnamese wives and dependent children.

According to Chambers, the commander of the Seventh Fleet was getting ahead of the game. "He had already begun to beef up the amphibious forces in the region in the event that they would be needed for the evacuations of Phnom Penh and Saigon." As the military and political situation continued to deteriorate, Chambers "received a heads-up from Commander Task Force Seventy Seven that his battle group might be needed in the South China Sea or the Gulf of Thailand to augment the U.S. Forces that were already on station, and that Chambers and his crew should make preparations to return to Vietnam."[15]

As Ambassador Martin's staff prepared to evacuate as many people as possible, Captain Chambers and the other commanding officers of the Seventh Fleet prepared to receive and process the evacuees.

While en route to Subic Bay, *Midway* was ordered to embark two Marine Corps helicopter squadrons that were based on the island of Okinawa for further transfer to USS *Hancock* (CV-19) and the helicopter carrier USS *Okinawa* (LPH-3). According to Chambers, "*Hancock* was just east of Guam and had entered Seventh Fleet's area of control. She had received orders to proceed to the South China Sea at best speed," and Chambers understood that "when *Hancock* arrived in the vicinity of the Philippines she would off load her tactical air wing and embark the Marine helicopter squadrons." Chambers and his crew were assigned "to ferry two squadrons from Okinawa to the Philippines. To make room in *Midway* for the Marines, Air Wing Five assets had to be positioned ashore at Subic Bay."[16]

On the morning of April 5, 1975, *Midway* anchored east of Okinawa in Buckner Bay and loaded aboard the aircraft and personnel from two Marine helicopter Squadrons, HML-367 and HMA-369. Meanwhile, "after the pickup, Midway departed Buckner Bay at a high speed of advance for a rendezvous with *Hancock* in the Mendoro Straits. On April 9, 1975, *Midway* transferred the Marines to *Hancock* in the mouth of the Mendoro straits."[17]

Chambers recalls that "upon completion of the transfer, *Hancock*, under the operational control of Commander Task Force Seventy Six, RADM D.B. Whitmire, proceeded to Southeast Asia to stand by for Operation Eagle Pull along with other ships of Task Force Seventy Six." Eagle Pull was the code name assigned to the operation that evacuated Phnom Penh, Cambodia.[18] *Midway* exited the Mindoro Straits, resumed its attack carrier posture and headed for Subic Bay. At the time, Captain Chambers thought that *Midway* was only hours away from receiving orders to proceed to the Gulf of Thailand or the South China Sea to join the carrier groups already on station off the coast of Vietnam. He admits that he was glad that it was *Hancock* that was becoming a helicopter carrier and not *Midway*. As the commanding officer of *Midway*, he wanted to get into the action, but also wanted to be involved as part of Seventh Fleet's Carrier Strike Force.[19]

On April 15, *Midway* entered Subic Bay for a scheduled 10-day upkeep period in the Philippines. Just three days later she was ordered to get underway in four hours and steam at maximum speed toward Vietnam. In anticipation of his mission's objective, Captain Chambers ordered the off-loading of over half of his aircraft wing before leaving port, as well as 500 officers and crewmen, to make room on board for the upcoming mission. Based on his new mission he needed a clean flight deck, but in the event the ship had to protect itself Chambers kept a sufficient number of tactical airplanes on the hanging deck in case he had to go into a defensive posture.

Even though Captain Chambers was allowed four hours to get underway,

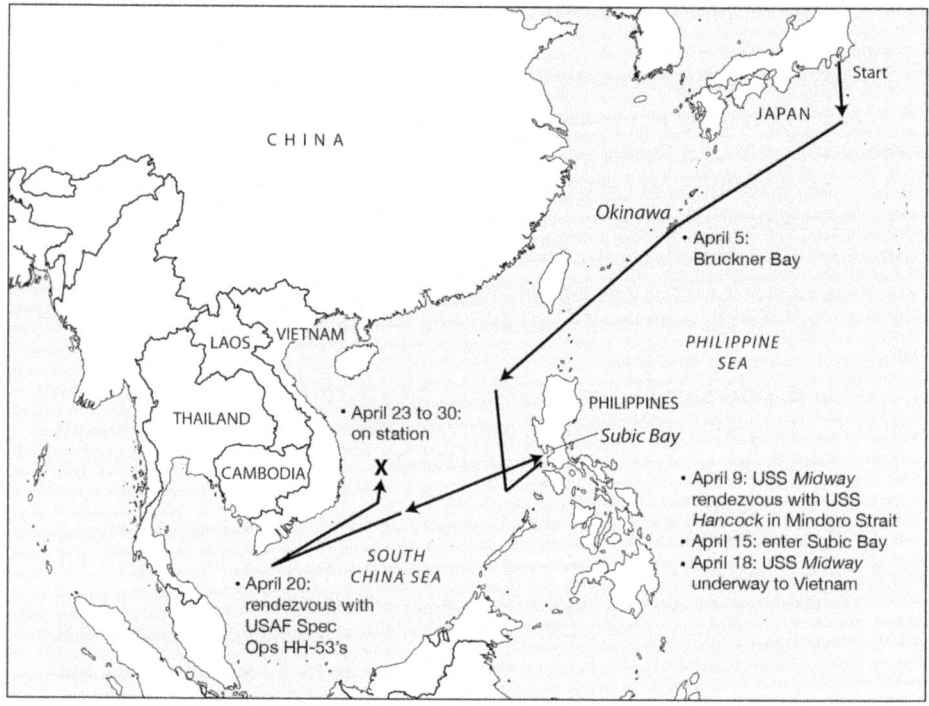

Map 3: USS *Midway* arrives off the coast of Vietnam.

the ship set sail in less time. The biggest challenge in setting sail was putting the engineering plant back together. The USS *Midway* class arrangement had twelve boilers compared to the eight boilers of most other earlier carriers. *Midway* immediately went to high-super heat steam, then gradually brought all 12 boilers on line so she could make max speed towards the South Coast of Vietnam.

Several days later, after steaming to a position off the southern tip of Vietnam, *Midway* embarked 10 U.S. Air Force H-53 helicopters. For the next eight days, the Air Force crewmen from the 56th Special Operations Wing, the 21st Special Operations Squadron and the 40th Aerospace Rescue and Recovery Squadron prepared for an operation that they knew would commence any minute.

The North Vietnamese were emboldened by their conquest of the city of Ban Me Thuot in the Central Highlands and no longer felt the need to hold back on their final offensive. The end was now in sight, particularly when Nguyen Van Thieu, under pressure from his allies, including the United States, resigned on April 21. The North's total control of all Vietnam was only days away. Preparations were now being made for an evacuation in Saigon. A group

South China Sea, 1975. The Air Force Sikorsky CH-53 Sea Stallion helicopters await airlift orders on USS *Midway's* flight deck (courtesy United States Navy).

South China Sea, 1975. After evacuating Saigon, the first to arrive aboard USS *Midway* was the former Minister of the Republic of Vietnam, Air Vice Marshal Nguyen Cao Ky (courtesy National Archives).

of sailors was selected and trained to process evacuees upon arrival aboard *Midway*. Made up of petty officers and non-rated men, the group was assigned to work on the flight and hangar decks in designated handling areas.

Just as the intelligence reports had envisioned, the resistance in Vietnam, both military and political, collapsed. Chambers recalls the morning of April 29 when he and his crew watched a South Vietnamese Air Force UH-1 helicopter land aboard *Midway* and, with deep sorrow, Chambers recognized Vice President General Nguyen Cao Ky of South Vietnam when he disembarked on Midway's flight deck.

As planned earlier that afternoon, the code to start the evacuation was aired on the Armed Forces Radio and all across the City of Saigon: the classic American holiday song "White Christmas," signaling the evacuation had begun and that time was of the essence. At 3:30 that afternoon, Captain Chambers received orders to execute Operation Frequent Wind. Upon Chambers' order, the helicopters lifted off of the flight deck and began the arduous journey of shuttling passengers from Saigon back to *Midway*.

South China Sea, April 29, 1975. At 15:30, Captain Chambers gives the orders; helicopters lift off USS *Midway* to execute Operation Frequent Wind (courtesy National Archives).

8. Operation Frequent Wind

As part of this operation, the carriers *Midway* (CV-41), *Hancock* (CV-19) and *Okinawa* (LPH-3) became part of the largest helicopter evacuation in United States history. Based on various sources, these aircraft carriers would be responsible for the immediate evacuation of as many as 20,000 Americans, foreign nationals and Vietnamese refugees from Saigon.

From the flight deck of USS *Midway*, nine H-53 helicopters departed for the designated landing zones in Saigon. On the original flights out, Marines were on board to help with the evacuation in Saigon and to ensure the safety of evacuees and of the American Embassy where evacuees arrived on buses to stand in line as they waited for helicopters to take them offshore to the awaiting ships.

For hours, the helicopter pilots went back and forth between *Midway* and Saigon. They stayed on board long enough to unload the evacuees only to depart and quickly return with another full load. On each return visit to the ship, they were asked the same question: "how many more?" Some of the

South China Sea, April 29, 1975. The first wave of helicopters evacuating from Saigon approach USS *Midway* (courtesy National Archives).

refugees who wanted to leave Vietnam via helicopter climbed the ladder at the United States Embassy in Saigon before being ferried to the awaiting aircraft carriers. In the final months and weeks before the evacuation, Graham Martin, American Ambassador to South Vietnam, was a crucial figure during the fall of Saigon.

While Captain Chambers and the other commanding officers of the awaiting ships were managing the situation offshore, Ambassador Martin and his staff were attempting to handle the situation on land, uncertain of the true numbers of anticipated evacuees. According to Martin, a man named Stuart Herrington who worked under Colonel Madison was helping to load people out in the yard—but, said Martin, "[Herrington] didn't know anything about anything other than loading." However, Herrington was "a guy who would always volunteer an answer whether he knew it or not." While pilots were returning and asking the Embassy staff how many additional people remained to evacuate, "Herrington was telling these pilots, 'You got 2,000 or 2,500 more.'"[20]

South China Sea, April 29, 1975. Evacuees from Saigon are offloaded onto the USS *Midway* (courtesy Naval History & Heritage Command Photo Archive, Naval Subject Collection).

Meanwhile, Admiral Noel Gayler was "just absolutely sitting on pins and needles, because he feared he was going to be the man in charge of a disaster...." Admiral Gayler was pressuring the crew members to "'evacuate the Americans! Evacuate the Americans! Evacuate the Americans!' And just come the hell out of there and just leave everybody else."[21]

Lieutenant General Brent Scowcroft of the U.S. Air Force had promised Martin that he would send 50 more helicopters to aid in the evacuation. They had rescued the intended Vietnamese and Koreans, carefully counted them and brought them into the inner compound. According to Martin, "We had no intention of bringing the people we had left in the outer compound," though they would be bringing "other people out—some of them were cabinet ministers and so on." But Stuart Herrington's message about 2,000 or 2,500 remaining evacuees reached the pilots, the admiral and CINCPAC before finally reaching Schlesinger in the Situation Room at the Pentagon. "Schlesinger," said Martin, "was being pushed by the Joint Chiefs to get it over with."[22]

As the helicopters were bringing evacuees on board, *Midway* sailors swiftly

South China Sea, April 30, 1975. Amongst the chaos onboard *Midway*, evacuees were quickly and professionally processed, ensuring all of their needs were addressed (courtesy United States Navy).

moved the evacuees to safety and processed their identifications. According to Captain Chambers, "those who needed medical attention were immediately attended to by the ship's medical staff. Everyone was fed by the supply department, and many of the sailors took tremendous pride in entertaining the small children with handmade toys." Chambers was absolutely surprised to see the caring and sensitive nature of his sailors with the children, some of whom were frightened by the whole ordeal. Chambers had never realized these gruff nineteen-year-old Navy men had a caring bone in their bodies.

The *Midway* "hotel" treated each evacuee as a guest and provided each with all the comforts expected of a gracious host. All of the sailors were sympathetic to the trauma being experienced by each evacuee—they were leaving behind their families and friends, their possessions and their homeland. As the evacuees arrived on *Midway*, Chambers said, "they were shown friendliness, sensitivity and compassion.... Our sailors executed their jobs with precision. They took their jobs seriously and helped each evacuee move through the process in a dignified manner."

A major fear for Chambers was that the helicopters coming in from Saigon with refugees might be overloaded and one or more would have an accident landing on the overcrowded flight deck. Chambers was concerned that such an incident would shut down the flight deck. Chambers thought he needed a lot of luck to pull off this operation without a hitch.

In his pre-briefing session with the Marines, Chambers gave orders for them to use deadly force if any mayhem broke out. After the incident in which Chambers forgot to bring proper identification to gain access to the engine room, nothing more was ever said of the incident; however, Chambers could tell the Marines held him in high esteem because of his respect for their position onboard and how he handled that particular moment. Chambers then instructed the Marines that there were to be no weapons brought on board, and he knew without question that they would handle that responsibility admirably. He then pointed to the Marine who stopped him at the engine room hatch when he didn't have his identification, looked at him as they shared a silent understanding and said to the Marine, "you are to be in charge."

Each passenger was checked for any weapons of any sort. If any were confiscated, since *Midway* didn't have the magazine space to store the weapons, they were tossed over the side of the ship. A reporter who was evacuated from Saigon had in his possession two pistols with very expensive pearl handles—purportedly family heirlooms. Chambers recalls looking on as LCDR Raymond Roper, after witnessing the reporter arguing with the Marines, calmly walked over and asked the reporter how he could help him, since the "staff" at "hotel" *Midway* was always eager to please. Roper tried to explain the circumstances of guns on board and asked if he would like a receipt for the guns. The offer pleased the reporter who then surrendered the weapons, so Roper took out his notepad and gave the reporter a receipt for two heirloom pistols.

Roper then handed the pistols over to Jim Turner who, with all of the professional decorum of a well-trained sailor, tossed the pistols over the side of the ship as the reporter, unaware of the ship's disposal methods for evacuee weapons, stood there in disbelief. As a few choice words were thrown his way, Roper walked away with a smile on his face. He knew that he had done a major favor for the reporter, and perhaps at some point the reporter would understand. Roper knew that the Marines had been seconds away from taking the pistols and either throwing them, and perhaps even the reporter, over the side of the ship. They took their assignments seriously, and the chaos of the ship did not allow for any melodrama on board.

Once the incident was over, Chambers turned his attention back to watch-

South China Sea, April 30, 1975. Passengers aboard a South Vietnamese helicopter await their turn for processing aboard the *Midway*, before being transported to the Philippines (courtesy United States Navy).

ing a steady stream of helicopters belonging to Vietnam, Air America[23] or the U.S. Army loaded to the brim and deftly flown by their pilots. Each of the huey helicopters were designed to hold 10 to 12 combat loaded soldiers or Marines but were now loaded with as many as 50 people, including small children and the elderly. On one such flight, when the sailors opened the doors, "they pulled fifty small children out of [the helicopter] and onto their feet. Parents who stayed behind had stacked their children on top of each other like firewood for the sixty-minute flight to safety aboard Midway."[24]

"The people in Saigon were doing a phenomenal job loading the helicopters with people because they always arrived full," says Chambers, "it created a logistical problem on our end." The helicopters were weighted down more than usual and their fuel needs had increased dramatically. The pilots would fly until their fuel was almost gone and would shut down on the flight deck without signal. Most of the helicopters could not be restarted once they shut down since Midway did not have the support gear to service them. Because of mass chaos, Chambers and his crew didn't have the resources to service or repair the helicopters that landed onboard.

South China Sea, April 29, 1975. As the evacuees arrived, mass chaos aboard the USS *Midway* **(courtesy National Archives).**

South China Sea, April 29, 1975. United States Naval officers talk with Vietnamese officers who arrive on USS *Midway* after being airlifted by Air Force HH-53 Jolly Helicopters (courtesy National Archives).

One of Chambers' biggest concerns was the flight deck. As bad as the logistical challenges were during the daylight hours, at night it was worse—everything was now done in the dark and there were no white lights on deck which only made the task more hazardous. The evening of April 29, *Hancock* suffered an accident on her flight deck and was forced to shut down flight deck operations for a period of time. An onboard crash was always a commanding officer's biggest fear. If an incident were to occur on *Midway*'s flight deck, Chambers would have had to shut down the flight deck and stop operations on board for an extended amount of time until the flight could be cleared for operations.

The tension and split-second decision making aboard *Midway* was staggering. With helicopters coming in at capacity from Saigon, the processing of refugees down below and the moving of refugees to the helicopters to take them to the support ships in company, the chaos was staggering. Chambers' subordinates marveled at their captain's unique ability to manage all of the divergent responsibilities in an orderly and coherent manner and admired his incredible ability to keep up with all of the chaos on deck.

During the evening of April 29, Chambers was informed that *Hancock*

South China Sea, April 29, 1975. The helicopters just kept coming and according to one observer "it seemed that sky was dotted with helicopters arriving from Saigon, looking to board the USS *Midway* as they awaited a landing space on deck" (courtesy Naval History & Heritage Command Photo Archive, Naval Subject Collection).

had shut down her flight deck due to an accident onboard. *Hancock* still had eight helicopters airborne that were low on fuel. *Midway* cleared two landing spots on her bow and proceeded to refuel *Hancock*'s helicopters. Once they landed, the Captain was told that the first helicopter to land only had eight minutes of fuel left—a potential catastrophe waiting to happen. All eight helicopters were eventually topped off and were able to return to *Hancock* when she resumed flight operations. Once *Hancock* cleared her flight deck of the crash site, she resumed taking on refugees.

One out of ten refugees needed immediate medical attention. Sailors gave up their bunks so fleeing brothers and sisters could stay together.[25] Although Captain Chambers and the men aboard *Midway* were tired, there was no time for rest or room for errors, so they operated on adrenaline. This is what they were trained to do. As the night progressed, the same question was asked of each returning flight: how many more? How many more?

But the helicopters just kept coming.

Chapter 9

"Bird Dog on Final"

By mid–April as the North Vietnamese moved further south toward Saigon, many of the city's residents quietly began the slow but steady process of evacuating the city. Many of the politically connected flew to the Con Son Airport, located on an island about 200 nautical miles south of Saigon, and then were transported to the Philippines for distribution to other locations around the world for refugee resettlement.

Some of the South Vietnamese Air Force pilots were assigned the detail in shuttling refugees from the city of Saigon, and others were assigned the detail in Con Son Island to help with the transfer of refuges to the Philippines. One such pilot was Major Bung Ly. As with the other pilots, Bung Ly understood that if the North Vietnamese moved any further south, they would be called upon to engage in an aggressive air campaign to protect the city at all costs. In preparation for the air campaign, some of the young pilots began the slow process of bringing their wives and children out of Saigon and relocated them to the safety of the island.

In addition to the Con Son Airport, the island was also home to the infamous Con Son National Prison for North Vietnamese prisoners of war and Viet Cong suspects. The prison was one of the largest prison of war facilities, was staffed by South Vietnamese military police and was supported by American military police as advisors. For the pilots, the small island was considered a safe temporary shelter for their families since it was controlled by the Americans.

As the North Vietnamese approached Saigon and the evacuation of Saigon took place, the pilots on Con Son Island were still awaiting word to begin their aerial assault against the North, unaware of what was going on 200 miles to the north. As they continued to wait on official word to begin an aerial assault, the pilots made the necessary plans for their families to be evacuated to the Philippines.

On April 30, 1975, without having direct communications from the mainland, Bung Ly and the other pilots began to hear the rumors that Saigon was about to be taken over by the North Vietnamese believed to originate from prisoners housed at the Con Son National Prison. Concerned for his family's safety, Major Bung Ly took the necessary steps for his family to be scheduled to depart on the next C-130 aircraft. He quickly learned that the flight would probably be the last to fly out of Con Son Airport.

The Lockheed C-130 is a reliable and sturdy plane that in normal circumstances can comfortably transport 100 paratroopers with their heavy gear and take off on relatively short runways such as the 6,000 foot runway at the Con Son Airport. But at the last moment before the plane was to take off, Bung Ly and the other pilots' worse fears were about to materialize: the C-130 had developed mechanical problems and was no longer air worthy. Trained at the U.S. Randolph Air Force Base in Universal City, Texas, Major Bung Ly made one of the hardest decisions of his life. He went to look for his family, boarded them on a small Cessna plane and began to fly in a northeast direction.

As the South Vietnamese pilots were just getting word that Saigon was about to fall, *Midway* was still in the process of recovering helicopters. In addition to the H 53's, there were a number of Bell Huey helicopters that were now involved in the evacuation process. Some of the Hueys belonged to the South Vietnamese Air Force, some belonged to Air America and some belonged to the U.S. Army. All of the helicopters were ferrying people from Vietnam to the ships at sea. But luck was not on their side as at any given time the helicopters would run out of gas and shut down on the nearest flight deck. During the operations, most of the smaller Hueys did not have radio communications with *Midway*'s control tower.

To aid the approaching helicopters, *Midway*'s tower personnel used their Aldis lamp to signal the approaching pilots. A green light meant the flight deck was open for landing, while a red light signaled that the flight deck was closed. Sometimes even without a signal the Hueys would land on deck and quickly discharge their passengers. If the helicopter had sufficient fuel for a return round trip, they would immediately depart to return to Vietnam and bring back more passengers. The dedication of the helicopter pilots was outstanding. However, in the end, when they were about to run out of fuel or had maintenance problems, they would shut down in the middle of an already crowded flight deck.

According to Captain Chambers, "The flight deck was chaotic, but at all times it was well-organized chaos, and the flight deck crew, the best in the business, did an absolutely outstanding job of managing chaos."

During all of these tactical maneuvers, with helicopters from the South

South China Sea, April 29, 1975. Organized chaos on the *Midway* fight deck (courtesy National Archives).

Vietnamese Air Force, Air America and the U.S. Army coming from the Saigon area, *Midway*'s lookouts spotted a Cessna OE-1 single-engine observation aircraft approaching the ship around 11 a.m. According to Chambers, when the Cessna approached *Midway*'s flight deck, it was extremely crowded with sailors, marines, evacuees and helicopters.

The pilot initially flew the Cessna "Bird Dog" across the flight deck and attempted to drop a note on deck, but unfortunately, during the first three attempts the note went over the side of the ship. On the fourth try, the pilot saw that his note remained onboard. The note hit the crash truck on deck which prevented it from going overboard. The note was rushed to the bridge for Captain Chambers to read. The note was written on a pilot's kneeboard card map of South Vietnam, and read, "*Can you move these Helicopter to the other side, I can land on your runway, I can fly 1 hour more, we have enough time to move please rescue me. Major Bung wife and 5 child.*"

Captain Chambers' initial thought was to encourage the pilot to return to Vietnam presuming that he had never made a carrier landing, and without a tailhook, the ship would need a very high wind over the deck or the plane

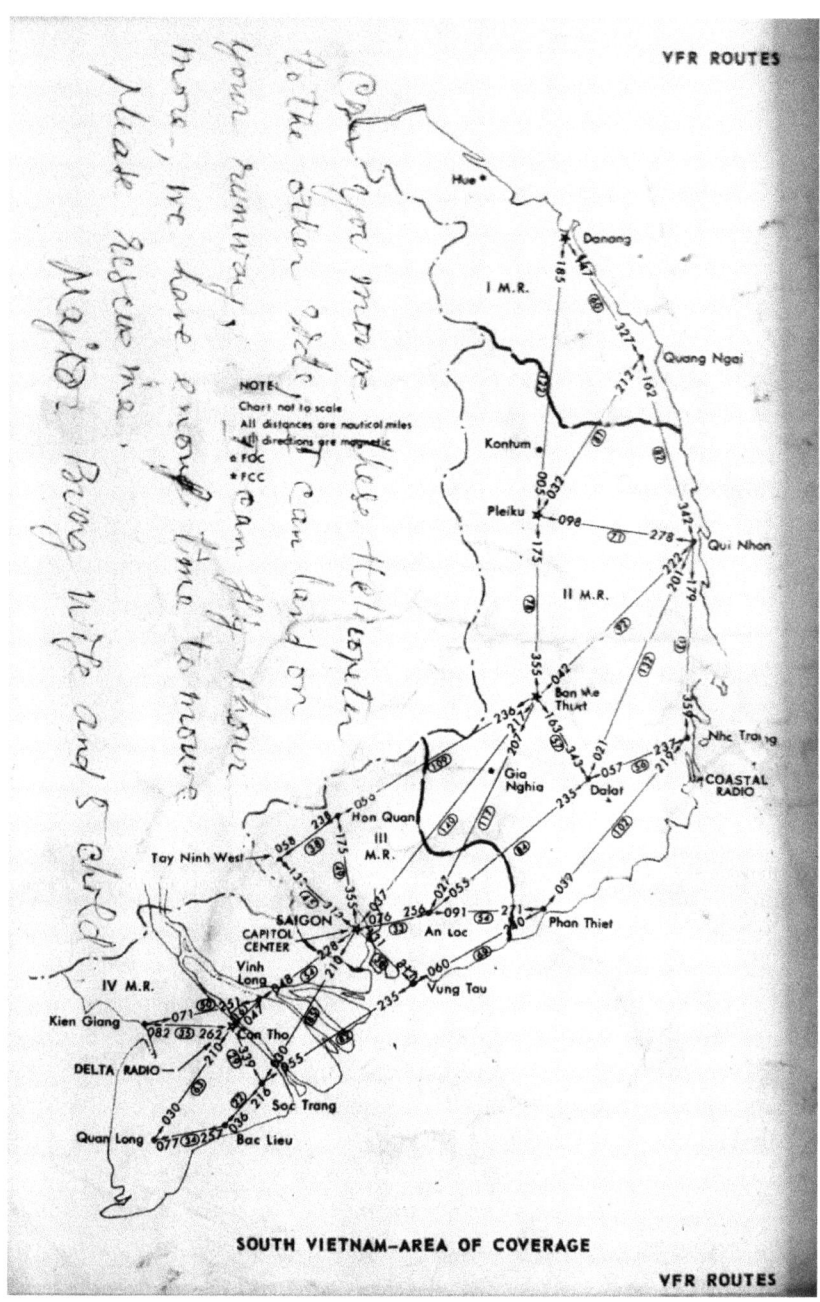

South China Sea, April 30, 1975. South Vietnamese pilot Major Bung Ly drops Pilot's Knee Board Card requesting permission to land aboard USS *Midway* (personal collection).

would run off the flight deck and over the side of the ship. However, Chambers realized that *Midway* was too far at sea and the pilot simply didn't have enough fuel to make a return flight back to the beach in South Vietnam. The Captain realized that the pilot wanted to land on the flight deck but had serious concerns about the pilot's ability to do so successfully. Chambers thought, "This is no place for a novice who has never seen the blunt end of a boat! How am I going to get out of this one?" He watched the airplane circling *Midway* through his binoculars. Chambers was hoping that once the pilot saw the condition of the flight deck he would either go somewhere else or he would ditch alongside the carrier.

Through binoculars, the ship could make out the pilot and a rear seat passenger who appeared to be holding a child. They could also see one person whose head appeared out of the baggage compartment. The passenger behind the pilot was apparently a woman whom they presumed to be the pilot's wife based on the note. She was not wearing a flight suit. Then, as the crew continued to watch the plane, it was determined that there were other people on board in the cargo area. Captain Chambers instructed the CDR Vern Jumper to try to communicate with the Bird Dog on all emergency frequencies with the hope that the pilot spoke enough English to understand them. Chambers had but one thought in mind: "Go away! I can't do a damn thing for you!"

South China Sea, April 30, 1975. Major Bung Ly circles the USS *Midway* as he attempts to communicate with the Control Tower by dropping three different notes on the flight deck (courtesy Naval History & Heritage Command Photo Archive, Naval Subject Collection).

The *Midway* crew quickly screened the evacuees on board while looking for an interpreter to help them communicate with the pilot. Chambers knew that even if the pilot spoke English, he might be so full of adrenaline that they would need to talk to him in his native language. They found a Vietnamese woman who spoke excellent English and rushed her to the control tower where they continued their attempts to communicate with the pilot on all emergency frequencies.

The Vietnamese interpreter in the control tower kept repeating the broadcast that the flight deck was clobbered (overcrowded) for fixed wing operations and that the pilot should find another place to land. As the Bird Dog continued to circle the flight deck, Chambers had to assume his tower did not have communication with the plane.

At this point in the operation Chambers' reporting senior was Rear Admiral Don Whitmire who was in command of Operation Frequent Wind. Chambers had a great deal of respect for Whitmire, a former all-American tackle at both Alabama and Navy, and, according to Chambers, a stand-up guy. Rear Admiral Bill Harris, who was on board *Midway* at the time, had been Chambers' boss prior to Operation Frequent Wind and would again assume that role when Frequent Wind was completed. Harris, a tough taskmaster, engendered little love from his subordinates.

Although Chambers had been aboard only a short time, it was obvious that Harris and Chambers did not see eye to eye on issues of priority and style of command. Many of Chambers' officers had noted the differences in the approach of the two men in handling crises, and respect for Chambers was growing daily among the crew. It was against this background that RADM Harris used the bridge's Announcement system for all on the bridge to hear and publicly instructed Chambers to tell the pilot to ditch the plane at sea and have the helicopters rescue him.

It was highly unusual for an admiral to publicly task a commander of a ship in the manner in which he did. Usually these discussions are conducted on the private sound power phone system where Harris could yell at Chambers and nobody else on the bridge would have been aware of the conversation or of any disagreements that the two men might have had. But Admiral Harris chose instead to use the 21 MC—the public announcement system—in order to intimidate Chambers to do what he wanted.

The Bird Dog circled the ship several times with his landing lights on which indicated that he wanted to land on board. As an experienced naval aviator, Chambers knew that a pilot of a fixed gear aircraft with that many people on board was not about to ditch his plane at sea. Chambers presumed that the pilot also knew that an aircraft ditched with wheels down almost always flipped over to an inverted position upon impact with the water. Chambers did not relish the idea that he would be a witness to an escape attempt by untrained civilians from an upside-down aircraft in the South China Sea. Ditching the aircraft would surely mean death for all aboard the plane because the pilot, in a vain attempt to save his wife and infant child, would also drown.

According to Chambers, he "surmised that even with all the activity on the flight deck, including offloading refugees and refueling helicopters, the pilot most likely was going to crash his plane on the flight deck in an attempt to save his family." With that thought in mind, Chambers ordered the crew to clear the helicopters and people out of the landing areas. Chambers says, "I just thought if I were in his shoes, I'm going to crash on deck as my only chance for survival. I've got no chance of survival if I try ditching." For himself, Chambers says, "My number one concern was the possibility of a disastrous fire on the flight deck so I needed to be concerned about the safety of my ship, my crew, the refugees, and now for this pilot and his family." Even though Chambers had been ordered not to clear the flight deck, he ordered the Air Boss, Vernon Jumper, to make a ready deck. He was thankful that the pilot had an hour of fuel left, as that would give the crew sufficient time to clear the flight deck.

Within 10 minutes of first spotting the Bird Dog in flight, the Captain explained to Vern Jumper that he was going to make an announcement via the general intercom of the ship and asked all flight deck personnel who weren't on watch to report to the flight deck. In response to Chambers' announcement, not only did all available flight deck personnel report to the flight deck, but also all hands from other *Midway* departments,

South China Sea, April 30, 1975. Captain Chambers communicating with USS *Midway* flight deck as "Bird Dog Lands"—Cesena aircraft circles the flight deck (courtesy Naval History & Heritage Command Photo Archive, Naval Subject Collection).

including the Marines, engineers, office personnel, the air wing and everyone else not actually on watch.

Ordinarily, the order to make a "ready deck" means moving aircraft and equipment from the landing area and placing it behind the "foul line." According to Chambers, the Air Boss had a problem because the entire flight deck was full of helicopters and equipment. Air Boss Jumper asked for clarification—was he really being authorized to push helicopters over the side to make a ready deck?

In a bold move, Captain Chambers said, "Yes, you are authorized to clear the flight deck." At this junction, with all of the men coming forward to provide assistance, they began what is now an historic moment in American history, symbolizing the end of the Vietnam War. Vietnamese helicopters, Air America helicopters and U.S. Army helicopters were shoved over the side of *Midway* into the South China Sea to make a ready deck for the Bird Dog, still circling and now very low on fuel.

As a former Air Boss, Chambers knew the task would not be easy, but he also knew that they were going to have to push a few of the helicopters over the side to make room, since they had neither time nor space to park all of the helicopters clear of the landing area and over the foul line. According to Chambers, he and CDR Jumper concluded that the cross deck pendants (arresting wires) might be a hindrance and had them removed from the flight deck. Likewise, they ruled out a barricade arrestment since the aircraft was not designed to take the stress. They were afraid that the wings might pull off and the fuselage would continue through the barricade.

Chambers' fear was that the Bird Dog would attempt to land and crash on deck, causing a massive fire. Under normal conditions, fire is one of the biggest dangers on ships at sea. With the chaotic, crowded conditions on *Midway*, even a small fire would have been catastrophic. Chambers knew that he was doing the right thing by shoving a number of helicopters overboard. He was protecting the integrity of the ship, the ship's other assets, and most of all, protecting the safety of the men and women who were now his responsibility on *Midway*.

As his men began to make a ready deck, Captain Chambers deliberately did not watch the operation, nor did he count the number of assets that went over the side of the ship. Although he knew he was doing the right thing, he naturally presumed that he was going to be in trouble because he was ignoring orders from RADM Harris not to make a ready deck. Since Chambers had authorized the crew to push as many helicopters over the side as necessary in order to clear the landing area, he wanted to be able to truthfully say that he did not know the number of assets lost over the side, stating,

9. *"Bird Dog on Final"* 149

South China Sea, April 30, 1975. Captain Chambers orders the *Midway* flight deck to be cleared of helicopters (courtesy United States Marine Corps).

I wanted to be able to sit in front of my court martial and say I pushed a few assets over the side. I don't know how many there were and I didn't count them and I could survive a lie detector test with that one because that was the absolute truth and we pretty much got the deck all squared away ... at least I wouldn't be accused of letting women and children drown without attempting to save their lives, and that I could sleep with.

In short order, the crew was able to clear the landing area for the Bird Dog, but just when the ship was about to give the Vietnamese pilot a green light, indicating that he had a clear deck, another group of Hueys landed on the flight deck. The new group of Hueys saw an open deck. They didn't have radio communication with the control tower and they didn't have permission to land, but they had been landing on *Midway*'s flight deck for the past 24 hours without signals, so they landed one more time.

During the intense moments of the operation, Chambers and Jumper were in communication with each other. Jumper shared his thoughts about Chambers:

[I had] tremendous respect for the Captain who was a former Air Boss and had first-hand knowledge of what my job was and the tremendous pressure that we were all under. As the Commanding Officer, he was very businesslike and a strong—dynamic leader, who he did not micromanage me or the other department heads as we each executed our responsibilities under extraordinary circumstances.[1]

According to Chambers, Jumper asked him what to do next, and the captain, knowing that the Bird Dog was running out of fuel and it would only be a matter of minutes before the pilot would try a landing, turned to the Air Boss and said, "Since we are going to get court-martialed anyway, what are a few more helicopters." The Air Boss proceeded to clear the deck, now slick with rain, for a second time. The wet condition on the deck was not an issue for landing helicopters, but for a small Cessna, piloted by someone who had never landed on an aircraft carrier, this condition could have posed serious problems.

Reacting quickly to the new environment, the captain contacted the chief engineer and informed him that he was going to need "twenty-five knots out of the old girl" in order to make enough wind over the deck to provide a headwind as breaking action for the Bird Dog. Airplanes designed to land on aircraft carriers are equipped with a device known as a "tail hook." During carrier landings, a pilot deploys his tail hook, which catches one of the heavy arresting cables strung across the flight deck and acts to stop the aircraft. The Bird Dog had no such device. If Captain Chambers was going to assist the pilot in making a successful landing he had to provide additional breaking action or the Bird Dog might run off the end of the runway and fall into the South China Sea.

9. "Bird Dog on Final" 151

Since *Midway* was only expecting to land helicopters during the evacuation operations, several of the steam boilers were taken offline for minor repairs. The engineer informed the captain that he didn't have enough steam for the main engines and that it would take too long to bring the boilers online in order to achieve the requested 25 knots.

Captain Chambers then ordered the chief engineer to shift the ship's electrical load from two of the four steam-driven generators to the ship's two emergency diesel generators, thereby making more steam available for the main engines. Chambers, during his years in the Navy, never missed an opportunity to volunteer to stand bridge watches on every carrier assignment. At that point in his career, Chambers had more bridge-watch time than any of his Naval Academy classmates—even the surface ship driver. He took advantage of every opportunity to watch and learn from knowledgeable skippers and senior officers. Seamanship and shipboard engineering plants were areas as familiar to him as flying. It was that attitude and knowledge that enabled Chambers to make the quick life and death decisions facing *Midway*.

South China Sea, April 30, 1975. After the flight deck becomes crowded once again with awaiting helicopters, Captain Chambers realizing that the Cessna was low on fuel, orders the *Midway* flight deck to be cleared of helicopters (courtesy Naval History & Heritage Command Photo Archive, Naval Subject Collection).

The ship answered the bell for 25 knots. The surface wind in the area was 15 knots. When added to the ship steaming at 25 knots, the wind over the deck was 40 knots. The captain did not know the approach speed for the airplane, but his guess was that it would land at a speed of 60 to 65 knots. Subtracting the 40 knots of headwind, the pilot now had a closing speed of 20 to 25 knots. Once the ship turned into the wind, the pilot had plenty of room to land without risk of running off the runway.

There was another danger to be considered, however. When there are high winds over the deck (40 knots is considered high wind over a flight deck), the airflow behind the ship tends to create a downdraft and turbulence. Experienced carrier pilots are used to the turbulence just behind the ship. However, the captain now had an inexperienced carrier pilot attempting his first carrier landing on a wet flight deck. Chambers had to provide high enough winds over the deck to prevent the pilot from overshooting the landing area, but the resulting danger was a significant amount of turbulence behind the ship, making it tougher for him to control his aircraft as it crossed through the turbulence.

Captain Chambers took the calculated gamble that if the Cessna's pilot applied enough power, it would get him through the turbulence. Because the Bird Dog had small wheels, the captain ordered the flight deck crew to remove the arresting cables, since the arresting gear was of no value to this airplane. The Bird Dog was now cleared to land. The Air Boss called the captain with these words: "...Bird Dog on Final."

While all of the activity and tension was taking place on the flight deck and in the control tower in anticipation of the pilot's landing, the remaining off-duty crew members had all gone up into the superstructure, called vulture's row, to observe the landing—and as it turned out, it was quite a show. Chambers recalls that he had done everything possible to prepare the ship for this extraordinary landing. The only thing he could remember thinking was that he hoped the Bird Dog had enough power to get through the turbulence in the groove behind the flight deck. Chambers said to himself, "Please God, let the Bird Dog make it." There were 43 knots of wind over the deck and Chambers believed that if the Bird Dog got over the ramp that he would have it made, even though the deck was rain soaked. As the Cessna approached, the entire flight deck went stone quiet. The seconds seemed like hours, and every movement of the plane was magnified.

According to Chambers, the Bird Dog rolled out on final approach. So far, he looked pretty good. Everyone on board was praying to themselves, "don't take the 'cut' (take off power) too soon!" All hands on deck held their breath. According to Chambers, "the young pilot, all things considered, made an absolute perfect landing. The South Vietnamese Air Force Major touched down

South China Sea, April 30, 1975. Major Bung Ly successfully lands Cessna O-1 on the USS *Midway* (courtesy Naval History & Heritage Command Photo Archive, Naval Subject Collection).

right on the spot which moments before was the location of the 'number three wire,' the arresting cable which was the target position for experienced carrier pilots." The Bird Dog bounced once and came to a stop at a right angle to the length of the island, amid a flight deck crew's wild cheering and arm waving.

As the pilot exited the plane, the crew was screaming and cheering. Everyone who had a hand in clearing the deck was so proud at that exact moment when the pilot had safely disembarked. Chambers recalls that none of them could have anticipated what was about to happen next. The young man turned around and stretched out his arms, and out came his wife holding an infant child in her arms. The whole ship erupted in applause. Then the pilot turned and pulled the rear seat forward and out came what Chambers describes as "four of the most beautiful and frightened young children you have ever seen. As each child emerged you could cut the silence with a knife. We didn't know what to expect next. Then all of a sudden, the ship erupted with such a loud roar of excitement, I'm sure the North Vietnamese heard us all the way back in Saigon."

South China Sea, April 30, 1975. Major Bung Ly taxies to a halt aboard USS *Midway*, with wife and five small children aboard (courtesy Naval History & Heritage Command Photo Archive, Naval Subject Collection).

Upon exiting the aircraft, as the pilot and his family were immediately surrounded by well-wishers, Captain Chambers admits that he gave a huge sigh of relief, and then issued a "well done to all hands! A fantastic feat!" Chambers had the pilot, Major Bung Ly, escorted to the bridge and personally congratulated him on his extraordinary display of airmanship. Chambers admits, "The young pilot's perseverance paid off. He had more guts than anyone I had ever known. He went beyond the point of no return with his wife and five children on board and with no assurance that he would find a place to land!" The Captain estimated that the four small children were probably in the hot baggage area of the fuselage, with little to no cooling air, for two or more hours. Chambers believed that their "father was a brave man. But seeing the faces of those small children, as a father myself, I knew those children were equally brave."

As the crew settled down and got back to all of the tasks still underway with the evacuation and rescue mission going on in Saigon, the pilot was escorted to the bridge to spend a few moments with the Captain. Chambers

9. "Bird Dog on Final" 155

South China Sea, April 30, 1975. Major Ly being interviewed aboard USS *Midway* (courtesy Naval History & Heritage Command Photo Archive, Naval Subject Collection).

recalled that because of all the other things going on at the time, he spent only a minute with this brave pilot. He welcomed him aboard, congratulated him for such a fine landing and expressed the hope that he, his wife and children were okay and could now grab a fine meal in safe surroundings as a reward for the ordeal that they had been through.

The crew of *Midway* was so impressed with this brave pilot that they gave him a pair of gold naval aviator wings, made him an honorary carrier pilot, and took up a collection for him that raised about $10,000 within a week.² South Vietnamese Major Bung Ly, his wife and his five children were eventually relocated to Orlando, Florida, and the contributions from the crew of *Midway* helped the family get settled in their new community.

After his brief meeting with Major Bung Ly, Chambers continued with the evacuation procedures, accepting helicopters filled with refugees from Saigon. Chambers knew that the evacuation was coming to an end when he was informed by one of the helicopter pilots that the American Ambassador to South Vietnam, Graham Martin, and some of his staff were now on board *Midway*. When Captain Chambers was informed that the ambassador and his staff were on their way up to the bridge to see him and to thank him for assistance in the evacuation of the embassy, Chambers was honored. But much to his surprise, when the ambassador and staff walked through the door, the delegation included his old friend and college roommate from Annapolis, Captain Hugh Benton from Virginia.

The two Naval Academy graduates had stayed in touch all those years, but had lost track of each other's locations in the rigmarole of their jobs. Chambers greeted the ambassador politely, and was elated to see his good buddy, knowing they were all safe and now under his care. That evening Ambassador Martin and his wife spent the night aboard *Midway* and slept in the captain's in-port cabin, while Captain Benton and other members of the ambassador's team slept below deck in the officer's quarters.

Ambassador Martin was the "last man standing"; now aboard *Midway*, Operation Frequent Wind was suspended. The War in Vietnam had come to an end.

The 11-year war was costly for the United States. The war caused riots on college campuses all across America as its youth marched in protest against the war effort. It stirred resentment in African American communities all across America as young Black men were disproportionately drafted and sent to war. It was a tremendous drain on the American treasury, and it was the cause of tremendous psychological trauma on the American public with the loss of American lives, physically maimed soldiers and soldiers affected by post-traumatic stress and drug-related addictions upon returning home.

In a 2011 Congressional Research Service Report, it was estimated that between 1965 and 1975, the Vietnam War cost $111 billion—at the war's peak, its cost was 2.3 percent of the Gross Domestic Product. At the time the Congressional Research Service Report was commissioned, in 2011, the cost of the war would have been equivalent to $738 billion present-day dollars.[3]

Chapter 10

Port of Sattahip

Once Operation Frequent Wind came to an official end after the evacuation of Saigon, Captain Chambers was ordered to proceed at best speed, which meant another full power run to the Gulf of Thailand. The purpose was to retrieve a number of Vietnamese F-5s and A-37 aircraft that had flown out of Vietnam to the U-Tapao Air Base in Thailand during the fall of Saigon. Almost half of the F-5 American-built planes were brand new with state-of-the-art equipment on board.

The newly formed government of Thailand asserted that any U.S. aircraft entering Thai airspace and landing without permission on a Thai airfield now belonged to the sovereign nation of Thailand. However, the U.S. government took the position that the airplanes were on loan to the Vietnamese Air Force and were still U.S. assets, and therefore property of the U.S. Air Force.

After traveling 900 nautical miles in 28 hours at 33 knots, Captain Chambers arrived at the Port of Sattahip in Thailand on May 3. While *Midway* was anchoring off the coast of Sattahip so that U.S. Air Force heavy lift helicopters could retrieve the disputed assets and place them aboard the *Midway*'s flight deck, a small Vietnamese fishing boat (roughly 30 to 40 feet long) fleeing the North Vietnamese advancement in Saigon pulled up alongside of *Midway*.

From *Midway*'s hangar deck, the crew could clearly see that the fishing boat was taking on water and had over 80 passengers, many of whom were signaling that they needed to come aboard *Midway*.

Meanwhile, the United States Air Force, not waiting for a resolution to the diplomatic dialogue between Thailand and the United States governments, began using Air Force heavy lift helicopters equipped with heavy duty slings to rescue the U.S. aircraft that had landed in Thailand and transfer them to *Midway*'s flight deck. Still aware of the sinking fishing boat, Chambers instructed *Midway*'s executive officer to bring the refugees onboard

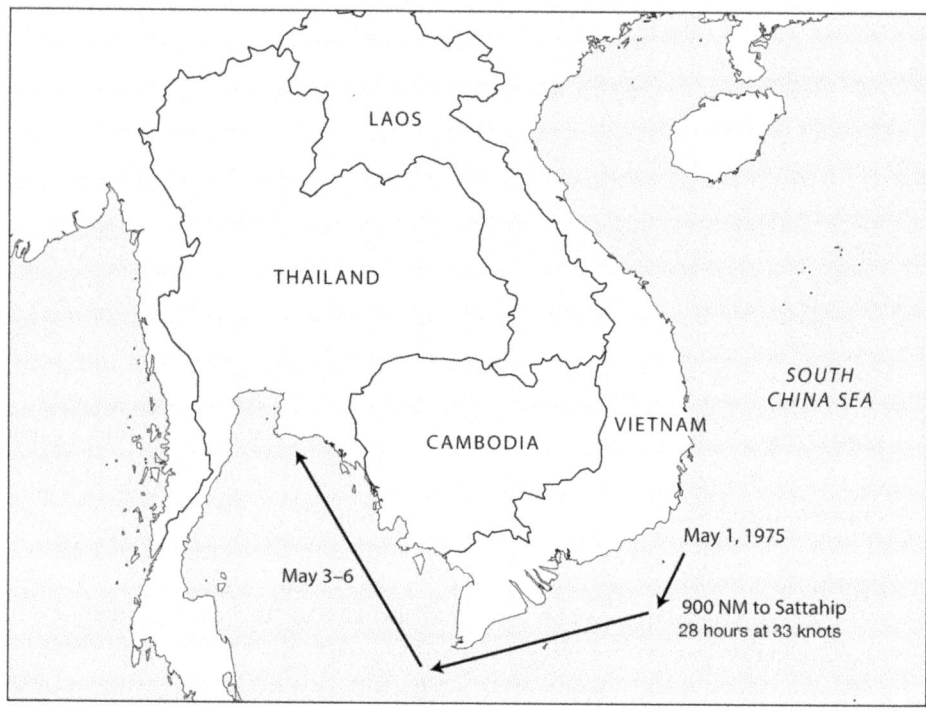

Map 4: USS *Midway* proceeds to Port Sattahip, May 1, 1975.

in the spirit of Operation Frequent Wind's intention, the rescue of Vietnamese refugees.

Rear Admiral Bill Harris (Commander CTG 77.4), who was still onboard *Midway* and once again Captain Chambers' boss, had his navigator check around the bearings. Harris informed the captain and the bridge that they were in Thai waters, not international waters, and therefore there was no requirement to rescue the refugees since the fishing boat was only three miles off the coast of Thailand.

Captain Chambers told his chief engineer to take the main engines off of jacking gear and be prepared to take steam to the turbines and to be prepared to answer all bells. He called the first lieutenant to the bridge, explained the situation and told him to man the forecastle to be prepared to veer chain (to let out a larger scope of the ship's anchor chain) so that the ship could maneuver itself away from Thai waters. Once the engineers got the engines back online, they twisted the ship using the propellers and veered the chain so that the whole ship was now in international waters.

As important as it was to save the lives of the 80 Vietnamese refugees stranded in international waters, the captain's primary objective was to make space aboard his ship to receive as many of the Air Force air assets as possible. At that point, Chambers instructed his executive officer to assist the small fishing boat that was alongside the gargantuan *Midway*. The refugees were brought onboard and a damage control team boarded the boat with instructions to dewater the vessel and to insure that it was sea worthy.

Meanwhile, Chambers went back to the larger mission at hand. He readied his flight deck to recover as many F-5 and A-37 aircraft as possible. As the Air Force was hauling the aircraft out on the slings and placing them on the flight deck, Chambers called back to the executive officer after a couple of hours to ascertain the status of the fishing boat. He was informed that the boat was taking on water and the damage control team was unable to stop the leak and couldn't dewater the vessel in order to make it sea worthy. Chambers ordered the executive officer to get his "damage control team and the refugees out of harm's way because [he] didn't want to get anyone hurt or to lose anybody over a piece of junk."

It was clear to Captain Chambers that the vessel would never make it to shore. Once again, Chambers made a critical decision and ordered that the 80

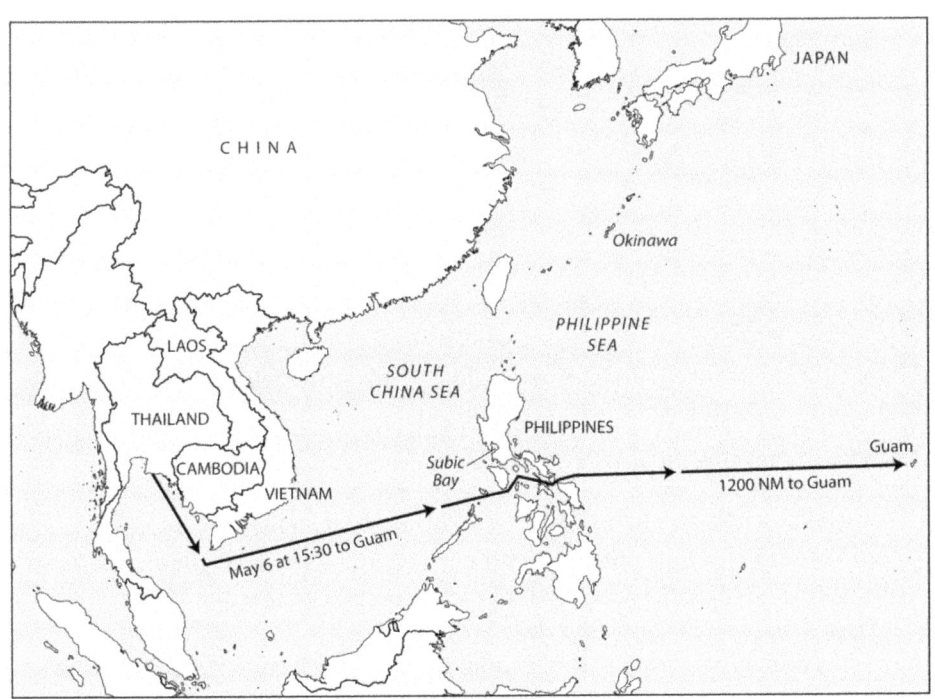

Map 5: USS *Midway* proceeds to Guam, May 6.

Gulf of Thailand, May 3–5, 1975. A CH-47 Chinook helicopter retrieving an asset from Thailand and placing it on the USS *Midway* (courtesy National Archives).

Vietnamese refugees be brought on board to safety. One by one, young and old were rescued from the fragile fishing boat and safely brought on *Midway*'s hangar deck where they received the same triage services as the evacuees from Saigon had received only four days earlier.

As Chambers returned to his primary goal of constantly clearing his flight deck in order to have as many U.S. aircraft placed on it as possible, the fishing boat began to sink. Admiral Harris had made inquiries and received word from the Commander U.S. Pacific Fleet that the crew should stop evacuating refugees, but since these particular Vietnamese refugees were already on board, the point was moot.

After recovering the aircraft from Thailand, Chambers was told to proceed to Guam in order to offload the remaining Vietnamese refugees, the helicopters, the Bird Dog and the Air Force jets.

Upon arriving in Guam, *Midway* spent the next 24 hours unloading over 50 South Vietnamese Air Force aircraft and over 100 American-made helicopters and other assets belonging to the U.S. Air Force. According to Chambers, "*Midway* took onboard over 100 Vietnamese F-5 fighter jets and 27 A-37 light bombers, all in a day's work."

In reflection, Chambers admits that this was a fairly hazardous task because "the United States Air Force helicopters were bringing these heavy jets out on slings and I didn't need one of those slings to break and have one of those jets weighing eight tons crash and caused a disaster on my flight deck." In 1975, in an article published by the U.S. *Midway* Public Affairs Office, Chambers wrote, "Upon departure from the Gulf of Siam on May 5, *Midway*'s flight deck looked as congested as a Japanese train at rush hour. Over 100 aircraft ... covered the flight deck en route to off-loading to their final destination in Guam."[1]

While Thailand and the United States were still disputing the ownership of the U.S. Air Force aircraft, Chambers received the jets on his flight deck and was ordered to transport the aircraft to Guam at full speed in order to return to Seventh Fleet operations as quickly as possible.

Chambers left the Gulf of Siam and commenced a full powered run toward Guam. He had to first navigate the 1,400 nautical mile journey to reach the treacherous Mindoro Strait in the Philippines. He navigated through the Mindoro Straits, arriving at dusk. He navigated at night through the dangerous San Bernardino Strait, a narrow body of water that connects the Samar Sea with the Philippine Sea. It took him over ten hours to navigate the 350 nautical miles of some of the most hazardous waters at full speed (33.5 knots), before he could complete the remainder of his 1,200 nautical mile journey and deliver his cargo in Guam.

On May 11, Chambers began to offload the U.S. Air Force jets obtained in Thailand. While in Guam offloading the aircraft and helicopters on the afternoon of May 12, 1975, Captain Chambers got word that there was yet another problem back in the Gulf of Thailand. *Midway* was instructed to turn around and reroute the ship to support the special operations forces rescuing the pirated U.S. cargo ship SS *Mayaguez* off the coast of Cambodia. *Midway* was urged to expedite offloading the airplanes in order to reach *Mayaguez* before the Cambodian naval forces could seize the vessel, reportedly for navigating in Cambodian waters.

Departing Guam on May 14, *Midway* commenced a full power run back to the Gulf of Thailand. Chambers knew that they might be in trouble meeting their objective. He realized that he needed to transit through the San Bernardino Strait again at night. Having just come through the strait only days earlier, Chambers knew the hazards of another full power run through those restricted waters.

The 350 nautical mile full power run through the San Bernardino Strait was dangerous during daylight hours due to the hundreds of small fishing boats taking advantage of the rich fishing grounds and strong currents in the straits. To do this at night was an extreme hazard. Having been lucky enough to get away with it the first time, Chambers was very concerned about the risk of having to make a second all-night passage that was above and beyond the call of duty. *Midway*'s wake could potentially swamp small boats during transit. After consulting with Admiral Harris, Chambers suggested that *Midway* be allowed to slow down as she went through the strait to avoid an accident. But intelligence reports were continuing to come in, and the admiral advised Captain Chambers to set sail at full throttle and continue with maximum speeds, despite the risk to the smaller fishing boats in the area.

As night fell, *Midway* continued at 33.5 knots through the strait with her whistle sounding the alarm to alert the fishing boats that they needed to get out of the way. Many of these fishing boats were nothing more than glorified rafts, sticks tied together and floating precariously on the water. Chambers was aware that in World War II during the Battle of Leyte Gulf in the Philippines Seas, the Japanese took an entire battleship force through the strait to attack the American transports anchored in Leyte Gulf. Recalling this, Chambers knew that if the Japanese had been successful maneuvering their forces through these straits at high speed, he could do the same with *Midway*.

Despite the size of *Midway*, the ship had tremendous maneuverability at full speed, and Chambers decided to use that to his advantage. Although the straits were dotted with small fishing boats, they tended to be clumped together in groups. According to Chambers, his destroyer escort complained all night about having to maneuver around all of the boats in the strait behind the carrier, but they made it through in record time, just as the admiral had requested.

The privately owned SS *Mayaguez* was en route from Hong Kong to Sattahip, Thailand, when it was fired upon by a Cambodian "swift boat." The Cambodian gunmen circled the merchant vessel and after machine gun firing, forced the captain to slow the vessel down. Once the swift boat fired rocket-propelled grenades toward the ship, the captain stopped the vessel at which point the ship was hijacked. The crew issued a distress call that was picked up on international radio channels. The *Mayaguez* and its forty-man crew was seized by the Cambodian gunboat approximately six or seven miles south of the Cambodian-claimed Island of Poulo Wai, which lies about 60 miles south/southwest of the Cambodian mainland. Cambodia had earlier seized, or attempted to seize, and then released other ships operating within its claimed territorial limit.[2] The *Mayaguez* sent out an SOS signal: "Have been fired upon and boarded by Cambodian armed forces at 9 degrees 48 minutes north/102 degrees 53 minutes east. Ship is being towed to unknown Cambodian port."[3]

During the next three days, the United States undertook a variety of diplomatic and military actions in an effort to secure the release of the ship and its crew. Some 66 hours after the seizure of the ship the Cambodians released the crew. The United States did not learn that the crew had been released until several hours after military actions were underway. A few hours thereafter, U.S. forces recaptured the *Mayaguez*.[4]

The capture of the SS *Mayaguez* was considered the last official battle of the Vietnam War, and several assets that were part of Operation Frequent Wind became part of the operation to recapture the *Mayaguez* and her crewmen. Once the Cambodians had control of *Mayaguez*, they took the ship and her crewmen to the Cambodian-controlled island of Koh Tang.

The USS *Coral Sea* (C-43) was the first United State asset to arrive on the scene and provided protective air strikes over Cambodia with the same Air Force helicopters used in Operation Frequent Wind. The Marines who protected the embassy and its staff during the evacuation of Saigon were now part of an assault on the island of Koh Tang with the objective to retrieve the ship and her crew.

Chambers got word of the Mayaguez incident on May 12 and *Midway*'s deck was not cleared to complete his refueling to return to the South China Seas until May 14. It took Chambers 85 hours at full speed to travel the 2,825 nautical miles to reach the Mayaguez rescue, including once again going through the treacherous San Bernardino and Mindoro Strait. By the time *Midway* reached the SS *Mayaguez*, the incident had already resolved itself. *Midway* served as a support vessel for a couple of days to the Special Operation Forces that rescued the SS *Mayaguez*.

Once *Midway* finally sailed back to Yokosuka, Japan, Chambers, who ran 10 miles per day on the flight deck for exercise, used his run to reflect on what had happened since that first time he stepped foot on *Midway*. Just about every sailor he met jokingly asked the same question in reference to the whirlwind of activities over the last 60 days: "Cap, is this how you start every assignment?"

Chambers, always ready with a quick retort, would reply, "Son, just wait until I tell you what we're going to be doing the next sixty days."

As *Midway* picked up speed and headed back to Yokosuka, Chambers looked over the bow at the vast open waters and silently wondered what would be in store for him when he finally reached base. He knew that he had stepped on a few toes during his cruise, but he also knew that he had done what he was trained to do and, most importantly, he had done what was right.

While in Apra Harbor in Guam, Admiral Bill Harris was advised that NBC's Today Show wanted to do an interview to recap the adventures of the *Midway* over the previous 60 days. It was expected that Admiral Harris would be interviewed. According to Chambers, he was relieved to be back in port so that he could get a couple hours of much needed sleep. He went to his stateroom only to discover that he was needed on the flight deck.

As Admiral Harris was about to be interviewed, a message was received from Commander U.S. Pacific Fleet that Chambers was to do the interview rather than Admiral Harris. This was a shock to all on board, and a shock to Chambers most of all. He had not slept for three nights, made apparent by his unshaved face and wrinkled clothes—in his own words, he "was a mess," but the steward's mates immediately brought Chambers a fresh uniform and a much needed razor and toiletries so he could clean up. According to Chambers, "The events happened so fast, from the time I was told to clean up and conduct the interview, so I didn't have much of a chance to process what I might be asked." Unfortunately, Chambers was not pleased with the interview "because the press was slanted. I was trying to get the conversation back to what really happened and they had a clear motive that was not consistent with the facts."

The interviewer concentrated on the events in Thailand and the removal of the disputed Vietnamese aircraft, using very purposefully worded questions that framed Chambers as a rogue captain who had violated international law by stealing airplanes that belonged to Thailand—a claim, says Chambers, which was "patently false."

Chambers, aware that the reporter was seeking a shocking story and personal fame at his expense, explained that the exercise was an approved operation and that he had acted under explicit orders from his commanders. Perturbed by the interviewer, and with his dry sense of humor, Chambers proceeded to say, "As you already know, everyone in the military understands that I did not take possession of the aircraft. However, it was the United States Air Force who placed them on the deck of my aircraft carrier in international waters." Although not smiling on camera, he was grinning on the inside as he watched the reporter's face turn red. The interview was cut short at that point.

Sometime later, unsure of how the interview had been edited by producers, Chambers received a long letter from his mother, Charlotte Chambers, asking him why he stole the airplanes in Thailand. Chambers shares that his mother "wanted to remind me that I was raised better than that." Months later, when Chambers had a chance to speak with his mother directly about the letter and the incident, he tried as best he could to explain what had actually happened. "No matter what I said or how I tried to explain it, she wasn't buying it." Chambers affectionately adds, "A mother's love will always keep a man grounded and humble."

Chambers' tour on *Midway* gave a bold and compassionate man a chance to shine. He was a man who was comfortable in his own skin, and broke barriers by setting the bar high for those who came after him—Black and white. He spoke with a soft voice, but his deeds, as witnessed by his superiors and subordinates, spoke loudly.

Captain Chambers was not afraid to take risks. But as he reflected over the last sixty days, he wondered to himself if he would be court-martialed and go down in history as having the briefest stint as commander of the USS *Mid-*

Subic Bay, Republic of the Philippines, December 1975. Secretary of the Navy William Middendorf arrives by helicopter for a tour of the USS *Midway* and is welcomed aboard by Captain Chambers, Commanding Officer (courtesy National Archives).

way. Once the evacuation was over and *Midway* returned to port, there was no court-martial or inquiry into the actions of Captain Chambers. What Chambers hadn't realized was that several of the other Seventh Fleet ships' captains had also tossed assets overboard during the evacuation for the exact same reasons he had, to facilitate the rescue effort and to protect the ships and the men and women on board.

The skill and mastery of Captain Chambers and all the men of *Midway* who were involved during those 60 days demonstrated the power of the United States military, and, as witnessed by several pieces of correspondence in the aftermath of the operation, is a testament to the dedication of all who were involved. For her role in Operation Frequent Wind, the USS *Midway* was awarded the Navy Unit Commendation and the Humanitarian Service Medal.

As history is the true judge of one's actions, Captain Chambers was commended for his quick thinking and his heroic actions. But what he really wanted was for his men to be recognized, rewarded and honored for their bravery and heroic actions on those two days in April 1975. In a 2010 recording for the USS *Midway* Museum, then-retired Rear Admiral Chambers expressed his disappointment that his men did not receive any medals for their heroism. According to Chambers, the ending of the war was an "embarrassment for the United States, and because of that, for all of the heroics that the crew did, there were no medals to recognize the individual or collective accomplishments in the evacuation and support of the evacuees."

Although the men of *Midway* did not receive any awards, their service and sacrifice was acknowledged by United States President Gerald Ford and Secretary of State Henry Kissinger, along with several military commanders[5]:

> The Honorable James R. Schlesinger
> Secretary of Defense
>
> Please convey to all personnel involved in the Vietnam evacuation operation my appreciation and respect for their superb performance.
>
> This operation was carried out under extremely adverse conditions. Its smooth and orderly accomplishment reflects great credit upon the men and women who participated in its planning and execution.
>
> I also join with their comrades in mourning the loss of those gallant men who gave their lives in this humanitarian task. To their families and loved ones goes our deepest sympathy.
>
> Their sacrifices, as well as the courage and determination of all the participating units, stand as a final example of the selfless dedication which has typified the performance of our armed forces through out our involvement in Indochina.
>
> They have my gratitude and that of the American people for the successful accomplishment of this difficult mission.
>
> Sincerely,
> Gerald R. Ford

Subic Bay, Republic of the Philippines, December 1975. Secretary of the Navy J. William Middendorf reads a citation for the meritorious service medal he presented to Captain Chambers in a ceremony on board the USS *Midway*. The medal was awarded to Chambers for his actions as commanding officer during the evacuation of Vietnam refugees (courtesy National Archives).

Up and down the chain of leadership, letters of appreciation were offered, including a letter from Secretary of State Henry Kissinger. Perhaps no one individual was more involved with the Vietnam War than Kissinger, who was President Richard Nixon's national security advisor and secretary of state, and continued as secretary of state under President Ford. On December 10, 1973, Kissinger and North Vietnam's Le Duc Tho were awarded the Noble Peace Prize for their work negotiating the Paris Peace Accords that were signed the previous year. Kissinger expressed his gratitude toward those involved in the evacuation:

> I want you to know how much I admire and appreciate the competent manner in which Operation Frequent Wind was carried out.

> The evacuation was an enormous undertaking of incredible technical complexity. Its success was due primarily to the extraordinary valor, coolness, and competence of the military people involved. Their performance was in the highest tradition of America's military services.
>
> ...To all those who participated in this operation, my admiration and gratitude for a job well done.
>
> Warm regards,
>
> Henry A. Kissinger

As the commander of the U.S. Seventh Fleet, graduate of the U.S. Naval Academy Admiral George P. Steele was extremely impressed with Captain Chambers' ability to think on his feet while under immense pressure during the evacuation of Saigon:

> The evacuation of U.S. citizens, together with Vietnamese and others from Vietnam, was accomplished with untold numbers of individual acts of valor. Those officers and men committed to or supporting the operation who were not personally subjected to danger displayed a uniformly high standard of dedication and professionalism.
>
> The Navy-Marine Corps team once again gave a superb performance under fire in the most grueling and exhausting circumstances. My hat is off to all of you.
>
> Thank you and well done.
>
> G. P. Steele
>
> Vice Admiral, U.S. Navy
>
> Commander, Seventh Fleet

Even Admiral Bill Harris, who was risk-averse himself, penned an appreciative letter to Captain Chambers and the crewmen of the USS *Midway*:

> To the crewmen of USS Midway:
>
> From my position onboard, I have observed with pride your performance through all phases of the complicated Vietnam evacuation operations, and I can unequivocally state that the results of your endeavors were superb.
>
> ... Particularly impressive was the flexibility shown by the flight deck crew handling the USAF [helicopters] LPH-style and in effecting an emergency respot to permit a safe ... landing of a Vietnamese [airplane] by which the determined pilot, his wife and five small children, arrived onboard unharmed.
>
> The entire crew of Midway can take great pride in their performance during the evacuation operations as they have been personally instrumental in preserving thousands of human lives and millions of dollars worth of aircraft.
>
> My personal "Well done" is extended to a dedicated crew who performed their duties with professionalism and efficiency and who, as true Americans, showed sincere compassion and concern for those who were displaced from their homeland by war and fear of retribution.
>
> Bravo Zulu.
>
> W. L. HARRIS
>
> Rear Admiral
>
> U.S. Navy Commander, Task Group 77.4

Chambers recognized that the decade-long war had come to an end. America was prepared to close the chapter on the Vietnam War and would now begin the long process of evaluating generals, battles and events. History would judge successes and failures of the war.

During their tour of the final days of Vietnam under Captain Chambers, the USS *Midway* received the *Battle Efficiency Award* and the prestigious *Captain Edward F. Ney Memorial Award* for the Best Large Vessel Afloat in the entire Navy. On July 2, 1976, Vietnam unified as a communist nation, the Socialist Republic of Vietnam.

During the week of August 18, 1976, the USS *Midway* and other Navy ships were off the coast of Korea as part of Operation Paul Bunyan. On August 18, two U.S. Army officers while in Korea's demilitarized zone were killed by North Korean soldiers. The incident caused an international crisis where the United States feigned a show of force in the area when it sent additional troops and ships to the area. While *Midway* and other Navy ships sailed off the Korean coast, Soviet Union and Chinese warships and submarines, at a safe distance, shadowed the U.S. ships. For all parties, tension was high. *Midway*'s Combat Information Center, along with the other U.S. Navy ships, scanned the activities of the Chinese and Russian ships. According to Scott McGaugh in his book *USS Midway: America's Shield*, "the intermittent sound of a Soviet guided-missile cruiser's radar had turned constant. Were the Soviets about to attack from only 1,500 yards behind *Midway*?"[6]

Having played the "game of chicken" with the Russians on several occasions, Chambers had little patience with the Soviets. He immediately ordered two F-4 Phantom jets into the air to let the Russians know he was not going to play this game. Chambers "ordered a flashing-light message to the Soviet ship demanding it turn off its radar. Minutes passed as the Phantoms circled high overhead and waited for instructions to attack. Finally the radar squeal stopped and the Soviet cruiser drifted away from *Midway*'s course."[7] On August 21, the United States symbolically sent soldiers in to finish cutting down the trees in the demilitarized zone. After the trees were cut down, tensions were deescalated, and *Midway* left the waters off Korea.

Despite the accolades Chambers and his crew received for all of their efforts aboard *Midway*, the only regret Chambers has over the whole experience was that his men did not get the medals he believed they justly deserved. As he explained, from the time that *Midway* picked up the H-53s for the Air Force until May 1 when they concluded the operations and headed to Thailand for the aircraft recovery, there were a number of truly heroic incidents that occurred where his men should have received medals for the way they conducted themselves.

The word from Washington, as near as he could tell, was that because the evacuation was classified, no medals would be given to anyone for anything that was done during that operation. Under any other circumstances, what the flight deck did to support the eight helicopters from the USS *Hancock* that night would have resulted in at least two or three of the men receiving Bronze Stars for the heroic way in which they handled the situation.

Flight operations normally run a twelve-hour day with a two-hour break at the end, during which the men are allowed to have some time off. However, during the operation the men worked 24/7. Many of them were half-asleep on watch but continued to provide extraordinary service to refugees and the pilots of helicopters that landed and took off from the flight deck. The amazing thing

August 1975. Although Captain Chambers, Commanding Officer, USS *Midway*, and Larry Grimes (left), Executive Officer, USS *Midway*, knew that there would not be any medals for the heroism of their men, they did throw an evening of celebration for a job well done for the crew upon return from "Frequent Wind" (personal collection).

was that not a single person was injured while on board. All injuries treated—often nothing more than scraped knees—had been received before the refugees arrived on board *Midway*, and the crew provided superb medical care, fed them and provided what support the refugees needed before they boarded the helicopters for other ship in company.

Right or wrong, Chambers knew that any award that he presented was going to be rejected. The word from up high was that there were to be no medals or awards. It was a decision that he had to live with, but in his mind, without question, his men deserved medals and awards because they went above and beyond what was expected of them. What was accomplished on *Midway* were not routine operations. A routine operation would have been the launch and recovery of attack aircraft fighters or the bombing of a port. Chambers believes that in the eyes of the American public, what the men did on *Midway* during Operation Frequent Wind was heroic in every sense possible.

Although Chambers' men never received medals or individual accolades for their service, their bravery during the evacuation and the profound sensitivity they displayed to the men, women, children and elderly who came aboard USS *Midway* in one of the largest evacuations in history would always be remembered.

Chapter 11

Rear Admiral

After the historic events of Operation Frequent Wind, Captain Chambers continued to serve his country with distinction. In 1977, he was appointed Rear Admiral in the United States Navy where he served as assistant chief of naval personnel, commander carrier group THREE, commander carrier group FOUR and vice commander, Naval Air Systems Command.

As the second African American to achieve a flag officer rank in the United States Navy, Rear Admiral Chambers stood on the shoulders of the African American men who had proudly served in the United States military since the nation's beginning—including his brother, Andrew Chambers, who served in the U.S. Army as a lieutenant general.

Despite the fact that their father had died when they were young, the Chambers brothers heard stories about his service during World War I from their grandfather, Clement Selden, and were inspired by their father's accomplishments. With his father's memory serving as a role model, Chambers moved confidently through the ranks of the United States Navy.

While at the Bureau of Naval Personnel, as a result of budget cuts, the Navy was required to reduce costs. The chief of navy personnel directed Chambers and a colleague, Rear Admiral Father John O'Connor, Chief of Navy Chaplains (who later became his Eminence Cardinal, John J. O'Connor, Archbishop of New York) to explore cost saving measures.

Rear Admiral Chambers and Rear Admiral O'Connor visited each and every isolated duty station around the world and met with Navy personnel to ascertain areas of potential cost savings. What became apparent and a major concern to Chambers was that overtime pay was provided to personnel assigned to duty stations that were the equivalent to the extra pay a man received if his tour was at sea. Chambers convinced O'Connor and the chief of navy personnel that "if it wasn't grey and underway it should not be considered as sea duty with the extra compensation."

11. Rear Admiral

What the admirals found out was that wives and family members were stationed at the duty stations on shore while men who were stationed at sea for extended months without their families received the same sea duty pay. Chambers contended that if a wife was stationed with her husband it was not sea duty, and it was not fair to a man who spent three or four years at sea without his wife and children that they receive the same compensation.

Admiral O'Connor, who grew up in a labor union family, with Chambers in agreement, helped to get the policy changed with the stipulation that current deployments would be grandfathered and that all new duty station assignments would adhere to a new policy that only at-sea duty would receive the extra compensation going forward.

Arlington, Virginia, November 1979. Rear Admiral Larry Chambers, Assistant Chief of Naval Personnel for Enlisted Personnel Development and Distribution in his office (courtesy National Archives).

While at the Bureau of Naval Personnel, Chambers was also instrumental in helping the Navy navigate the sensitive waters of women in the Navy. The Navy, by providing sailors, supports the National Science Foundation while it conducts scientific experiments in Antarctica. As part of the Navy's support role, during the summer months of what is referred to as the "tour of season" while the experiments were being set up when there was plenty of daily transportation going in and out, there were plenty of female sailors present. However, during the dead cold of winter it becomes so frigid that transportation equipment freezes and breaks down, making it difficult to retrieve someone from the test sites in the event that someone has to be removed. Essentially, they are stuck there until the weather changes and equipment can get in there.

As the Bureau of Naval Personnel was trying to make a decision as to whether or not they wanted to put female sailors as support in the Antarctica during the "dark of winter" a sexual harassment incident happened at the site.

Chambers was tasked to conduct an investigation where he flew down to Antarctica to conduct his investigation.

Chambers was stuck "on the ice" for about a week as he conducted his interviews. Since he continued to run his 10 miles per day, the only place he could see where he could run was on the frozen ice runway. After a couple of days of running, Chambers noticed that he was being monitored on camera. When he made an inquiry to the commanding officer, the reply was that if the admiral wanted to run in minus 40 degrees in the pitch darkness they needed to monitor his activities. The facility's manager was concerned that in the event he fell, he wasn't going to have some "dumb ass Admiral die and freeze on his watch."

As Chambers conducted his investigation there happened to be a woman on site who was a Senior Researcher from the National Science Foundation who made a recommendation that the campus infrastructure was not yet ready to accommodate a coed living environment when there was nothing to do but get into trouble.

Chambers, after freezing out in the cold in below zero temperatures for a week, agreed with the counsel he was given and concluded his investigation. There were much better places in which young female sailors and aviators would enjoy being stationed. While at the Bureau of Naval Personnel Chambers was instrumental in helping to enhance the careers of a number of women, including Rosemary Bryant Mariner who became the first women military test pilot.

Chambers spent a lot of time with her, preparing her for the challenges she may encounter as the first woman. He shared with her the personal challenges he encountered at the Naval Academy, and the horrendous treatment endured by Benjamin Davis at West Point and Wes Brown at the Academy. As a mentor he was proud of Mariner, for the more he shared with her the challenges she would encounter with some of the men, particularly those who were not as good as she was, the more determined she was in succeeding. Chambers said that her attitude was "send me on."

What was more interesting about Mariner was that Chambers did not know her prior to being randomly selected to be one of the women to become a test pilot. Under the direction of Chambers, the Bureau of Naval Personnel took affirmative action in identifying qualified women such as Mariner, who had more than 2,000 flight hours as a civilian even before she went to Navy flight school. After talking to her commanding officers, Chambers believed that she was unique in that she was as good as any man in the flight squadron, and probably better than most.

When the commanding officer informed Chambers that he didn't want

11. Rear Admiral

Arlington, Virginia, November 1979. Yeoman Second-Class Cooper working with Rear Admiral Larry Chambers, Assistant Chief of Naval Personnel for Enlisted Personnel Development and Distribution in his office (courtesy National Archives).

her in his squadron, Chambers advised him of her qualifications and that he had six vacancies, and if he still didn't want her he would not fill any of his vacancies. While there was an exchange of words, it was clear that Chambers was not going to back down. The commanding officer relented, and in a short period of time, Mariner outshined the men in the program. In a few short years Mariner became the first woman to fly the A-7E Corsair, a front-line light attack aircraft. When she retired in 1997, she retired as captain after having been the first woman to command an operational squadron and having commanded Tactical Electronic Warfare Squadron Thirty Four during Operation Desert Storm.

In August 1979, Rear Admiral Chambers was made Commander of Carrier Group 3 in the Indian Ocean. The kid who attended segregated Dunbar High School, graduated at the top of his class from the Naval Academy, received a master's in aeronautical engineering from the Naval Postgraduate School, served as an aviator in attack squadrons aboard several aircraft carriers throughout the Vietnam War and was a combat information control officer had gained substantial experience in naval operations. Chambers was a Navy man who served as the Air Boss aboard the USS *Oriskany*, and as the commanding officer of the USS *White Plains* and the USS *Midway*; there was no question as to his superior qualifications and his suitability to take a command as rear admiral.

As commander of a carrier group, Chambers was responsible for the naval assets under his control in order to ensure primary offensive fire power in time of war or conflict. There are 10 carrier groups worldwide, each being responsible for the command and control of the international and border area of waters in which it is assigned. Chambers' command consisted of 6 ships, including 2 destroyers, a guided missile cruiser, several frigates and over 6,000 personnel and 85 planes.

As a result of his unique experience and knowledge of the waters in that region of the world and their geopolitical implications, Chambers had now become one of the major naval leaders in the faceoff with the Russians over the Persian Gulf.

Admiral Chambers was involved with Operation Eagle Claw, the failed attempt to rescue 52 diplomats held captive in the United States Embassy in Tehran, Iran. The capture of the American diplomats started with the overthrow of Mohammad Reza Pahlavi as the Shah of Iran on July 27, 1980.

As naval commander in the Indian Ocean, Chambers had the unique opportunity to meet the national and military leaders of India, Oman, Saudi Arabia, Somalia and Pakistan, as well as Iran's Shah Mohammad Reza Pahlavi. In an attempt at strong international relations, Chambers would often provide world leaders with tours of the aircraft carriers, explain the assets onboard and in order for them to have a better understanding of the ship's capacity, allow them to watch certain drills his men would conduct.

The question of how he came to power clouded the Shah's entire rule, and the manner in which he governed overshadowed any of his accomplishments. The Shah remained in power after a 1953 coup during the highly controversial Operation Ajax where the United States provided military aid and support to the Shah during and after the coup, and provided economic aid for Western-style programs and initiatives.

After the coup attempt with the Shah securely perched on the monarch, many Western social and economic reforms were introduced. Iranian religious scholars were highly critical and denounced these reforms as being anti–Islam. A popular Imam known as Ayatollah Khomeini "made a bold anti–Shah speech before a hundred thousand people at a mosque in Qom, after which he was arrested and imprisoned." The impassioned and articulate Khomeini was forced into exile after another speech in October 1964 when he fused "Islam to Iranian nationalism and appealing to Iranians to fight for a clerical form of government."[1]

Eventually, many Iranians, young intellectuals and religious clerics alike came to see the Shah's programs as synonymous with political oppression.

Meanwhile, the exiled Khomeini lectured freely about corruption in Iran and became more effective than when he had been censored in Iran. Khomeini said what Iranians were thinking but afraid to say for fear of retribution. Khomeini became the face of the religious uprising and pending revolution against the Shah of Iran.

By December 1978, foreign diplomats could sense a major shift in the attitudes and events in Iran, and "on December 11, 1978, Amnesty International published a new report accusing Iranian authorities of 'systematic torture of political prisoners,'" a claim contradicted by the Shah. Seven days after the Amnesty's publication, "Ayatollah Khomeini called for a general strike in Iran. He took the opportunity to criticize President Carter's human rights policy."[2]

All across Iran, mass political demonstrations continued, strikes were called in the oil fields and living conditions deteriorated rapidly as citizens went cold and hungry due to the lack of oil for heat and cooking. In protests all across Tehran, portions of the city were set ablaze, and "On December 24, 1978, the Marine guards at the U.S. Embassy ... used tear gas to repel an attack by ... students. The demonstrators broke down the gate and threw burning tires into the compound ... before military reinforcements arrived."[3]

By the end of December, Iran was in turmoil and showed no signs of defusing tensions when on "New Year's Eve, after a series of meetings with U.S. ambassador Sullivan, Shah Mohammad Reza Pahlavi made the dramatic announcement that he would be leaving Iran temporarily" for health reasons.[4] On January 16, 1979, Shah Mohammad Reza Pahlavi and his family left Iran for Egypt. Within two days, "one and a half million Iranians assembled in the streets of Tehran for the largest demonstration in Iranian history. A ten-point statement was read by Muslim clerics and their political allies" in an attempt to unify the country.[5]

Upon hearing that the Shah and his family had left Iran, Ayatollah Khomeini took advantage of the Shah's absence and flew back to his homeland to take control of the country, and

> On Thursday, February 1, 1979, Khomeini boarded an Air France jet in Paris and returned to Iran after fourteen years of exile, to a sea of rapturous supporters, a tsunami of affection ... Khomeini declared the Pahlavi monarchy null and void and appointed ... [a] prime minister of a provisional government." After a long illness and "a long and humiliating journey around the world, the shah finally went to Egypt, where he died on July 27, 1980. The monarchy was over. Khomeini was the sole, absolute law of the land. A sacred tyranny of unfathomable proportions was now fast upon the nation.[6]

Upon Khomeini's return, the Shah's loyalists were quickly rounded up and tried for "crimes committed." Retribution was on the minds of many, and although the Shah had been displaced, tensions in Iran continued to escalate. Not wanting to waste time in establishing control and Islamic law, Khomeini quickly developed a powerful presence in Iran.

On February 14, 1979, President Carter was notified that protestors in Iran had once again stormed the U.S. Embassy, capturing and injuring two Marines. While protests and violence aimed at any Western presence or support in Iran persisted, Khomeini continued to act as the voice and leader for the people. By April 1, 1979, Khomeini pushed through a national referendum that formed the Islamic Republic of Iran to be ratified in November.

On September 29, 1979, in the waters off of Hong Kong, Vice President Walter Mondale was escorted across the flight deck of the USS *Midway* by Rear Admiral Chambers and presiding Commanding Officer Captain T.F. Brown. Mondale and other U.S. dignitaries, including U.S. Senator Patricia Schroeder, were on a fact-finding mission, concerned about the continuously escalating tensions and anti–Western sentiment in Iran, particularly in Tehran.

Soon after the Shah was overthrown, the U.S. allowed the ailing Mohammad Reza Pahlavi to come to the states for medical treatment. The Shah "had been diagnosed with lymphoma in 1978 ... State Department Medical Director Dr. Eben Dustin recommended that he be brought to the Cornell University Medical Center in New York for diagnosis and treatment."[7] The offer to come to the states was a diplomatic crisis for the Carter administration because they

Hong Kong, September 1979. Captain T. F. Brown, Commanding Officer of the USS *Midway* (left), Vice Admiral Sylvester R. Foley, Commander, 7th Fleet (center right), and Rear Admiral Larry Chambers, Commander, Carrier Group Three, walk across the flight deck with U.S. Vice President Walter F. Mondale on the USS *Midway* (courtesy National Archives).

knew it would do nothing to assuage the violent protests in Iran. The secretary of state at the time, Cyrus Vance, recalled that "'we were faced squarely with a decision in which common decency and humanity had to be weighed against possible harm to our embassy personnel in Tehran.'"[8]

While the Carter administration tried to keep the full extent of the Shah's illness under wraps, followers of the Ayatollah Khomeini were weary of the United States' presence and suspicious of its endgame. They believed that since Carter campaigned on a platform of ending international human rights abuses, the U.S. should hand over the Shah to Iran to be tried for crimes and human rights violations committed under his reign.

Khomeini and other elder statesmen, clerics and Iranian intellectuals believed that the Shah's absence was just a ploy, similar to the CIA ploy in 1953 when the U.S. and British governments executed Operation Ajax, which restored the Shah to the monarchy and "set off a series of unintended consequences." In his book *All The Shah's Men: An American Coup and the Roots of Middle East Terror*, Stephen Kinzer surmised that the effects of Operation Ajax gave "Mohammad Reza Shah the chance to become dictator. He received enormous amounts of aid from the United States—more than $1 billion in the decade following the coup—but his oppressive rule turned Iranians against him ... their anger exploded in a shattering revolution led by Islamic fundamentalists."[9]

By the end of October in 1979, Iranian citizens were resolute in their fury over the Shah being admitted into the United States, "and street protests ... engulfed Tehran. The main target of these rallies was the U.S. embassy compound, where irate crowds burned effigies and shouted anti-shah and anti–American slogans."[10] A frequent speaker at these demonstrations was Ayatollah Khomeini, who would incite the crowds with his anti–American rants and demands that the Shah return to pay for committing atrocities against the Iranian people.

Much of Khomeini's disdain for the United States was residual anger from Operation Ajax, during which the Central Intelligence Agency (CIA) overthrew the "highly popular government of Muhammad Mossadeq and thus laid the groundwork for the establishment of the autocratic rule of the Muhammad Reza Shah Pahlavi" regime[11]:

> In the back of everybody's mind hung the suspicion that, with the admission of the Shah to the United States, the countdown for another coup d'etat had begun ... "such was to be our fate again, we were convinced, and it would be irreversible. We now had to reverse the irreversible."[12]

With tensions in Iran ever increasing, on November 4, 1979, the unexpected happened—an angry mob of Islamic college students stormed the

United States Embassy in Tehran and gained control of the facility. The students seized 65 embassy staff, setting in motion a series of events that once again involved Rear Admiral Chambers in a historic evacuation of American hostages, later to be known as the Iranian Hostage Crisis.

President Carter, upon being made aware of the events unfolding in Tehran, "was disturbed to learn that [Iranian] students with the [subsequent] encouragement of Khomeini had taken over our embassy and captured fifty or sixty of our people."[13] Carter and several of his senior advisors were amazed at the brazen steps taken by the demonstrators, but equally amazed that the actions were state sanctioned:

> It was an unprecedented act for a host government to support invasion of the sovereign diplomatic territory of another nation and hold diplomatic staff members hostage. Initially, I expected the Iranian students to release the hostages quickly; it was inconceivable to us that the militants would hold our embassy personnel for any length of time. We had no way of knowing, of course, that this disturbing incident would evolve into the most important event of my last year as president. We had received assurances from Prime Minister Bazargan and Foreign Minister Ebrahim Yasdi of Iran that our embassy would be protected. Their only condition was that the shah refrain from making any political statements while in our country, and the shah accepted this restriction.[14]

After 48 hours had elapsed and the demonstrators still held the hostages, President Carter sent an urgent letter to Ayatollah Khomeini requesting a meeting with Ramsey Clark, a former United States' Attorney General under President Johnson, and William G. Miller, President Carter's U.S. Secretary of the Treasury. In the letter, President Carter, on behalf of the American people, requested the safe release of "all Americans presently detained in Iran and those held with them...." Carter further stressed that Ayatolla Khomeini "recognize the compelling humanitarian reasons, firmly based in international law, for doing so."[15] In response, and in solidarity with those oppressed in the United States, 13 hostages were released, including women and racial minorities.

After all diplomatic channels and economic sanctions failed to release the remaining hostages by April 11, 1980, the Carter administration decided to rescue them. Carter informed his leadership team in a meeting that "a team of expert paramilitary people now report that they have confidence in their ability to rescue our people." At that point, the chairman of the Joint Chiefs of Staff, David Jones, spread out a large map on the table, and Secretary of Defense Harold Brown elaborated on the various stages of the mission. All present at the meeting seemed to be in agreement. Vice President Walter Mondale said he was inclined to attempt the rescue. Zbigniew Brzezinski (United States National Security Advisor) spoke glowingly about the members of the Delta team and their previous training and backgrounds. At one point, he reminded the group that the nights would be getting shorter as summer approached so the operation should be undertaken as soon as possible. Brzezinski also proposed that in addition to the rescue, Iranian prisoners be taken in retaliation.[16]

Absent from the meeting was Secretary of State Cyrus Vance who was on State Department travel. Upon his return, he "raised questions about the dangers and political consequences of such an operation."[17] Vance was appalled by the risk associated with the operation and would later resign:

> While Secretary of State Cyrus Vance was away on a trip to Florida, Carter agreed to a complex mission that involved eight helicopters flying south of Tehran, where they would land and rendezvous with C-130 aircraft that would be carrying supplies for the soldiers and the hostages. A rescue team would drive into Tehran from the landing base, raid the building where the hostages were held, and depart on C-141 airplanes. Carter agreed to the plan on April 11. The mission was top secret. When he learned about the mission upon his return to Washington, Vance told Carter that he would formally resign once the operation was complete, regardless of the outcome. He explained, "I was convinced that the decision was wrong and that it carried great risks for the hostages and our national interests."[18]

Rear Admiral Chambers had his own frustrations about the mission, though for different reasons than Vance. Chambers admits that his opinion on the incidents surrounding Operation Eagle Claw are clouded because of the length of time it took President Carter to make a decision about the rescue of the Iranian hostages and how Chambers' men sat idle in the Indian Ocean for more than three months while the Carter Administration made up its mind as to what to do.

In Washington there were two schools of thoughts, and Carter weighed each option. The first was to do nothing and wait for the events internal to Iran to resolve themselves over time, hoping that the hostages would be set free. The second was to go into Tehran clandestinely and rescue the hostages. Carter initially took the first option hoping to invoke sanctions and political pressure on the Iranian government.

Chambers and his men from the U.S. Navy and Marine Corps, along with the resources of the U.S. Air Force and the U.S. Army, waited for orders. For 110 days there were two carrier task groups sitting dormant in the Indian Ocean, creating an enormous supply line challenge. As the men sat and waited, they constantly needed food, fuel and ammunition for training exercises. Although there was no word from official channels in Washington, the Navy knew what would be expected of them if called upon, and they trained every day until word came.

Carter finally came around to the second school of thought, and the administration planned Operation Eagle Claw, which would put Chambers and his men on track to rescue Iran's hostages. Operation Eagle Claw needed

Indian Ocean, 1980. Rear Admiral Chambers, Commander, Carrier Group 3 (right), with Captain Ming Chang (left), Chief of Staff, Carrier Group Three, and Commodore Jack Gelke, on the bridge of the aircraft carrier USS *Coral Sea* (CV-43) (courtesy Naval History & Heritage Command Photo Archive, Naval Subject Collection).

total darkness in order to successfully execute. The closer the execution date got to the equinox the less darkness they had. Chambers believed that the rescue plan was reasonable and could have been executed well if it had been implemented long before it actually was. In hindsight, Chambers feels that for Operation Eagle Claw to have had any real chance of success, it should have started much sooner. As the Battle Group Commander for the Coral Sea Battle Group, Chambers was responsible for providing tactical air support for Operation Eagle Claw. According to the African American publication *Jet Magazine*, in an article referring to Chambers, "never before in modern U.S. history [had] a Black officer ever been assigned such a critical military role, and in position where the slightest decision [could have affected] the future of mankind."[19] The operation played out as follows:

> The sole objective of the operation was to position the rescue team for the subsequent effort to withdraw the American hostages, which required my approval before [the team] executed the rescue itself. No such approval was requested or given because, as described below, the mission was aborted.
>
> Beginning approximately 10:30 a.m. EST on April 24, six U.S. C-130 transport aircraft and eight RH-53 helicopters entered Iran airspace. The C-130 aircraft carried a force of approximately ninety members of the rescue team equipped for combat, plus various support personnel. There was room for all the hostages.

From approximately 2:00 to 4:00 p.m. EST the transports and six of the eight helicopters landed at a remote desert site in Iran approximately two hundred miles from Tehran, where they disembarked the rescue team, commenced refueling, and began to prepare for the subsequent phases.

During the flight to the remote desert site, two of the eight helicopters developed operating difficulties. Of the six helicopters that landed, one developed a serious hydraulic problem and was unable to continue with the mission. The operational plans called for a minimum of six helicopters in operational condition able to proceed from the desert site. When the number of helicopters available to continue dropped to five, it was determined that all our people could not be extracted from Tehran and the operation could not proceed as planned. Therefore, on the recommendation of Delta Force commander Beckwith and my military advisors, I canceled the mission.

During the process of withdrawal, one of the helicopters accidentally collided with a C-130 aircraft, which was preparing to take off, resulting in the death of eight personnel and the injury of several others. Altogether, U.S. forces remained on the ground approximately three hours. The five remaining C-130s took off about 5:45 p.m. EST and departed from Iran airspace without further incident.[20]

According to Chambers, once the tactical decision was made, "the CIA had set up an intermediate airfield for the helicopters to be refueled in route to Tehran. All was going well." After the helicopters made it to the intermediate airfield, they were serviced with enough fuel to make it to the embassy in Tehran, pick up the hostages and return "to a second outlying field in more neutral territory where the hostages and their rescuers were to be flown out of Iran in C-130 aircraft. The helicopters were then to be abandoned at the intermediate airfield."

As the Battle Group Commander, Chambers' Flag Ship was the USS *Coral Sea*, where several of the marine fighter attack squadron aircraft were stationed. The *Coral Sea* and the USS *Nimitz* were responsible for providing the overall protection of the operation. As an aviator himself, Chambers knew the aviators and the rescuers who flew on the helicopters. They were well trained professionals who were fluent in the Persian language known as Farsi, knew the terrain well, had strong survival skills and could have survived in the most demanding of environments.

When the aircraft returned to base, Chambers was informed that "while refueling at the intermediate airfield, the on-scene commander observed a series of trucks in a convoy passing by on a nearby road," and they assumed that they had been discovered. Because of that, "they decided to abort the mission since the rescue helicopters only enough fuel to pick up the hostages and return to the airfield with the rescuers and the hostages, and not enough fuel to return to *Nimitz*."

Chambers believes that the indecisiveness of the White House regarding when to rescue the hostages led to the chain of events that eventually caused the operation to be aborted. But in that moment, the helicopters needed

Indian Ocean, February 1980. Rear Admiral Larry Chambers, Commander, Carrier Group Three, with Captain Ming B. Chang, his Chief of Staff, aboard USS *Coral Sea* (CV-43). Chang is the first and only Chinese-American Chief of Staff in the United States Navy (courtesy National Archives).

enough fuel to get back to safety aboard the aircraft carriers. During the refueling process, according to Chambers, a desert sandstorm engulfed their airfield, causing visibility to drop to near zero. While repositioning the helicopters to obtain the necessary fuel, one of the helicopters collided with one of the C-130's. Eight American servicemen were killed in the accident, which caused Operation Eagle Claw to be aborted.

The aftermath of the aborted mission was devastating, and "the official Iranian reaction to the failed rescue attempt was to claim that God had delivered a great victory over the United States. Iranian newspapers published photographs of the abandoned and burned aircraft and of the bodies of the dead U.S. servicemen."[21]

The Iranians captured sensitive and classified information from the damaged helicopters left behind. They repeatedly paraded the blindfolded hostages before mass demonstrations and the awaiting press. They would burn the American flag, as well as an effigy of President Carter, doing anything and everything that would publicly humiliate the Americans.

11. Rear Admiral

At the conclusion of the operation, there was a series of debriefs, inquiries and investigations. Chambers had to fly to Hawaii and meet with the Deputy Director for the Commander in Chief, U.S. Pacific Fleet (CINCPAC) Ed Briggs for a series of interviews. Admiral Briggs was selected as number one on the Naval Academy's golf team while he was a midshipman. He knew that Chambers liked to play golf and invited him to play a round at the private Navy Marine Golf Club in Hawaii where he could conduct the debrief with just the two of them; then they would go in an meet with the commander in chief U.S. Pacific Fleet.

The deputy commander obviously did not know how competitive Chambers was about his golf game or how much he had missed hitting a golf ball on dry land. Chambers, an avid golf player, would try to hit golf balls as often as he could. While on ship, Chambers would often join the sailors on board and hit golf balls off the fan tail into the ocean. Not to be outdone by the Naval Academy's golf team number one midshipman, always disciplined and normally up by 5 a.m. each morning, Chambers was at the country club's driving range

Pacific Ocean, 1982. Rear Admiral Larry Chambers, Commander, Carrier Group 3, is greeted by his officers on board the USS *Kitty Hawk*, CV 63 (courtesy National Archives).

as soon as it opened. To loosen up, Chambers hit golf balls for three straight hours before their scheduled tee time.

Once he and Briggs had talked about the operation and played a round of golf, Chambers birdied on the last three holes. After the two of them met with the commander, Briggs jokingly shared that he could not believe that the "old timer," after being stationed at sea for more than 110 days, could swing a golf club the way that he did, and that even though Briggs was stationed at sea for as long as Chambers had been, Chambers still beat him. The levity of the golf game helped to diffuse an otherwise very serious conversation.

Epilogue

On April 29, 2015, the world celebrated the 40th Anniversary of Operation Frequent Wind, the successful evacuation of over 200,000 refugees from South Vietnam's capital city, Saigon. Many will reflect on the operation, known today as the "Fall of Saigon," and on the impressive, significant career of Retired Rear Admiral Chambers. The key decisions he made saved countless lives, and many of the descendants of the Fall of Saigon evacuees owe their very existence to him. It was those decisions, heralded today by many, that Chambers thought would get him court-martialed—not because the decisions were wrong, but because he was at odds with Rear Admiral Bill Harris, his immediate superior. For Chambers, the events during his tenure in the Pacific were amazing, given where he came from and his impressive journey throughout his career.

Rear Admiral Chambers' career, along with the growing number of African American contemporaries, was in part grounded in the personal sacrifices of the over 10,000 African American men who served in the Revolutionary War, such as Peter Salem who fought in the Battle of Bunker Hill, and of the men who served in the United States Colored Troops such as the Colored Massachusetts 54th Regiment during the Civil War. African Americans have contributed much to this nation's global power and success—despite America's history of subjugation, oppression and violence toward people of color.

During his tenure aboard the USS *Midway*, a period of racial strife within the nation, Chambers was embraced by his subordinates although he is an African American, and they protected their commander at a time when he needed their support. During the change of command a year and a half after Operation Frequent Wind, several of the *Midway* crewmen came up to congratulate Chambers for his service. Many of his former crewmen had tremendous respect for him and his exemplary leadership during the evacuation of Saigon. Then, and only then, did the crewmen reveal that they had deliberately sunk the small fishing boat rather than save it in order to keep Captain Chambers out of trouble after the commander of the Pacific Fleet ordered Seventh Fleet assets to stop refugee rescues.

At the time of the incident, the former crewmen knew that Chambers, the constant straight shooter, would have court-martialed his crewmen had he known of their direct disobedience of his lawful order to repair the refugee boat. However, at this point and the passage of time, as their former captain, Chambers thanked them for trying to protect him. Well aware of the consequences, the crewmen laughed and informed their former captain that they had waited to confess their actions until after his change of command so that they wouldn't get into any trouble.

At the conclusion of Operation Frequent Wind, the Vietnamese refugees who embarked on USS *Midway*'s fight deck on April 29 and 30, 1975, were eventually transported to Guam for continued processing and then transported onward to temporary immigration centers in the United States.

As part of Operation New Life, on May 23, 1975, President Ford signed the Indochina Migration and Refugee Act, providing funds for the resettlement of over 130,000 Vietnamese refugees in the United States. The refugees supported by immigration agencies and charitable organizations resettled in cities such as Atlanta, Houston, Los Angeles, New York, San Francisco and Northern Virginia. The state of Florida became home to Major Bung Ly, the gutsy Vietnamese pilot who flew the Bird Dog plane aboard USS *Midway*.

Over the years Chambers reflected on the many events that occurred as part of Operation Frequent Wind, including the brief encounter with Major Ly. In April 2014 Chambers and Major Ly were invited to attend the 40th Annual

Subic Bay, Republic of the Philippines, December 1975. In recognition of his tremendous leadership during Operation Frequent Wind, the crew of the USS *Midway* dedicated this caricature to Captain Chambers in the 1976 USS *Midway* Cruise Book (courtesy United States Navy).

Sun 'n' Fun Air Expo in Lakeland, Florida. In a ceremony honoring the two men for heroic acts in aviation, each was presented a museum quality model of the "Bird Dog" airplane Major Ly landed aboard *Midway* that historic day of April 29, 1975. At a brief reception before the event, the two men had the opportunity for the first time to sit and talk about the moments just before Major Ly approached and landed onboard *Midway*.

Chambers was finally able to satisfy his own curiosity about what the major had really intended to do in that situation—only to find out that the two men had been thinking along the same lines. Ly shared that there was no way he was going to land the plane in the water with his wife and young children onboard. For Ly, the only chance for his family to survive was to land on the aircraft carrier; no matter what he had to do, he was going to land. Ly told Chambers, "I was going to crash land onboard had you not cleared the runway! You saved my life, my family's life, and the lives of the people on the flight deck."

During the formalities of the event, when asked what he thought of Cham-

The year 1983. Two brothers share a special moment together, Rear Admiral Larry Chambers and his younger brother Major General Andrew Chambers (personal collection).

bers' bold actions, Major Bung Ly replied without hesitation or forethought that Chambers was the bravest man he had ever known. Chambers provided a similar compliment to Ly. Chambers was humbled that Ly believed he was brave since he personally felt he was only doing his job. All Chambers and his crew did was toss over the helicopters to make a ready deck to save the little Bird Dog and to provide the necessary space to make a safe landing. Chambers believed that the true bravery belonged to the pilot who landed a plane onboard an aircraft carrier for the first time ever with such perfection.

Also present at this occasion were Mrs. Ly and four of the five children who were in the Bird Dog that day. Now grown and successful professionals with children of their own, each of the children expressed their gratitude with hugs for everyone. Incidentally, it was at this introduction that Chambers learned that Mrs. Ly could not swim.

On March 1, 1984, following his final naval assignment with the Naval Air Systems Command in Arlington, Virginia, Rear Admiral Chambers retired after a long and distinguished military career. His career was further distinguished by being awarded the Bronze Star, the Meritorious Service Medal, the China Service Medal and the Vietnam Service Medal with three Bronze Stars.

Upon his retirement from the USN, RADM Chambers was employed by the Unisys Corporation in Reston, Virginia, where he was responsible for developing new markets for Mine Countermeasures and Electronic Warfare in the Far East and the Pacific Rim.

Chambers' younger brother, Andrew, retired from the United States Army as a lieutenant general with major military awards including the Distinguished Service Medal with oak leaf cluster, the Defense Superior Service Medal, the Legion of Merit, Soldier's Medal, a Bronze Star with "V" Device, the Meritorious Service Medal with oak leaf cluster, Air

Charlotte, North Carolina, 2014. Rear Admiral Chambers and Mrs. Sarah Jones Chambers (personal collection).

Epilogue

The year 2015. Rear Admiral Larry Chambers, still very busy, but enjoying retirement (personal collection).

Medal with three oak leaf clusters, Army Commendation Medal with two oak leaf clusters, Combat Infantryman Badge, Master Parachutist Badge and Army General Staff Identification Badge.

Mrs. Charlotte Chambers was a strong African American woman who, after the death of her husband, sacrificed for her five small children. Americans and citizens from all over the world have much to thank her for, as she raised five successful and productive Americans, two of whom became national heroes.

A Personal Note from the Author

Thank you Rear Admiral Larry Chambers (Ret.) and Mrs. Sarah Jones Chambers and your children Celeste, Mia, Roger, Leila, Christopher and John for your service, your endurance and your perseverance.

Chronology

1929

June 10   Lawrence C. Chambers (known as Larry) is born as the third of five children in Bedford, Virginia, to Lawrence E. Chambers and Charlotte H. Selden Chambers.

1940

September 27   Civil rights and African American labor leaders meet with President Franklin D. Roosevelt to demand the end of racism in the American military.

October 24   President Roosevelt mandates the use of African American pilots and aircraft mechanics.

December 14   NAACP's *The Crisis* magazine cover depicts a U.S. Army training airplane in flight over Randolph Field, Texas, with the caption "FOR WHITES ONLY."

1941

June 25   President Roosevelt issues Executive Order 8802 ending racial discrimination in the hiring practices of the defense industries and the War Department and decrees that African Americans be admitted to training in the Army Air Corps.

December 7   Attack on Pearl Harbor: Government of Japan attacks United States Pacific Naval Fleet by bombing U.S. military installations at Pearl Harbor.

December 8   United States enters World War II in response to attack on Pearl Harbor.

1944

September 5   Chambers begins attending the segregated Paul Laurence Dunbar High School (originally named the Preparatory High School for Colored Youth) in Washington, District of Columbia.

1945

April 12   President Roosevelt dies of a cerebral hemorrhage. Vice President Harry S Truman becomes President of the United States.

May 8   President Truman's first order of business is overseeing, with England's Winston Churchill and the Soviet Union's Joseph Stalin, the Allied victory in Europe.

July 28   Japanese Emperor Hirohito rejects Allied overtures to surrender.

August 6, 9   Atomic Bomb: President Truman orders the dropping of atomic bombs over Japanese cities.

September 8   Emperor Hirohito surrenders. World War II comes to an end. Japan surrenders its colonies: Korea is divided at the 38th parallel, with the Soviet Union controlling northern Korea and the United States controlling southern Korea as trustees with the intent to establish an independent Korean nation.

October 24   United Nations is formed to maintain international peace and security.

1947

March 12   Truman Doctrine: President Harry Truman states doctrine to suppress communist insurgency in Eastern Europe.

1948

June 17   Chambers graduates as class valedictorian from Dunbar High School where he served as Colonel of the JROTC program.

June 26   Executive Order 9980: President Harry S Truman issues order ending racial segregation in the United States federal workforce.

Executive Order 9981: President Harry S Truman issues order ending racial segregation of the United States Armed Services.

June 30   Chambers begins attending the United States Naval Academy in Annapolis, Maryland.

August 15   Republic of Korea (South Korea) is established.

1949

April 4   NATO: Twelve nations sign the North Atlantic Treaty establishing North Atlantic Treaty Organization (NATO).

May 8   West German Constitution is approved.

June 14   State of Vietnam is formed.

1950

January 5   President Truman vows the United States will not get involved in the dispute between People's Republic of China (mainland China) and the Republic of China (Taiwan) over the Taiwan Strait.

June 25   North Korean forces cross the 38th parallel to invade South Korea which begins the Korean War.

June 27   First Taiwan Strait Crisis: President Truman sends U.S. Navy's Seventh Fleet to Taiwan Straight to neutralize any potential conflict between Mainland China and Taiwan.

1952

June 6 Ensign Chambers graduates from the United States Naval Academy in Annapolis, Maryland, ranked academically in the top ten percent of his class. He is the second African American to graduate from the Academy.

June 7 Ensign Chambers assigned to the heavy cruiser USS *Columbus* (CA-74).

November 6 Ensign Chambers assigned to Naval Air Station at Pensacola, Florida, to begin pilot training.

1953

March 14 Nikita Khrushchev becomes the First Secretary of the Central Committee of the Communist Party of the Union of Soviet Socialist Republics (Soviet Union).

July 27 Korean War Truce.

August 15 Democratically-elected Iranian Prime Minister Mohammad Mossadeq is overthrown in CIA-backed coup known as Operation Ajax.

December 6 Ensign Chambers promoted to Lieutenant (junior grade).

1954

January 25 Berlin Conference: International conference to discuss settlement issues of the Korean War and to facilitate peace between France and its French colonies in Indochina continues until February 18, 1954.

April 7 Falling Domino Principle: President Eisenhower projects that if one nation comes under the influence of communism then the entire region will become communist and the United States must intervene to protect surrounding nations and American interests.

April 26 Geneva Conference: International conference to resolve outstanding issues from the Berlin Conference on the Korean peninsula and to restore peace in Indochina continues until July 20, 1954.

April 29 President Eisenhower proclaims no United States intervention in Vietnam.

June 6 Lieutenant (junior grade) Chambers receives navy wings and becomes a naval aviator. Assigned to Anti-Submarine Squadron 37 aboard USS *Princeton* (CVS-37).

July 20 Korean cease-fire agreement is reached.

July 21 Final Declaration of Geneva Conference: Known as the Geneva Accords the declaration separates Vietnam into two zones (North Vietnam and South Vietnam) on a temporary basis at the 17th parallel.

September 12 U.S. Joint Chiefs of Staff recommend use of nuclear weapons against China. U.S. Seventh Fleet on ready alert.

1955

February 12 President Eisenhower sends advisors to South Vietnam.

May 31 U.S. Supreme Court, in narrow ruling, issues an order for school integration to proceed "with all deliberate speed."

June 1 Lieutenant (j.g.) Chambers assigned to Attack Squadron 215 (VA-215) on board USS *Bon Homme Richard* (CVA-31).

December 1 Rosa Parks, civil rights activist, is arrested for refusing to sit in the "Colored Section" of a bus in Montgomery, Alabama.

1956

July 1 Lieutenant (j.g.) Chambers is promoted to Lieutenant.

October 29 Suez Canal Crisis: Efforts are made to maintain Western control of the Suez Canal and to prevent Soviet Union occupation. Crisis continues until November 7, 1956.

1957

January 5 Eisenhower Doctrine: President Dwight Eisenhower announces doctrine to intervene militarily in the Middle East to protect legitimate governments from communist subversion.

April 10 Lieutenant Chambers assigned to the Naval Postgraduate School in Monterey, CA.

1958

January 8 Cuban revolutionaries capture Havana, the capital city.

August 23 Second Taiwan Strait crisis over the Quemoy and Matsu islands.

September 12 U.S. Supreme Court orders Little Rock, Arkansas, to integrate public schools.

December 31 Cuban President Fulgencio Batista informs his cabinet of his pending departure at a New Year's Eve party.

1959

January 1 Cuban President Fulgencio Batista flees Cuba.

January 7 Fidel Castro's revolutionary Cuban government recognized by the U.S.

August 2 Lieutenant Chambers receives masters in aeronautical engineering from Naval Postgraduate School in Monterey, California.

August 5 Lieutenant Chambers ordered to Stanford University in Palo Alto, California, for postgraduate studies in physics.

1960

September 1 Lieutenant Chambers assigned to Attack Squadron 125 based at Moffett Field in Sunnyvale, California, pending further assignment to Attack Squadron 22 (VA-22) aboard USS *Midway* (CV-41).

1961

January 20 President John Kennedy announces doctrine to contain and reverse communism in the Western Hemisphere.

Chronology

April 17 Bay of Pigs Invasion: United States attempts a military invasion of Cuba and fails on April 19, 1961.

May 9 Vice President Lyndon Johnson undertakes a tour of Southeast Asian countries where he meets South Vietnam's President Ngo Dinh Diem.

June 3 Vienna Summit: The first meeting between U.S. President Kennedy and Soviet Premier Khrushchev to discuss Cold War issues, including disarmament.

June 4 Berlin Crisis: Soviet Union demands withdrawal of Western armed forces from West Berlin. Crisis continues until November 9, 1961.

July 1 Fidel Castro's Cuba nationalizes foreign oil refineries.

Lieutenant Chambers designated Officer in Charge, Attack Squadron 22 (Detachment Romeo), onboard USS *Kearsarge* (CVS-33).

July 22 Cuba nationalizes sugar refineries.

July 25 President Kennedy speaks to the American public on the pending Berlin crisis.

September 1 Lieutenant Chambers promoted to Lieutenant Commander.

September 17 Cuba nationalizes U.S. banks.

August 13 Operation Rose: East Germany installs barbed wire, defining its territorial borders.

August 20 Construction of the Berlin Wall begins; East Germany intends to divide East and West Berlin.

August 23 East Germany institutes restrictions on travel between East and West Berlin.

1962

July 23 International Agreement on the Neutrality of Laos is signed at Geneva, promising Laotian neutrality.

September 8 Soviet Union begins to deploy strategic missiles to Cuba secretly.

January 12 Operation Ranch Hand begins. U.S. planes spray herbicides and defoliants, e.g., Agent Orange, over South Vietnam until 1971.

October 14 Cuban Missile Crisis: Confrontation between the United States and the Soviet Union over Soviet ballistic missiles deployed in Cuba.

October 23 Soviet President Nikita Khrushchev stops Soviet ships in route to Cuba.

October 15 Chambers deployed as Officer-in-Charge of VA 22 Detachment "R" on board USS *Kearsarge* (CVS-33).

1963

May 8 Buddhists demonstrate in South Vietnam after the display of religious flags is prohibited.

September 2 Kennedy criticizes the Diem regime in an interview with Walter Cronkite, citing the Buddhist repression and claiming that Diem is out of touch.

August 23   Dr. Martin Luther King delivers "I Have a Dream" speech in Washington, D.C.

November 1   South Vietnamese President Ngo Dinh Diem is murdered during military officers' coup d'état.

November 26   President Johnson reverses Kennedy's course of action regarding Vietnam, orders Secretaries of State and Defense and the Chairman of the Joint Chiefs of Staff to expand war effort in Vietnam.

December 1   Lieutenant Commander Chambers assigned to the Naval Postgraduate School, Monterey, CA (Assistant Curriculum Officer, Aeronautical Engineering programs).

1964

January 8   President Johnson introduces legislation to address national poverty and to leverage federal funds to combat poverty at the state and local levels.

July 2   Johnson signs the landmark Civil Rights Act of 1964, known as the Great Society.

July 31   North Vietnamese islands located in the Gulf of Tonkin are attacked by South Vietnamese gunboats.

August 7   United States Congress passes the Gulf of Tonkin Resolution.

November 1   South Vietnamese Viet Cong insurgents attack the Bien Hoa Air Base.

1965

March 2   U.S. and South Vietnamese Air Forces join together for Operation Flaming Dart and strike military bases in North Vietnam.

June 1   Johnson Doctrine, an extension of Eisenhower and Kennedy Doctrines, continues containment and reversal of communism in the Western hemisphere and dictatorships worldwide.

July 28   President Johnson commits the United States to a major war in Vietnam by dispatching more than 125,000 more troops.

August 6   President Johnson signs Voting Rights Act.

October 23   Battle of the Ia Drang Valley begins, the first major land battle between U.S. and North Vietnamese regular forces.

November 14   Additional 100,000 American troops are sent to Vietnam.

1966

February 4   U.S. Senate Foreign Relations Committee, chaired by Senator J. William Fulbright, holds televised hearings on the Vietnam War.

February 6   President Johnson convenes a conference in Honolulu on the Vietnam War.

March 15   Vietnamese Buddhists and students protest against the Saigon government.

July 1 Lieutenant Commander Chambers is promoted to Commander.

August 23 Secretary of Defense, Robert McNamara, announces the Project 100,000 program to accept previously rejected mental group four or unqualified men into military service.

1967

January 1 Commander Chambers assigned to the USS *Ranger* (CV-61) as the Combat Information Center Officer.

January 8 Operation Cedar Falls takes place in the Iron Triangle region, northeast of Saigon.

February 22 Operation Junction City begins in War Zone C near the Cambodian border.

April 4 Dr. Martin Luther King delivers anti-war speech before Clergy and Laity Concerned about Vietnam group.

September 3 Nguyen Van Thieu is elected president of South Vietnam.

September 29 President Johnson offers to stop the bombing of North Vietnam if it will agree to start negotiations, known as the "San Antonio Formula."

October 16 Anti-war activists hold demonstrations throughout the United States.

October 21 March on the Pentagon, demonstration against the Vietnam War.

1968

January 20 North Vietnamese forces besiege an American Marine base at Khe Sanh. The siege is lifted on April 14.

January 30 North Vietnamese launch Tet Offensive against cities throughout South Vietnam.

February 20 Senate Foreign Relations Committee begins hearings on the 1964 Gulf of Tonkin incident.

February 28 President Johnson is informed that General Westmoreland needs an additional 206,000 troops.

March 16 A platoon of U.S. soldiers slaughter hundreds of unarmed villagers in the hamlet of My Lai.

March 25 Johnson reconvenes the "Wise Men," a collection of six government advisors who counsel against additional troop increases and recommend a negotiated peace in Vietnam.

March 31 President Johnson announces unilateral halt to all U.S. bombing north of the 20th parallel.

President Johnson announces his withdrawal from the presidential race.

April 4 Dr. Martin Luther King is assassinated in Memphis, Tennessee.

May 12 Johnson Administration begins peace negotiations between the United States and North Vietnam in Paris.

August 1 Commander Chambers assigned as Commanding Officer Attack Squadron Fifteen (VA-15) on board USS *Franklin D. Roosevelt* (CV-42).

October 31 President Johnson announces a complete bombing halt over North Vietnam, ending Operation Rolling Thunder.

1969

January 25 Initial four-way plenary session takes place in Paris among the United States, North Vietnam, South Vietnam and the NLF.

March 18 President Nixon orders Operation Menu, the secret bombing of communist bases in Cambodia.

June 8 President Nixon announces that 25,000 U.S. troops will be withdrawn by the end of August.

July 25 President Nixon promulgates the Nixon Doctrine: Asian governments are expected to wean themselves off U.S. military aid in the war on communism, known as Vietnamization.

August 4 Secret negotiations begin in Paris between U.S. special envoy Henry Kissinger and North Vietnam's Xuan Thuy.

October 15 The Moratorium, the largest anti-war demonstration in American history, takes place across the country.

November 3 President Nixon's "Silent Majority" speech defends his Vietnam War policies.

November 15 Mobilization draws more than 250,000 people to Washington, D.C., in protest of the Vietnam War.

1970

March 27 South Vietnamese attack communist bases inside Cambodia for the first time.

February 1 Commander Chambers assigned as Air Operations Officer USS *Oriskany* (CV-34).

April 30 American forces invade the Fishhook region of Cambodia.

May 4 Ohio National Guard troops fire into a crowd of student demonstrators on the campus of Kent State University, killing four and wounding nine.

May 9 Anti-war demonstrators protest Kent State massacre and call for the immediate withdrawal of all U.S. troops from Indochina.

June 24 U.S. Senate repeals the Gulf of Tonkin Resolution.

June 30 U.S. ends the nation's role in the Cambodian operation.

1971

January 1 Congress forbids the use of U.S. ground troops in Laos or Cambodia.

February 8   Operation Lam Son: South Vietnamese forces invade Laos to cut supply routes down the Ho Chi Minh Trail.

June 13   *New York Times* publishes what becomes known as the Pentagon Papers.

December 26   President Nixon orders resumption of U.S. bombing of North Vietnam.

1972

February 21   President Nixon begins historic visit to China.

March 30   North Vietnam conducts Easter Offensive, a three-pronged attack across the demilitarized zone, into the central highlands of South Vietnam.

May 8   President Nixon retaliates and orders the bombing of tactical assets and the mining of all North Vietnamese ports as part of Operation Linebacker.

May 22   President Nixon and Soviet General Secretary Leonid Brezhnev meet in Moscow for a summit conference.

June 17   Democratic National Committee break-in at the Watergate Hotel in Washington, D.C.

July 1   Commander Chambers is promoted to Captain and assigned to Naval Air Systems Command as Program Manager A-7E program (PMA-235).

October 8   Secret meetings in Paris between U.S. and North Vietnam produce tentative settlement of the war.

October 22   President Thieu rejects the proposed settlement.

December 14   United States ends peace talks with the North Vietnamese.

December 18   President Nixon orders Operation Linebacker II, the destruction of North Vietnamese industrial infrastructure.

December 28   North Vietnam agrees to resume negotiations if the United States stops bombing above the 20th parallel.

1973

January 8   Henry Kissinger and Le Duc Tho resume negotiations in Paris and reach agreement similar to the previous October agreement.

January 23   President Nixon announces the signing of the Paris Accords, which goes into effect on January 27, 1973.

January 27   Nixon announces the end of the U.S. military draft.

February 1   Secret letter from Richard Nixon to Pham Van Dong promises postwar reconstruction aid to North Vietnam.

February 12   Release of U.S. prisoners of war begins.

March 29   Last U.S. troops and prisoners of war leave South Vietnam.

June 1   Captain Chambers assigned to USS *White Plains* (AFS-F) as Commanding Officer.

1974

August 9 Richard Nixon resigns as president.
Vice President Gerald Ford becomes president.

1975

March 28 Captain Chambers assumes command of USS *Midway* (CV-41).

March 31 Captain Chambers and crew of *Midway* leave Yokosuka, Japan, for a routine cruise with visits scheduled for Subic Bay in the Philippines and Hong Kong.

April 15 *Midway* enters Subic Bay for a scheduled ten-day upkeep period in the Philippines.

April 18 USS *Midway* ordered to proceed to the coast of Vietnam.

April 20 *Midway* is joined by ten Air Force H-53 helicopters from the 56th Special Operations Wing, the 21st Special Operations Squadron, and the 40th Aerospace Rescue and Recovery Squadron.

April 21 Under pressure from the United States, Nguyen Van Thieu, President of South Vietnam, resigns.

April 29 Captain Chambers receives the signal to begin the evacuation known by the code name "Frequent Wind."

April 30 Rescue of South Vietnamese Air Force Major flying a single-engine plane from Con Son Island seaward in search of safety with his wife and five children on board.

May 1 *Midway* ordered to sail to the Gulf of Thailand.

May 5 Rescue of 84 additional evacuees.

May 6 *Midway* ordered to sail to Guam via the Mindoro and San Bernardino Straits.

May 12 Captain Chambers receives orders to proceed to the Gulf of Thailand to support rescue of the pirated U.S. commercial vessel SS *Mayaguez*.

December 8 President Gerald Ford promulgates the Ford Doctrine to strengthen U.S. position in South-East Asia against communist aggression.

1976

July 2 Vietnam becomes unified, communist nation, now known as the Socialist Republic of Vietnam.

December 1 Captain Chambers promoted to Rear Admiral upon detachment from USS *Midway*.

1977

January 5 Rear Admiral Chambers' first flag assignment was as Assistant Chief of Naval Personnel for Personnel Distribution.

1979

January 16 Shah Mohammad Reza Pahlavi and his family flee Iran for Egypt.

February 1   Ayatollah Khomeini returns to Iran after fourteen years in exile.

February 14   Iran protestors storm U.S. Embassy, injuring two Marines.

April 1   Khomeini pushes through a national referendum to establish Islamic Republic of Iran.

August 1   Rear Admiral Chambers assigned as Commander Carrier Group 3, embarked on USS *Coral Sea* (CV-43).

November 4   Iranian militants seize United States Embassy in Tehran.

November 14   President Carter issues Executive Order 12170, freezing Iranian government assets held within the United States until the end of the hostage crisis.

1980

January 23   President Jimmy Carter promulgates the Carter Doctrine which protects countries of the Persian Gulf from outside interference.

January 27   Canadian covert operation rescues six American diplomats.

April 24   U.S. aborts Operation Eagle Claw, an attempt to rescue 52 American hostages.

September 12   Ayatollah Khomeini announces conditions for release of American hostages.

November 4   Ronald Reagan wins 1980 presidential election.

1981

January 19   Iranian hostage crisis ends with signing of Algiers Accords.

March 1   Rear Admiral Chambers is assigned to Naval Air Systems Command in Arlington, Virginia, as Vice Commander.

1983

September 1   Rear Admiral Chambers assigned additional duties as Commander Carrier Group 4, embarked on USS *Nimitz* (CVN-68).

1984

March 1   Rear Admiral Chambers retires from the United States Navy.

Chapter Notes

Chapter 1

1. Air America, an American passenger and cargo airline covertly owned by the United States government and used by the CIA for intelligence operations in China.
2. Author interview with Admiral Lawrence C. Chambers, Sun City, Florida, July 27, 2014.

Chapter 2

1. William Raspberry, "The Final Indignity for Dunbar High," *Washington Post*, March 21, 1977.
2. "A Very Special Monument: The Dunbar High School First Street." *New Yorker*, March 20, 1978, 101.
3. *Ibid.*, 106.
4. *Ibid.*, 106.
5. *Ibid.*, 101.
6. *Ibid.*, 107.
7. Samuel L. Broadnax, *Blue Skies, Black Wings: African American Pioneers of Aviation* (Lincoln: University of Nebraska Press, 2008), 10–11.
8. *Ibid.*, 11.
9. Robert J. Jakeman, *The Divided Skies: Establishing Segregated Flight Training at Tuskegee, Alabama, 1934–1942* (Tuscaloosa: University of Alabama Press, 1992), 62.
10. Broadnax, *Blue Skies, Black Wings*, 9–10.
11. Von Hardesty, *Black Wings: Courageous Stories of African Americans in Aviation and Space History* (New York: HarperCollins, 2008), 63.
12. *Ibid.*
13. Jakeman, *The Divided Skies*, 184–185.
14. *Ibid.*, 197.
15. *Ibid.*, 191.
16. Hardesty, *Black Wings*, 65.
17. Ric Murphy, *Freedom Road: An American Family Saga from Jamestown to World War* (Bloomington, IN: AuthorHouse, 2014), 336.
18. *Ibid*, 338.
19. *Ibid.*

Chapter 3

1. William T. Bowers, William M. Hammond, and George L. MacGarrigle. *Black Soldier White Army: The 24th Infantry Regiment in Korea* (Washington, D.C.: Center of Military History, 1996), 36–37.

2. Lurita Doan, "On race, Harvard still must learn," *Los Angeles Times*, 2 August 2009, accessed April 25, 2014.

3. Morris J. MacGregor, Jr., *Integration of the Armed Forces, 1940–1965* (Washington, D.C.: Center of Military History, 1981). Superintendent Documents Number D-114.2: In 8/940–65. 58.

4. Ibid., 59.

5. Executive Order 8802, Prohibition of Discrimination in the Defense Industry, signed by President Franklin D. Roosevelt, June 25, 1941, made available by the National Archives and Records Administration.

6. "Academics," *United States Naval Academy*, accessed July 15, 2014, https://www.usna.edu/Academics/.

7. Ibid.

8. Robert J. Schneller, *Blue & Gold and Black: Racial Integration of the U.S. Naval Academy* (College Station: Texas A&M University Press, 2008), 40.

9. Ibid., 55.

10. Ibid., 69–70.

11. Stanley Sandler, *The Korean War: No Victors, No Vanquished* (Lexington: University Press of Kentucky, 1999), 18–19.

12. Ibid., 24–25.

13. Brian Catchpole, *The Korean War* (New York: Carroll & Graff, 2000), 4–5.

14. Bruce Cumings, *The Korean War: A History* (New York: Modern Library, 2011), 11.

15. Catchpole, *The Korean War*, 7–13.

16. Cumings, *The Korean War*, 11.

17. U.S. Department of State, Office of the Historian, *Milestones: 1945–1952, The Truman Doctrine, 1947*. http://history.state.gov/milestones/1945-1952/TrumanDoctrine. Accessed May, 6, 2013.

18. Jesse Walker, "D.C. Grad Ranks High at U.S. Naval Academy, Ensign Lawrence Chambers Jr. Stands 119 in Class of 783" *The Afro-American Newspaper*, June 14, 1952.

19. Schneller, *Blue & Gold and Black*, 99.

Chapter 4

1. James Carroll, *House of War: The Pentagon and the Disastrous Rise of American Power* (Boston: Houghton Mifflin, 2006), 276.

2. Michael D. Gordon, *Red Cloud at Dawn: Truman, Stalin and the End of the Atomic Monopoly* (New York: Farrar, Straus, and Giroux, 2009), 26–27.

3. USS *Midway* (CVA) Cruise Book, United States Navy, 1961, 4.

4. Evan Thomas, *Ike's Bluff: President Eisenhower's Secret Battle to Save the World* (New York: Little, Brown, 2012), 394.

5. Jim Newton, *Eisenhower: The White House Years* (New York: Doubleday, 2011), 156–157.

6. Ibid., 157.

7. Thomas, *Ike's Bluff*, 155.

8. Ibid., 158.

9. Ibid., 157.

10. Carroll, *House of War*, 190.

11. Mitchell K. Hall, ed., *Vietnam War Era: People and Perspectives* (Santa Barbara, CA: ABC, 2009).

12. Cong Minh Bui, *A Distant Cause: A History and the Vindication of the Vietnam War* (Bloomington, IN: Xlibris Publishers, 2006), 41–54.

13. Jean Edward Smith, *Eisenhower in War and Peace* (New York: Random House, 2012), 611.

14. Ibid., 614.

15. Minh, *A Distant Cause*, 54.

16. *The Final Declarations of the Geneva Conference, July 1954*. Gravel (ed.), Viet Nam War Documents, Vol. 1, 279–282. Accessed May 18, 2014. http://faculty.vassar.edu/robrigha/.

17. Hall, *Vietnam War Era: People and Perspectives*, 41.
18. Norman Polmar and Dana Bell, *One Hundred Years of World Military Aircraft* (Annapolis, MD: Naval Institute Press, 2004), 301.
19. Ibid., 303.
20. Dwight D. Eisenhower, "Special Message to the Congress on the Situation in the Middle East," January 5, 1957, *The American Presidency Project*, http://www.presidency.ucsb.edu/ws/?pid=11007.
21. Michael Korda, *IKE: An American Hero* (New York: HarperCollins, 2007), 714.
22. Aleksandr Fursenko and Timothy Naftali, *Khrushchev's Cold War: The Inside Story of an American Adversary* (New York: W. W. Norton, 2006), 363.
23. Ibid., 364.
24. Ibid., 376.
25. Ibid., 379.
26. Ibid., 383.
27. Max Frankel, *High Noon in the Cold War: Kennedy, Khrushchev, and the Cuban Missile Crisis* (New York: Random House, 2004), 222.
28. Ibid., 20.
29. Robert A. Divine, *The Cuban Missile Crisis* (New York: Marcus Weiner Publishing, 1988), 18.
30. Ibid., 3.
31. Polmar and Bell, *One Hundred Years*, 375–378.

Chapter 5

1. Mark Atwood Lawrence, *The Vietnam War: A Concise International History* (New York: Oxford University Press, 2008), 63.
2. Stanley Karnow, *Vietnam: A History. The First Complete Account of Vietnam at War* (New York: Viking Press, 1983), 250.
3. MacGregor, *Integration of the Armed Forces*, 522.
4. Karnow, *Vietnam: A History*, 277.
5. Albert Marrin, *America and Vietnam: The Elephant and the Tiger* (New York: Viking, 1992), 79.
6. Ibid., 84.
7. Ibid., 85.
8. Michel Lind, *Vietnam: The Necessary War: A Reinterpretation of America's Most Disastrous Military Conflict* (New York: Free Press, 1999), 16.
9. Lloyd C. Gardner, *Pay Any Price: Lyndon Johnson and the Wars for Vietnam* (Chicago: Ivan R. Dee, 1995), 212.
10. Lind, *Vietnam: The Necessary War*, 17.
11. Naval History and Heritage Command, *Monthly Summaries 1966*, April, 1.
12. Gardner, *Pay Any Price*, 219.
13. Karnow, *Vietnam: A History*, 435.
14. Lyndon B. Johnson, "Address Before Joint Session of Congress" (speech, Washington, D.C., November 27, 1963), The American Presidency Project, http://www.presidency.ucsb.edu/ws/?pid=25988.
15. Gardner, *Pay Any Price*, 269.
16. Lawrence, *The Vietnam War*, 105.
17. Ibid., 105.

Chapter 6

1. MacGregor, *Integration of the Armed Forces*, 522.
2. Deborah Shapley, *Promise and Power: The Life and Times of Robert McNamara* (Boston: Little, Brown, 1993), 384.

3. *Ibid.*, 384.
4. MacGregor, *Integration of the Armed Forces*, 523.
5. Shapley, *Promise and Power*, 386.
6. *Ibid.*, 388–389.
7. Martin Luther King, "I Have a Dream" (speech, Washington, D.C., August 28, 1963), The Martin Luther King, Jr., Research and Education Institute, https://kinginstitute.stanford.edu/king-papers/documents/i-have-dream-address-delivered-march-washington-jobs-and-freedom.
8. Lind, *Vietnam: The Necessary War*, 181.
9. *Ibid.*, 182.
10. Hall, *Vietnam War Era*, 150–151.
11. *Ibid.*, 156.
12. Marrin, *America and Vietnam*, 156.
13. *Ibid.*, 157.
14. Lawrence, *The Vietnam War*, 121–122.
15. Marrin, *America and Vietnam*, 170.
16. Gardner, *Pay Any Price*, 403–404.
17. *Ibid.*, 461.
18. Hall, *Vietnam War Era*, 164.
19. Conrad Black, *Richard M. Nixon: A Life in Full* (New York: PublicAffairs, 2008), 568.
20. *Ibid.*, 569.
21. *Ibid.*, 591.
22. Elizabeth Drew, *Richard M. Nixon* (New York: Times Books, 2007), 66.
23. Richard M. Nixon, *The Memoirs of Richard M. Nixon* (New York: Grosset and Dunlap, 1978), 345–470.
24. Black, *Richard M. Nixon*, 670.
25. Karnow, *Vietnam: A History*, 611.

Chapter 7

1. Nixon, *The Memoirs of Richard M. Nixon*, 394.
2. Drew, *Richard M. Nixon*, 71.
3. *Ibid.*
4. Jacob Van Staaveren, *Interdiction in Southern Laos, 1960–1968*, (Washington, D.C.: Center for Air Force History, 1993), 301.
5. *Ibid.*, 97.
6. Karnow, *Vietnam: A History*, 636.
7. Karnow, *Vietnam: A History*, 637.
8. Nixon, *The Memoirs of Richard M. Nixon*, 584–585.
9. Black, *Richard M. Nixon*, 796.
10. Black, *Richard M. Nixon*, 797.
11. John Lehman, *On Seas of Glory: Heroic Men, Great Ships, and Epic Battles of the American Navy* (New York: Simon & Schuster, 2002), 342.
12. Nixon, *The Memoirs of Richard M. Nixon*, 345.
13. *Ibid.*, 605–606.
14. Karnow, *Vietnam: A History*, 637.
15. Richard Nixon, *No More Vietnams* (Westminster, MD: Arbor House Publishing, 1985), 105–106.
16. Black, *Richard M. Nixon*, 840.
17. Nixon, *The Memoirs of Richard M. Nixon*, 733.
18. Lehman, *On Seas of Glory*, 343.
19. Lawrence, *The Vietnam War*, 164–165.

Chapter 8

1. Drew, *Richard M. Nixon*, 117.
2. Lawrence, *The Vietnam War*, 165.
3. *Ibid.*, 165–166.
4. Douglas Brinkley, *Gerald R. Ford* (New York: Times Books, 2007), 88.
5. *Ibid.*
6. Larry Engelmann, *Tears Before the Rain: An Oral History of the Fall of South Vietnam* (New York: Oxford University Press, 1990), 33.
7. Lawrence, *The Vietnam War*, 166.
8. *Ibid.*, 166–167.
9. Engelmann, *Tears Before the Rain*, 53.
10. At the time of Chambers' *Midway* command, only men served on the vessel.
11. *USS Midway by the Numbers*, USS *Midway* Museum, San Diego, California, 2013.
12. Author interview with Vernon Jumper, San Diego, California, September 20, 2015.
13. *Foundation Magazine* 14, no. 2 (Fall 1993): 35.
14. Justin Corfield, *The History of Vietnam* (Westport, CT: Greenwood, 2008), 100.
15. *Foundation Magazine*, 35.
16. *Ibid.*
17. *Ibid.*
18. *Ibid.*
19. *Ibid.*
20. Engelmann, *Tears Before the Rain*, 58–59.
21. *Ibid.*
22. *Ibid.*
23. Air America was a passenger and cargo airline covertly owned by the United States government and managed by the CIA during the Vietnam War.
24. Scott McGaugh, *USS Midway: America's Shield* (Gretna, LA: Pelican Publishing Company, 2011), 134.
25. *Ibid.*

Chapter 9

1. Author interview with Vernon Jumper, San Diego, California, September 20, 2015.
2. Author interview with Admiral Lawrence C. Chambers, Sun City, Florida, July 27, 2014.
3. Stephen Daggett, "Costs of Major U.S. Wars," *Congressional Research Service*, June 29, 2010, 2.

Chapter 10

1. Captain L.C. Chambers, Commanding Officer, *Spectrum Special* 1, no. 13 (Spring 1975).
2. Comptroller General of the United States, "The Seizure of the Mayaguez: A Case Study of Management," *Departments of State and Defense, National Security Council*, May 11, 1976, 61–62.
3. Command History Branch, Office of the Joint Secretary, "Commander in Chief Pacific Command History: Appendix VI—The SS Mayaguez Incident," CINCPAC, 1975, 3.
4. Comptroller General of the United States, *The Seizure of the Mayaguez*, 59.
5. Correspondence copied from Spectrum Special Newsletter, Spring 1975.
6. McGaugh, *USS Midway*, 135.
7. *Ibid.*

Chapter 11

1. Robert Wright, *Our Man in Tehran: The True Story Behind the Secret Mission to Save Six Americans During the Iran Hostage Crisis and the Foreign Ambassador Who Worked with the CIA to Bring Them Home* (New York: Other Press, 2011), 22–23.
2. Ibid., 62.
3. James Buchan, *Days of God: The Revolution in Iran and Its Consequences* (New York: Simon & Schuster, 2013), 204
4. Wright, *Our Man in Tehran*, 63.
5. Ibid., 70.
6. Hamid Dabashi, *Iran: A People Interrupted* (New York: New Press, 2008), 162–163.
7. Wright, *Our Man in Tehran*, 101.
8. Cyrus Vance, *Hard Choices: Critical Years in America's Foreign Policy* (New York: Simon & Schuster, 1983), 371.
9. Stephen Kinzer, *All the Shah's Men* (Hoboken, NJ: John Wiley, 2003), 202.
10. Wright, *Our Man in Tehran*, 103.
11. Ervand Abrahamian, *The Coup: 1953, the CIA, and the Roots of Modern U.S.–Iranian Relations* (New York: New Press, 2013), 1–2.
12. Kinzer, *All the Shah's Men*, 203.
13. Jimmy Carter, *White House Diary* (New York: Farrar, Straus and Giroux, 2010), 367.
14. Ibid.
15. Jimmy Carter to Ayatollah Ruhollah Khomeini, November 6, 1979, in *The U.S. National Archives*. Declassified April 22, 1985.
16. Betty Glad, *An Outsider in the White House: Jimmy Carter, His Advisors, and the Making of American Foreign Policy* (Ithaca, NY: Cornell University Press, 2009), 263.
17. Ibid., 264.
18. Julian E. Zelizer, *Jimmy Carter* (New York: Henry Holt, 2010), 107.
19. "Admiral Chambers Heads Persian Gulf Naval Force," *Jet Magazine*, March 13, 1980, 57.
20. Jimmy Carter, *White House Diary*, 421.
21. Wright, *Our Man in Tehran*, 323.

Bibliography

Books

Abrahamian, Ervand. *The Coup: 1953, the CIA, and the Roots of Modern U.S.–Iranian Relations.* New York: New Press, 2013.
Binkin, Martin, and Mark J. Eitelberg. *Blacks and the Military.* Washington, D.C.: Brookings Institution, 1982.
Black, Conrad. *Richard M. Nixon: A Life in Full.* New York: Perseus Books Group, 2007.
Bowers, William T., William M. Hammond, and George L. MacGarrigle. *Black Soldier White Army: The 24th Infantry Regiment in Korea.* Washington, D.C.: Center of Military History, 2016.
Brinkley, Douglas. *Gerald R. Ford.* New York: Times Books, 2007.
Broadnax, Samuel L. *Blue Skies, Black Wings: African American Pioneers of Aviation.* Lincoln: University of Nebraska Press, 2008.
Buchan, James. *Days of God: The Revolution in Iran and Its Consequences.* New York: Simon & Schuster, 2013.
Cannon, James. *Gerald R. Ford: An Honorable Life.* Ann Arbor: University of Michigan Press, 2013.
Carroll, James. *House of War: The Pentagon and the Disastrous Rise of American Power.* Boston: Houghton Mifflin, 2006.
Carter, Jimmy, *White House Diary.* New York: Farrar, Straus and Giroux, 2010.
Catchpole, Brian. *The Korean War.* New York: Carroll & Graff, 2000.
Corfield, Justin. *The History of Vietnam.* Westport, CT: Greenwood Press, 2008.
Cumings, Bruce, *The Korean War: A History.* New York: Modern Library, 2011.
Dabashi, Hamid. *Iran: A People Interrupted.* New York: New Press, 2007.
Divine, Robert A. *The Cuban Missile Crisis.* New York: Marcus Weiner Publishing, 1988.
Drew, Elizabeth. *Richard M. Nixon.* New York: Times Books, 2007.
Drury, Bob, and Tom Clavin. *Last Men Out: The True Story of America's Heroic Final Hours in Vietnam.* New York: Free Press, 2011.
Engelmann, Larry. *Tears Before the Rain: An Oral History of the Fall of South Vietnam.* New York: Oxford University Press, 1990.
Frankle, Max. *High Noon in the Cold War: Kennedy, Khrushchev, and the Cuban Missile Crisis* New York: Random House, 2004.
Furgurson, Ernest B. *Westmoreland: The Inevitable General.* Boston: Little, Brown, 1968.
Fursenko, Aleksandr, and Timothy Naftali. *Khrushchev's Cold War: The Inside Story of an American Adversary.* New York: W. W. Norton, 2006.
Gardner, Lloyd C. *Pay Any Price: Lyndon Johnson and the Wars for Vietnam.* Chicago: Ivan R. Dee, 1995.
Glad, Betty. *An Outsider in the White House: Jimmy Carter, His Advisors, and the Making of American Foreign Policy.* Ithaca, NY: Cornell University Press, 2009.

Gordon, Michael D. *Red Cloud at Dawn: Truman, Stalin and the End of the Atomic Monopoly.* New York: Farrar, Straus, and Giroux, 2009.
Hall, Mitchell K., ed. *Vietnam War Era: People and Perspectives.* Santa Barbara, CA: ABC, 2009.
Hardesty, Von. *Black Wings: Courageous Stories of African Americans in Aviation and Space History.* New York: HarperCollins, 2008.
Jakeman, Robert J. *The Divided Skies: Establishing Segregated Flight Training at Tuskegee, Alabama, 1934–1942.* (Tuscaloosa: University of Alabama Press, 1992.
Karnow, Stanley. *Vietnam: A History. The First Complete Account of Vietnam at War.* New York: Viking Press, 1983.
Kinzer, Stephen. *All the Shah's Men.* (Hoboken, NJ: John Wiley, 2003.
Korda, Michael. *IKE: An American Hero.* New York: HarperCollins, 2007.
Langguth, A.J. *Our Vietnam: The War 1959–1975.* (New York: Simon & Schuster, 2000.
Lanning, Lt. Col (Ret) Michael Lee. *The African American Solider: From Crispus Attucks to Colin Powell.* Secaucus, NJ: Carol Publishing Group, 1997.
Lavalle, Lt. Colonel A.J.C., ed. *Last Flight from Saigon.* Washington, D.C.: CreateSpace Independent Publishing Platform, 2012.
Lawrence, Mark Atwood. *The Vietnam War: A Concise International History.* New York: Oxford University Press, 2008.
Lehman, John. *On Seas of Glory: Heroic Men, the Great Ships, and Epic Battles of the American Navy.* New York: Simon & Schuster, 2002.
Lind, Michel. *Vietnam The Necessary War: A Reinterpretation of America's Most Disastrous Military Conflict.* New York: Free Press, 1999.
MacGregor, Morris J., Jr. *Integration of the Armed Forces, 1940–1965.* Washington, D.C., Center of Military History, United States Army, 1981. Superintendent Documents Number D-114.2: In 8/940–65.
Marrin, Albert. *America and Vietnam, the Elephant and the Tiger.* New York: Viking, 1992.
McGaugh, Scott. *USS Midway: Americas' Shield.* Gretna, LA: Pelican Publishing Company, 2011.
Mersky, Peter, and Norman Polmar. *The Naval Air War in Vietnam.* Annapolis, MD: Nautical and Aviation Publishing Company, 1981.
Minh, Bui Cong. *A Distant Cause: A History and the Vindication of the Vietnam War.* Bloomington, IN: Xlibris Publishers, 2006.
Mollenhoff, Clark R., *The President Who Failed: Carter Out of Control.* New York: Macmillan Publishing Co., Inc., 1980.
Murphy, Ric. *Freedom Road: An American Family Saga from Jamestown to World War.* Bloomington, Indiana. AuthorHouse, 2014.
Newdick, Thomas. *Aircraft of the Cold War: 1945–1991.* London: Amber Books, Ltd., 2010.
Newton, Jim. *Eisenhower: The White House Years.* New York: Doubleday, 2011.
Nixon, Richard. *No More Vietnams.* Westminster, MD: Arbor House Publishing, 1985.
Nixon, Richard M. *The Memoirs of Richard M. Nixon.* New York: Grosset and Dunlap, 1978.
Polmar, Norman, and Dana Bell. *One Hundred Years of World Military Aircraft.* Annapolis, MD: Naval Institute Press, 2004.
Reef, Catherine. *African Americans in the Military.* New York: Facts on File, 2010.
Robbins, Mary Susannah. *Against the Vietnam War: Writings by Activists.* Lanham, MD: Rowman & Littlefield, 2007.
Sandler, Stanley. *The Korean War: No Victors, No Vanquished.* Lexington: University Press of Kentucky, 1999.
Schneller, Robert J. *Blue & Gold and Black: Racial Integration of the U.S. Naval Academy.* College Station: Texas A&M University Press, 2008.
Shapley, Deborah. *Promise and Power: The Life and Times of Robert McNamara.* Boston, MA: Little, Brown, 1993.
Smith, Jean Edward. *Eisenhower in War and Peace.* New York: Random House, 2012.
Sorely, Lewis. *Westmoreland: The General Who Lost Vietnam.* Boston, MA: Houghton Mifflin Harcourt, 2011.
Stewart, Allison. *First Class: The Legacy of Dunbar, America's First Black Public High School.* Chicago: Lawrence Hill Books, 2013.

Summers, Anthony. *The Arrogance of Power: The Secret World of Richard Nixon.* New York: Penguin, 2001.
Thomas, Evan. *Ike's Bluff: President Eisenhower's Secret Battle to Save the World.* New York: Little, Brown, 2012.
Vance, Cyrus. *Hard Choice: Critical Years in America's Foreign Policy.* New York: Simon & Schuster, 1983.
Walton, Ben L. *Great Black War Fighters: Profiles in Service.* Houston, TX: Strategic Book Publishing and Rights, Co., 2012.
Westmoreland, William C. *A Soldier Reports.* Garden City, NY: Doubleday and Congress, 1976.
Wright, Robert. *Our Man in Tehran: The True Story Behind the Secret Mission to Save Six Americans During the Iran Hostage Crisis and the Foreign Ambassador Who Worked with the CIA to Bring Them Home.* New York: HarperCollins, 2011.
Wright, Robin. *The Last Great Revolution: Turmoil and Transformation in Iran.* New York: Knopf, 2000.
Zelizer, Julian E. *Jimmy Carter.* New York: Henry Holt, 2010.

Electronic Sources

Eisenhower, Dwight D. "Special Message to Congress on the Situation in the Middle East." Speech, Washington, D.C., January 5, 1957. *The American Presidency Project.* http://www.presidency.ucsb.edu/ws/?pid=11007.
"Milestones: 1945–1952, the Truman Doctrine, 1947." U.S. Department of State, *Office of the Historian.* Accessed May, 6, 2013. https://history.state.gov/milestones/1945-1952/truman-doctrine.
Paust, Jordan J. "More Revelations About Mayaguez (And Its Secret Cargo)," *Boston College International and Comparative Law Review* 4, no. 1 (March 1981). Accessed May 2, 2015.

Government Publications

Chambers, Captain L.C., Commanding Officer, *Spectrum Special* 1, no. 13 (Spring 1975).
Command History Branch, Office of the Joint Secretary. "Commander in Chief Pacific Command History: Appendix Vi—The SS Mayaguez Incident." *CINCPAC,* 1975. http://www.kohtang.com/documents/PDFs/DOD/cincpac-command-history-1975-appendix-vi.pdf.
Comptroller General of the United States. "The Seizure of the Mayaguez: A Case Study of Management." *Departments of State and Defense, National Security Council.* May 11, 1976. 59, 61–62.
Daggett, Stephen. "Costs of Major U.S. Wars." *Congressional Research Service.* June 29, 2010.
"Executive Order 8802: Prohibition of Discrimination in the Defense Industry." *The National Archives.* June 25, 1941.
Foundation Magazine 14, no. 2 (Fall 1993): 35.
Gravel, Mike, ed. "The Final Declarations of the Geneva Conference, July 1954." *Viet Nam War Documents,* Vol. 1. 279–282. Accessed May 18, 2014. http://faculty.vassar.edu/robrigha/.
Johnson, Lyndon B. "Address Before Joint Session of Congress." Speech, Washington, D.C., November 27, 1963. *The American Presidency Project.* http://www.presidency.ucsb.edu/ws/?pid=25988.
Mattingly, Robert N. *M Street-Dunbar High School, Autobiographic Memories, 1897–1954.* Washington Public School, Washington, D.C. May, 1974.
McGuire, Grayson. *Alumni Night, Paul Laurence Dunbar High School.* Washington Public School, Washington, D.C. November, 1945.
Toal, Mark J., Major. "The Mayaguez Incident: Near Disaster at Koh Tang." *Marine Corps War Combat Development Command.* 1998.
USS *Midway* (CVA) Cruise Book. United States Navy. 1961.
"USS *Midway* by the Numbers." USS *Midway* Museum. San Diego, California. 2013.

Van Staaveren, Jacob. *Interdiction in Southern Laos, 1960–1968.* Washington, D.C., *Center for Air Force History*: 1993. Appendix 5.

Magazines and Newspaper Articles

"Admiral Chambers Heads Persian Gulf Naval Force." *Jet Magazine,* March 13, 1980, 57.

Doan, Lurita. "On Race, Harvard Still Must Learn." *Los Angeles Times,* August 2, 2009.

King, Reverend Martin Luther, Jr. "Declaration of Independence from the War in Vietnam." *Ramparts Magazine,* May 1967.

Llorens, David. "High Reenlistment Is Rooted in Economics and Psychodynamics." *Ebony Magazine.* August 1968.

National Association for the Advancement of Colored People. *The Crisis Magazine* 47, no. 11. Cover Image. 1940.

Raspberry, William. "The Final Indignity for Dunbar High?" *Washington Post,* March 21, 1977.

"A Very Special Monument: The Dunbar High School First Street." *New Yorker Magazine,* March 20, 1978.

Walker, Jesse. "D.C. Grad Ranks High at U.S. Naval Academy, Ensign Lawrence Chambers Jr. Stands 119 in Class of 783." *The Afro-American Newspaper,* June 14, 1952.

Index

A-4 Skyhawk 73, 83, 106
A-7 Corsair 83, 106, 175
A-7E Aircraft Procurement Program 106, 201
A-37, Dragonfly 157, 159, 161
Abrams, Gen. Creighton 97
AD-6 Skyraider 59
Agent Orange 89, 197
Agricultural and Technical 3, 30
Air America 10, 138, 142, 143, 148, 205n1, 209n23
Air Boss 94, 102, 122, 123, 127, 147, 148, 150, 152, 175
Air Wing Five 129
Airborne Early Warning Squadron 60
Aircraft Procurement Program 106
Alexis, Lucien, Jr. 35
Ali, Muhammad 91
Allied Forces 42, 65
Allied Nations 48–49
Amnesty International 177
Antarctica 173–174
Arabia 176
Arkansas 29, 196
Arlington, Virginia 173, 175, 190
Armed Forces Qualification Test 87
Armed Forces Radio 128, 132
Armed Forces, U.S. 28–29, 32–33, 35–36, 49, 62, 77, 87, 92
Army Air Corps 29, 30–31, 33, 193
Assistant Curriculum Officer 198
Atlanta, Georgia 188
Atlantic Fleet 72
Atwood, Henry O. 37–39, 41, 88–89, 96
Australians 128

B-52 Boeing 105
Baltimore Afro American 45
Ban Me Thuot, Vietnam 118, 130
Bancroft, Sec. of Navy George 35
Barin Field, Alabama 53
Batista, Fulgencio 67, 196
Battle of Bunker Hill 187

Bay of Pigs 67, 197
Bedford, Virginia 10, 12–15, 17–20, 22–23, 193
Beijing, China 55–56, 106
Benton, Capt. Hugh 39, 56
Berlin, Germany 32, 65–71, 74, 78, 95–96, 107, 195, 197
Berlin Crisis 77, 197
Bird Dog 141, 143, 145–148, 150–153, 161, 188–190
USS *Bon Homme Richard* (carrier) 59–61, 196
Boston, Massachusetts 28, 62–63
Brezhnev, Leonid 105, 201
Briggs, Ed 185–186
Brinkley, Douglas 117
Brotherhood of Sleeping Car Porters 30, 36
Brown, Harold 180
Brown, T.F. 178
Brown, Wesley 33, 37–41, 88, 174
Brzezinski, Zbigniew 180–181
Buddhists 82
Bundy, McGeorge 71, 79
Bureau of Naval Personnel 172–174
Bureau of Navigation 36
Burma 57

C-130 Lockheed 142, 181–184
C-141 Boeing 181
Cadet Board 37
Cadet Corps 26, 28, 37, 39
Cambodia 6, 9, 56, 75, 98–102, 104, 118, 128–129, 161–163, 199–200
Camp Lejeune 96
Campbell, Gordon 47, 86
Canada 94
Capitol Hill 93
Caribbean Sea 71
Carrier Group 3, 175, 182, 185, 203
Carter, Jimmy 45, 177–181, 184, 203; and Khomeini, Ayatollah 179; and Operation Eagle Claw 181; and Pahlavi, Mohammad Reza 178; and U.S. Embassy in Tehran 178, 180

215

Index

Castro, Fidel 67, 70, 71
Central Highlands 80, 118, 130, 201
Central Intelligence Agency 3, 66–67, 71, 179, 183, 195, 205n
CH-47 Chinook 160
CH-53 Sea Stallion 131
Chambers, Andrew 13–15, 26, 28, 62, 172, 189, 190
Chambers, Charlotte (daughter) 14–15
Chambers, Charlotte 10, 11–13, 14–16, 19, 21, 23–24, 26, 165, 191
Chambers, Janet *see* Murphy, Janet 63
Chambers, Lauretta 14–15
Chambers, Lawrence, Sr. 10–11
Chambers, Melvin 13–15
Chance Vought Corporation (LTV) 83
Chang, Ming 182, 184
Charlotte, North Carolina 190
Chicago and Democratic National Convention 97
China 6, 40, 42, 47–48, 52–57, 60–61, 64–66, 76, 78, 80, 98, 103–106, 194–195, 201
Christmas bombing 105
Churchill, Winston 34, 194
Civil Pilot Training Program 30, 33
Clark, Ramsey 180
CNN 128
Cold War 6, 44–46, 48, 50, 53, 74, 77–78, 197
USS *Columbus* (warship) 46–47, 50, 86, 195
Combat Information Center 3, 82–85, 123, 125
Combat Stores Ship (AFS) 3, 108, 201
Communism 6, 42–45, 48, 57–58, 62, 66, 74, 76, 80, 195–196, 198, 200
Communist Party of the Soviet Union 61
Con Son, Vietnam: airport 141, 142; Con Son Island 141; National Prison 141, 142
concentration camps 16, 89
Congressional Research Service Report 156
USS *Constellation* (carrier) 96
containment policy 43, 57
USS *Conway* (destroyer) 67
Cooper-Church Amendment 102
USS *Coral Sea* (carrier) 163, 182–184, 203
Corcoran Art Gallery 20
Cornell University Medical Center 178
Cortez Peters Business School 14
The Crisis Magazine 30, 193
Cuba 65–67, 70–74, 77–79, 196–197
Cuban Missile Crisis 71, 73, 197
Czechoslovakia 29, 103

Dallas, Texas 78, 83
Da Nang, Vietnam 96, 118
Davis, Benjamin O., Jr. 38, 41, 88, 174
Dawson, William Levi 33, 36, 39
Defense Center of Military History 36
Defense Condition Five 71
defense readiness condition (DEFCON) 3, 71
Delaware State College 30
Delta Force 183

Democratic National Convention 97
Detachment Romeo 68, 71, 78, 197
Diem, Ngo Dinh 75–78, 197–198
Dien Bien Phu 57, 59, 61
Doan, Laurita Alexis 35
Dominican Republic 79–80
drones 62
Dulles, John Foster 55
Dunbar High School 6, 23–27, 33, 37, 39, 88, 96, 175, 193–194
Dustin, Dr. Eben 178

East Germany 65, 67–69, 197
Easter Offensive 104, 201
USS *Eaton* (destroyer) 67
Egypt 62, 177, 202
Eisenhower, Dwight D. 45, 52, 55–59, 62, 65–67, 75, 80
El Centro, California 56, 62
Elks National Home 15
Ellington, Duke 21
USS *Essex* (carrier) 67
Executive Order 8802 31, 37
Executive Order 9981 35, 46

F-4 Phantom 127, 169
F-5 Northorp 157, 159, 161
Falling Domino Principle 57, 66, 195
Federal Bureau of Investigation (FBI) 3, 99
54th Massachusetts Colored Infantry Regiment 16
56th Special Operations Wing 10, 130, 202
First World War *see* World War
Florida 50, 54, 71, 155, 181, 189, 195
Foley, VADM Sylvester R. 178
Foley, Alabama 53
Ford, Gerald R. 45, 116–118, 120, 166–167, 188, 202, 214
40th Aerospace Rescue and Recovery Squadron 10, 130, 202
40th Annual Sun 'n' Fun Air Expo 188–189
USS *Franklin D. Roosevelt* (carrier) 94, 200
Fulbright, J. William 82, 199

Gayler, ADM. Noel 135
Gelke, Jack 182
Geneva Agreement 58
Geneva Conference 57, 195
Georgia 29
Great Britain 30, 42, 65
Great Society 81, 95, 198
Grimes, Larry 170
gross domestic product 156
Gulf of Tonkin 79, 94, 102, 198–200

H-53 Sikorsky 10, 131, 133, 139, 169, 182, 202
Hampton Institute 30
USS *Hancock* (carrier) 10, 129, 133, 139–140, 170
Hanoi, Vietnam 80, 93, 95, 105–107, 117–118

Index

Harris, ADM Bill 125, 146, 148, 158, 160, 162, 164, 168, 187
Harvard University 28, 35
Hawaii 70, 96, 108, 119, 185
Henry, Alice *see* Selden, Alice
Henry, Gladys (Selden) 17
Herrington, Stuart 134–135
High School Cadet Corp 33
Hill, T. Arnold 30
Hiroshima, Japan 34
Hitler, Adolf 29, 49
Ho Chi Ming Trail 94
Hong Kong 9, 25, 162, 178, 202
Hoover, J. Edgar 99
Houston, Texas 188
Howard College 30
Howard Theater 21
Howard University 25, 33, 62–63
Hue, South Vietnam 118

Ia Drang, Battle of 81
Illinois 29, 33
India 176
Indian Ocean 62, 175–176, 181–182, 184
Indochina Migration and Refugee Act 188
Indochina Military Assistance and Advisory Group 57
Indochina Theater 80
Indonesia 57
Iranian Hostage Crisis 180–181, 203
Islamic Republic of Iran 178, 203
Island of Poulo Wai 163

Japan 9, 31, 34, 42–43, 49, 64–66, 74, 90, 108, 125, 126, 163, 193–194, 202
Jet magazine 182
Jews 16, 35
Jim Crow South 7, 16
Johnson, Lyndon B. 45, 69, 76, 78–83, 87, 94–95, 97, 105, 109, 180, 197–200
Joint Chiefs of Staff 79, 180, 195, 198
Jones, David 180
Jumper, Vernon 123, 145, 147–148, 150
Junior Reserve Officer Training Corps (JROTC) 3, 194

Karnow, Stanley 78, 80, 103
USS *Kearsarge* (warship) 68, 71–73, 85, 197
Kennedy, John F. 45, 65, 66–71, 73–74, 76–81, 87, 196–198
Kent State University 99, 200
Kentucky 29
Khomeini, Ayatollah 176–180, 203
Khrushchev, Nikita 61, 65–71, 73, 77, 105, 195, 197
Kidd, ADM Isaac, Jr. 72
King, Martin Luther, Jr. 89–92, 95, 198–199
Kissinger, Henry 98, 101, 107–108, 116, 120, 166–168, 200–201
USS *Kitty Hawk* (carrier) 96

Knee Board Card 114
Koh Tang, Cambodia 163
Kola Peninsula 72
Korea, Democratic People's Republic of 43
Korean War 42, 47, 50, 52–53, 56, 59, 64, 194, 195
Ky, Nguyen Cao 131–132

Lakeland, Florida 189
Laos 6, 56, 75–76, 94, 100, 102–104, 197, 200–201
leukemia 6, 64
Leyte Gulf, Battle of 162
Los Angeles, California 188
Ly, Major Bung 141, 144–145, 153–155, 188–190

MacGregor, Morris J., Jr. 36
USS *Maddox* (destroyer) 79
Malaysia 57
Mao Zedong 103
March on Washington 91
Mariner, Rosemary Bryant 174–175
Marrin, Albert 93
Martin, Graham 120, 128, 134–135, 155–156
Maryland 33, 35, 46, 90, 96, 116, 194
Mason-Dixon Line 20
Massachusetts 54th Regiment 187
Massachusetts Institute for Technology 28
Matsu 52–54, 64–66, 196
SS *Mayaguez* (cargo) 161–163, 202
McCarthy, Eugene 53
McGaugh, Scott 169
McNamara, Robert 87–90, 92–95, 199
McNamara's Project 100,000 87–88, 90, 92, 199
Mediterranean Sea 62
Mekong Delta 80
Memphis, Tennessee 95–96, 199
Middendorf, William 165, 167
Middle East 45, 62, 74, 98, 179, 196
USS *Midway* (carrier) 1, 5, 9–11, 16, 63–66, 74–75, 101, 118–140, 142
Midway Museum 9, 166
Military Assistance and Advisory Group 59
Military Assistance and Advisory Group-Indochina 57
Miller, William G. 180
Mindoro Strait 129, 161, 163, 202
Mississippi 29, 35
Mondale, Walter 178, 180
Monterey, California 62–63, 82, 85, 122, 196, 198
Moscow, Russia 70, 105–106, 201
Mossadeq, Muhammad 179, 195
Murphy, Janet 6, 62–64
USS *Murray* (destroyer) 67
Museum of Natural History 20
Muslim 177
My Lai Massacre 94, 99, 199

NAACP *see* National Association for the Advancement of Colored People
Nagasaki 34
National Air Museum 21
National Association for the Advancement of Colored People (NAACP) 30, 33, 36, 193
National Council of Negro Women 36
National Defense Act 26
National Liberation Front (NLF) 82
National Science Foundation 173–174
National Security Advisor, U.S. 71, 78, 167, 180
National Security Council 54, 57
National Urban League 30
Naval Academy 2, 7, 28, 33, 35, 37–39, 42, 44–47, 50–51, 86, 88, 96, 122, 151, 156, 168, 174–175, 185, 194–195
Naval Air Forces Pacific 119
Naval Air Systems Command (NavAir) 3, 106, 172, 190, 201, 203
Naval Postgraduate School 62–63, 74, 82, 85, 122, 175, 196, 198
Naval Tactical Data System 123
Nazis 69
NBC's Today Show 164
New York 29, 37, 39, 172, 178, 188
New York Times 101, 201
The New Yorker 24–25
New Zealand 128
Ney, Edward F,. 115
USS *Nimitz* (carrier) 183, 203
99th Fighter Squadron 31–32
Nixon, Richard M. 45, 65–66, 97–99, 101–118, 115–117, 167, 200–202
North Atlantic Treaty Organization (NATO) 44, 59, 73, 194
North Carolina A&T College 30
North Korea 12, 47–48, 83–84, 103, 169, 194
North Vietnam 5–6, 9–10, 59, 74–76, 79–83, 92–95, 97–99, 101–108, 116–118, 123, 130, 141–153, 157, 167, 195, 198–201
Northern Virginia 188
Norwegian Sea 72

O'Connor, RADM John 172, 173
OE-1 Cessna 143
Ohio 29, 99, 200
USS *Okinawa* (amphibious assault) 129, 133
Okinawa, Japan 9, 59, 96, 129
Oman 176
Operation Ajax 176, 179, 195
Operation Eagle Claw 176, 181–182, 184, 203
Operation Flaming Dart 79, 198
Operation Frequent Wind 1, 5, 7, 10, 23, 124, 132, 146, 156–158, 163, 166–168, 170–172, 187–188, 202
Operation Game Warden 80
Operation Lam Son 102, 104, 201
Operation Linebacker 6, 104–105, 107, 201
Operation Menu 98–99, 200
Operation New Life 188

Operation Rolling Thunder 6, 94, 97, 200
Operation Rose 69, 197
Operational Readiness Inspections 70
USS *Oriskany* (carrier) 94, 102, 122–123, 175, 200
Orlando, Florida 155
Oswald, Lee Harvey 78

Pacific Naval Fleet 31, 193
Pacific Seventh Fleet 49
Pahlavi, Reza 176–179, 202
Pakistan 176
Paris, France 97, 101, 107–108, 116, 177, 199–201
Paris Peace Accords 9, 101, 108, 167
Parks, Rosa 196
Pearl Harbor 31, 164, 193
Peking, China 105
Pennsylvania 29
Pensacola, Florida 6, 51, 55, 195
Pentagon 52, 72, 86, 95, 120, 135, 199, 201
People's Assembly 42
Phi Beta Kappa 25
Philippine Sea 112, 161
Phuoc Long, Battle of 117
Port of Sattahip 157
Powell, Adam Clayton 36–37
Prague, Czechoslovakia 29
Preparatory High School for Colored Youth 24, 193
USS *Princeton* (carrier) 53–54, 60, 195
Project 100,000 87–88, 90, 92, 199
Provisional People's Committee 42
Psychological Examining 29
USS *Pueblo* (research) 83–84
Puerto Ricans 96
Pullman porters 25

Qom, Iran 176
Quemoy 52–54, 64–66, 196
Qui Nhon, Vietnam 79

Randolph, A. Phillip 30, 35
Randolph Air Force Base 142
USS *Ranger* (carrier) 76, 83, 84–85, 89, 94, 106, 123, 199
Reagan, Ronald W. 45, 203
Red China 52
Red Sea 62
Red Tail Pilots 31–33
Republic of China 42, 52–53, 194
Reserve Officer Training Corps 26–28, 37, 194
Revolutionary War 187
Rhee, Syngman 43
Rhodes, James 99
Romani 35
Roosevelt, Eleanor 28, 30
Roosevelt, Franklin D. 28, 30–31, 34, 36, 193
Roper, Malakai 15
Roper, LCDR Raymond 136

Russian Man-o'-War 84
Russian Military Security Force 68
Russo-Japanese War 42

Saigon, Vietnam 1, 5–6, 9–10, 80, 82, 93, 96, 101, 104, 107, 117–120, 123, 128, 130–134, 136, 138–143, 153–155, 157, 160, 163, 168, 187, 198–199
Saint Cyprian's Church 62
Salem, Peter 187
San Bernardino Strait 161–163
San Diego, California 119
San Francisco, California 188
Saudi Arabia 176
USS *Schenectady* (war ship) 112
Schlesinger, James R. 135, 166
Schneller, Robert J. 37–38, 40
Schroeder, Patricia 178
Scowcroft, Brent 135
Sea of Japan 42, 72
Second World War *see* World War II
Selden, Bernice 14
Selden, Bob 18
Selden, Charlotte *see* Charlotte Chambers
Selden, Clement 13–14, 16, 21, 26, 40, 172
Selden, Eugene 14
Selden, Gladden (Gladys) 13, 16, 21, 26
Selden, Theodore 19
Selden, William 14
Senate Foreign Relations Committee 81, 94, 198
Seoul, South Korea 42–43
17th parallel 57, 74, 195
Seventh Fleet 49, 53, 55, 64–65, 85, 108–109, 114–115, 119, 128–129, 161, 166, 168, 188, 194–195
USS *Shangri-La* (carrier) 67
Shaw, Robert Gould 16
Shelepin, Alexander 68
Sierer, Pason 39
Silent Majority Speech 99, 200
Single Integrated Operational Plan (SIOP) 52, 70
Sino-Japanese War 42
Situation Room 135
Socialist Republic of Vietnam 169, 202
Somalia 176
South China Sea 9, 11, 54–56, 109–112, 114, 119, 122, 128–129, 131–135, 137, 139–140, 143–145, 147–151, 153–155, 163
South Korea 42–43, 48, 114, 128, 194
South Vietnam 1, 5–6, 9–10, 58–59, 74–80, 82–83, 93–95, 97–99, 101–105, 107–108, 116–118, 120, 128, 132, 134, 137, 141–145, 152, 153, 155, 161, 187, 195, 198
Soviet Union 6, 34, 42–43, 45, 48–49, 52, 56–58, 61–62, 65–71, 73, 76, 79, 103, 105–106, 169, 194–197
Staaveren, Jacob Van 102
Stalin, Joseph 34, 42–43, 49, 61, 69, 194

Steele, ADM George P. 168
Stewart, Alison 26
Straits of Florida 71
Strategic Air Command (SAC) 56, 71
Subic Bay 9, 125, 129, 165, 167, 188, 202
Suez Canal 62, 196
Sung, Kim Il 42–43
Supplementary Foreign Assistance Act 102
Switzerland 58
Syphax, William 24

Taiwan 52–56, 61, 65–66, 194, 196
Taiwan Strait 53, 194
Task Force Seventy Seven 128
Taylor, Reeves 33
Tehran, Iran 176–180, 183, 203
Tet Offensive 93–94, 199
Thailand 56–57, 128–129, 157–158, 160–162, 164–165, 169, 202
Thieu, Nguyen Van 107, 118, 130, 199, 201, 202
Third World 69, 71
38th parallel 42, 47–48, 194
Tho, Le Duc 107–108, 167
USS *Threadfin* (submarine) 67
332nd Fighter Group 31
Thuy, Xuan 101, 200
Truman, Harry S 34–35, 42–45, 49, 57, 65, 74, 193–194
Turkey 73
USS *Turner Joy* (destroyer) 79
USS *Tuscaloosa* (cruiser) 112
Tuskegee Airmen 27–28, 31–32, 38
Tuskegee Army Airfield Flying School 31
Tuskegee Institute, Alabama 30, 31, 33
20th Parallel 95, 107, 199, 201
25th Amendment 116–117
21st Special Operations Squadron 10, 130, 202

U-Tapao Air Base 157
UH-1 Iroquois 132
Uniform Code of Military 114, 124
United Kingdom 42
United Nations 34, 42–43, 47–48, 58, 194
United Nations' Security Council 43
United States: African Americans 20, 27–30, 33–35, 41, 46, 81, 87, 90, 92, 95, 187, 193; Air Force 1, 6, 10, 55, 76–77, 79–80, 87, 94, 102, 104–105, 119, 130–132, 135, 139, 141–143, 152, 157, 159, 161, 163–164, 169, 181, 198, 202; Armed Forces 28–29, 32–33, 35–36, 49, 62, 77, 87, 92; Army 10, 28–33, 35, 62, 66, 77, 80, 87–88, 92, 98, 138, 142–143, 148, 169, 172, 181, 190, 193; black teachers 24–25; Blacks Only 20; Civil Rights 28–30, 33–34, 36, 38, 81, 87–88, 90–92, 95, 193, 196; Civil Rights Act 81, 196, 198; civil rights groups 30, 34, 87, 92; Congress 30, 33, 36–37, 43, 57, 62, 66, 79, 80–81, 99, 101, 103, 115–118, 120, 198, 200; discrimination 31–32, 35–37, 45, 89,

193; Embassy 93, 118, 128, 133–134, 156, 163, 176–180, 183, 203; Jim Crow South 7, 16; March on Washington 91; Marine Corps 9, 35, 37, 64, 77, 80, 87, 89, 92, 96, 129, 133, 136–138, 143, 149–149, 168, 163, 178, 181, 203; National Security Advisor 71, 78, 167, 180; Navy 35, 106; Secretary of Defense 87, 94–95, 166, 180, 199; Secretary of State 55, 116, 166–167, 179, 181; Secretary of the Treasury 180; segregation 5, 20, 24, 28, 33, 35–36, 40, 51, 89, 90, 98, 194; State Department 178, 181; Supreme Court 20, 102, 195–196; War Department 13, 15–16, 23, 31, 193; Whites Only 20

United States Colored Troops 187

United States Naval Academy 2, 7, 28, 33, 35, 37–39, 42, 44–47, 50–51, 86, 88, 96, 122, 151, 156, 168, 174–175, 185, 194–195

U.S. Pacific Command (CINCPAC) 119, 135, 185

Universal City, Texas 142

Vance, Cyrus 179, 181

Veterans of Foreign Wars 87

Vienna Summit 67, 77, 197

Vietnam: Chinese influence 56–57, 59, 78, 80, 103; Communist North 58; French control 56–57, 59; proxy war 76; Russian involvement 78, 80, 103; Vietnamization 98, 101, 117, 200; *see also* North Vietnam; South Vietnam

Vietnam, Democratic Republic of 56, 58, 74

Virginia 10–15, 17–23, 39, 46, 156, 173, 175, 188, 190

Waikiki 76

Walden, Arthur 21

Walden, Oscar 21

War on Poverty 87

Washington, D.C.: Dunbar High School 6, 23–27, 33, 37, 39, 88, 96, 175, 193, 194; 14th Street 95–96; March on Washington 91; Rock Creek Park 20; Shaw neighborhood 16; U Street 95–96

West Germany 65, 69

West Point 37–39, 88, 174

West Virginia 23

West Virginia State College 30

Westmoreland, Gen. William 80–82, 93–94, 97, 199

White, Walter 30

White House 28, 36, 73, 76, 86, 93, 97, 116–117, 120, 183

Whites Only 20

USS *White Plains* (escort carrier) 108–112, 114–115, 119, 123, 176, 201

Whiting Field 51

Whitmire, ADM Don 129, 146

Wilson, RADM Russell 35

Wilson, Woodrow 26

World War I 10–11, 28, 29, 36, 62, 89, 172

World War II 9, 23, 26, 28, 29, 31, 34, 36, 42, 45, 47–50, 52, 56, 59, 62, 65–66, 69, 87, 95–96, 107, 162, 193–194

Yasdi, Ebrahim 180

Yellow Sea 42

Yokosuka, Japan 9, 64–65, 74, 90, 108, 125, 126, 163–164, 202

Yuma, Arizona 56

www.ingramcontent.com/pod-product-compliance
Ingram Content Group UK Ltd.
Pitfield, Milton Keynes, MK11 3LW, UK
UKHW041953140426
5217IPUK00015B/775